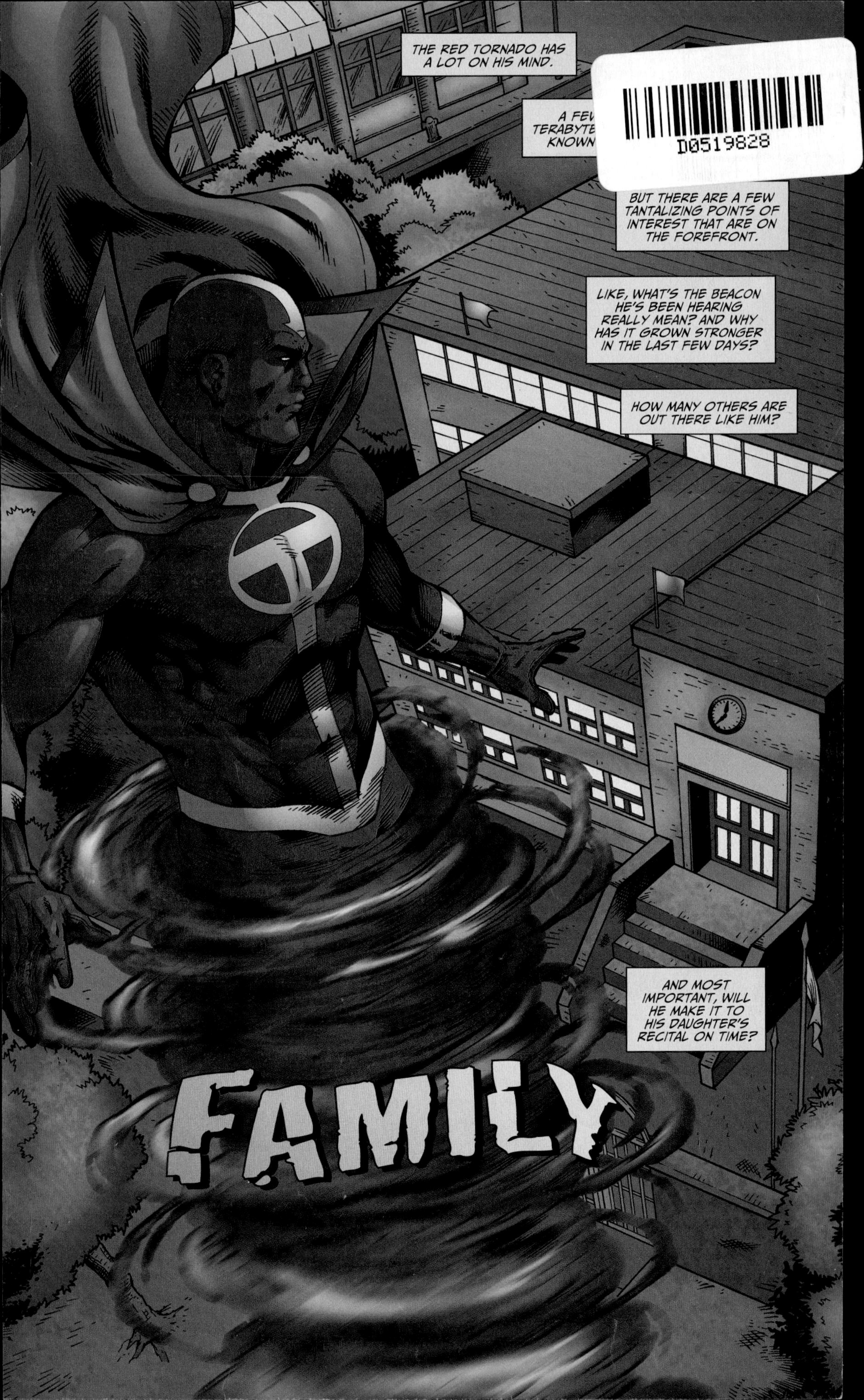
THE RED TORNADO HAS A LOT ON HIS MIND.
BUT THERE ARE A FEW TANTALIZING POINTS OF INTEREST THAT ARE ON THE FOREFRONT.
LIKE, WHAT'S THE BEACON HE'S BEEN HEARING REALLY MEAN? AND WHY HAS IT GROWN STRONGER IN THE LAST FEW DAYS?
HOW MANY OTHERS ARE OUT THERE LIKE HIM?
AND MOST IMPORTANT, WILL HE MAKE IT TO HIS DAUGHTER'S RECITAL ON TIME?
FAMILY

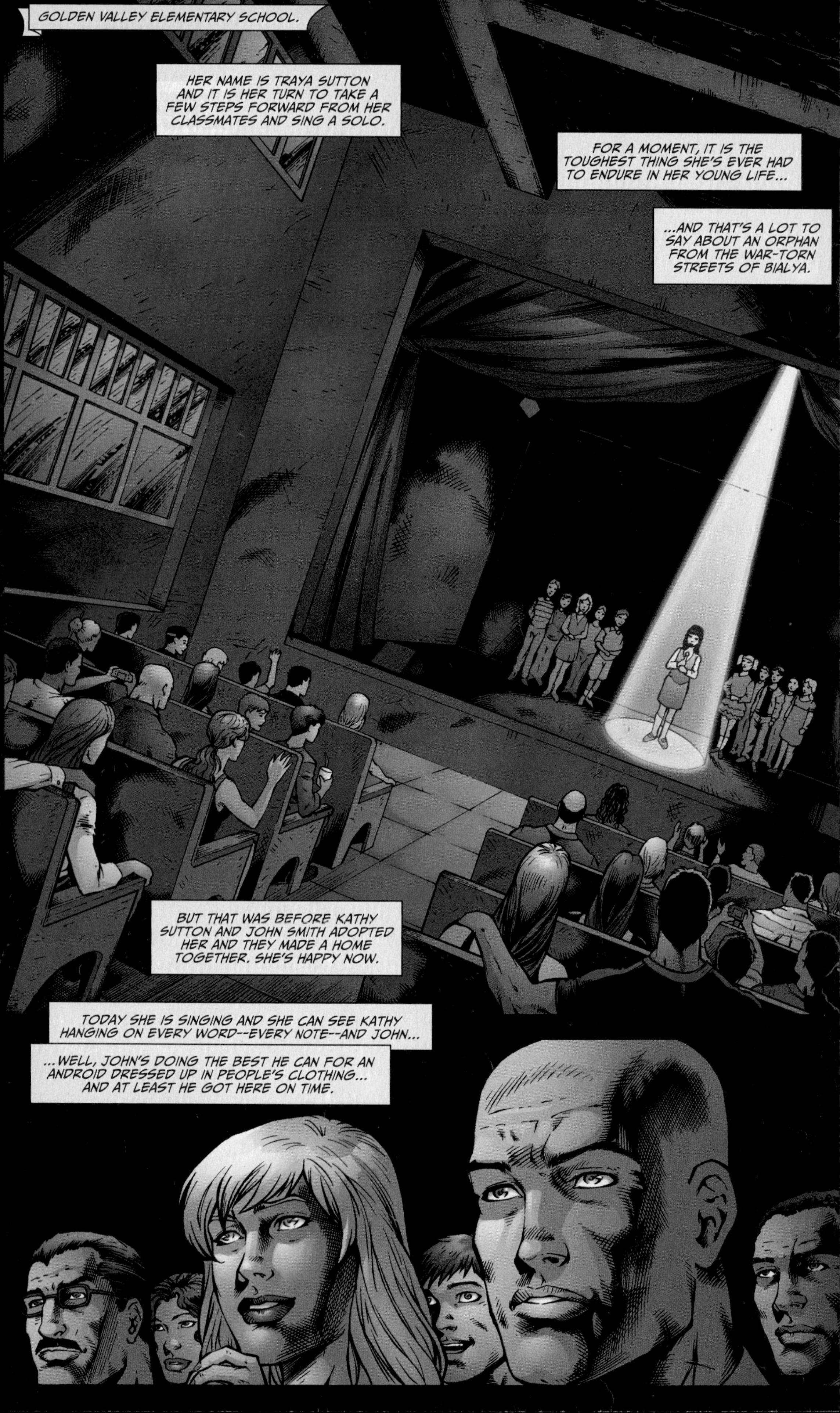
GOLDEN VALLEY ELEMENTARY SCHOOL.
HER NAME IS TRAYA SUTTON AND IT IS HER TURN TO TAKE A FEW STEPS FORWARD FROM HER CLASSMATES AND SING A SOLO.
FOR A MOMENT, IT IS THE TOUGHEST THING SHE'S EVER HAD TO ENDURE IN HER YOUNG LIFE...
...AND THAT'S A LOT TO SAY ABOUT AN ORPHAN FROM THE WAR-TORN STREETS OF BIALYA.
BUT THAT WAS BEFORE KATHY SUTTON AND JOHN SMITH ADOPTED HER AND THEY MADE A HOME TOGETHER. SHE'S HAPPY NOW.
TODAY SHE IS SINGING AND SHE CAN SEE KATHY HANGING ON EVERY WORD--EVERY NOTE--AND JOHN...
...WELL, JOHN'S DOING THE BEST HE CAN FOR AN ANDROID DRESSED UP IN PEOPLE'S CLOTHING... AND AT LEAST HE GOT HERE ON TIME.

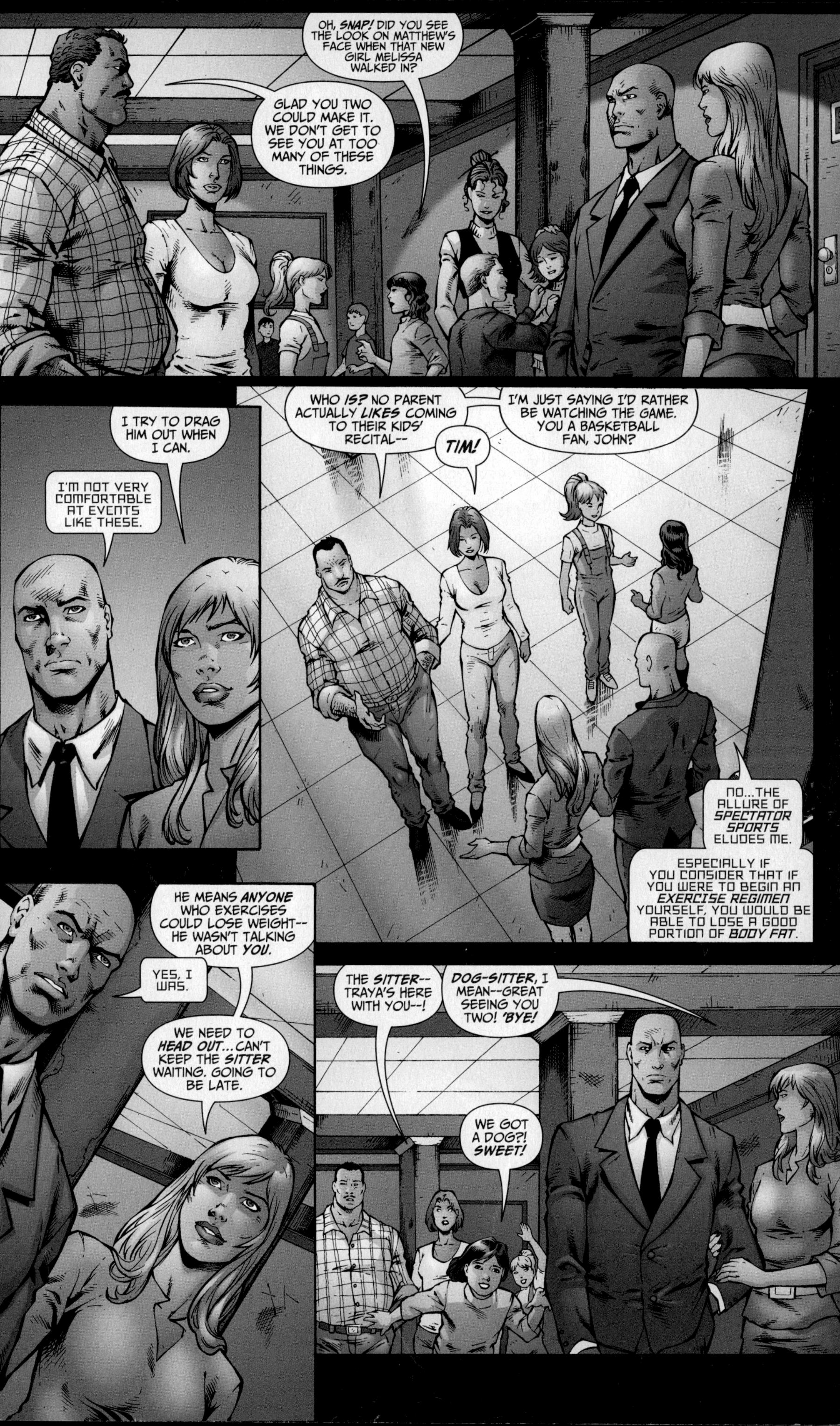
OH, SNAP! DID YOU SEE THE LOOK ON MATTHEW'S FACE WHEN THAT NEW GIRL MELISSA WALKED IN?
GLAD YOU TWO COULD MAKE IT. WE DON'T GET TO SEE YOU AT TOO MANY OF THESE THINGS.
I TRY TO DRAG HIM OUT WHEN I CAN.
I'M NOT VERY COMFORTABLE AT EVENTS LIKE THESE.
WHO IS? NO PARENT ACTUALLY LIKES COMING TO THEIR KIDS' RECITAL--
TIM!
I'M JUST SAYING I'D RATHER BE WATCHING THE GAME. YOU A BASKETBALL FAN, JOHN?
NO...THE ALLURE OF SPECTATOR SPORTS ELUDES ME.
ESPECIALLY IF YOU CONSIDER THAT IF YOU WERE TO BEGIN AN EXERCISE REGIMEN YOURSELF, YOU WOULD BE ABLE TO LOSE A GOOD PORTION OF BODY FAT.
HE MEANS ANYONE WHO EXERCISES COULD LOSE WEIGHT--HE WASN'T TALKING ABOUT YOU.
YES, I WAS.
WE NEED TO HEAD OUT...CAN'T KEEP THE SITTER WAITING. GOING TO BE LATE.
THE SITTER--TRAYA'S HERE WITH YOU--!
DOG-SITTER, I MEAN--GREAT SEEING YOU TWO! 'BYE!
WE GOT A DOG?! SWEET!

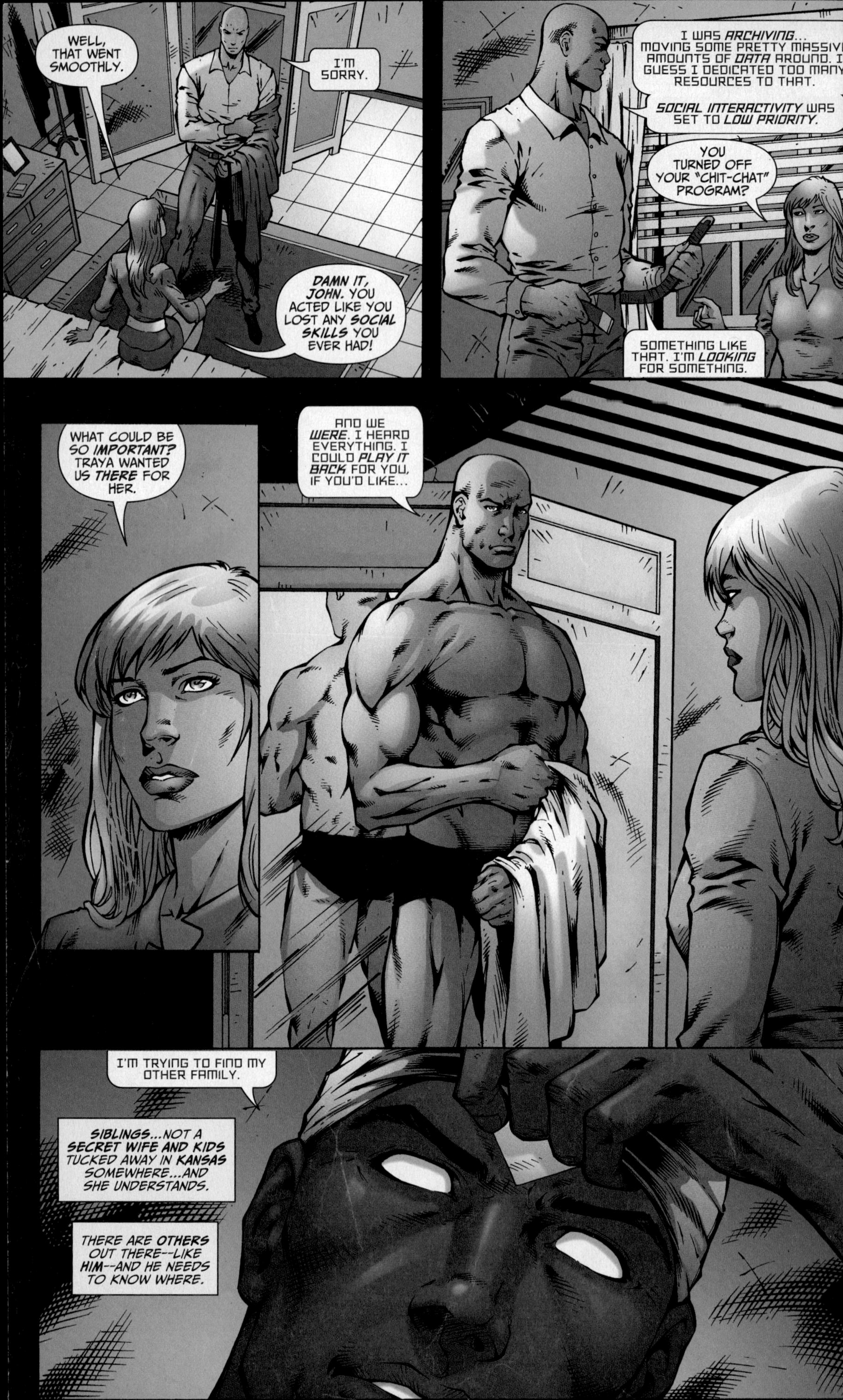

WELL, THAT WENT SMOOTHLY.
I'M SORRY.
DAMN IT, JOHN. YOU ACTED LIKE YOU LOST ANY SOCIAL SKILLS YOU EVER HAD!
I WAS ARCHIVING... MOVING SOME PRETTY MASSIVE AMOUNTS OF DATA AROUND. I GUESS I DEDICATED TOO MANY RESOURCES TO THAT.
SOCIAL INTERACTIVITY WAS SET TO LOW PRIORITY.
YOU TURNED OFF YOUR "CHIT-CHAT" PROGRAM?
SOMETHING LIKE THAT. I'M LOOKING FOR SOMETHING.
WHAT COULD BE SO IMPORTANT? TRAYA WANTED US THERE FOR HER.
AND WE WERE. I HEARD EVERYTHING. I COULD PLAY IT BACK FOR YOU, IF YOU'D LIKE...
I'M TRYING TO FIND MY OTHER FAMILY.
SIBLINGS...NOT A SECRET WIFE AND KIDS TUCKED AWAY IN KANSAS SOMEWHERE...AND SHE UNDERSTANDS.
THERE ARE OTHERS OUT THERE--LIKE HIM--AND HE NEEDS TO KNOW WHERE.

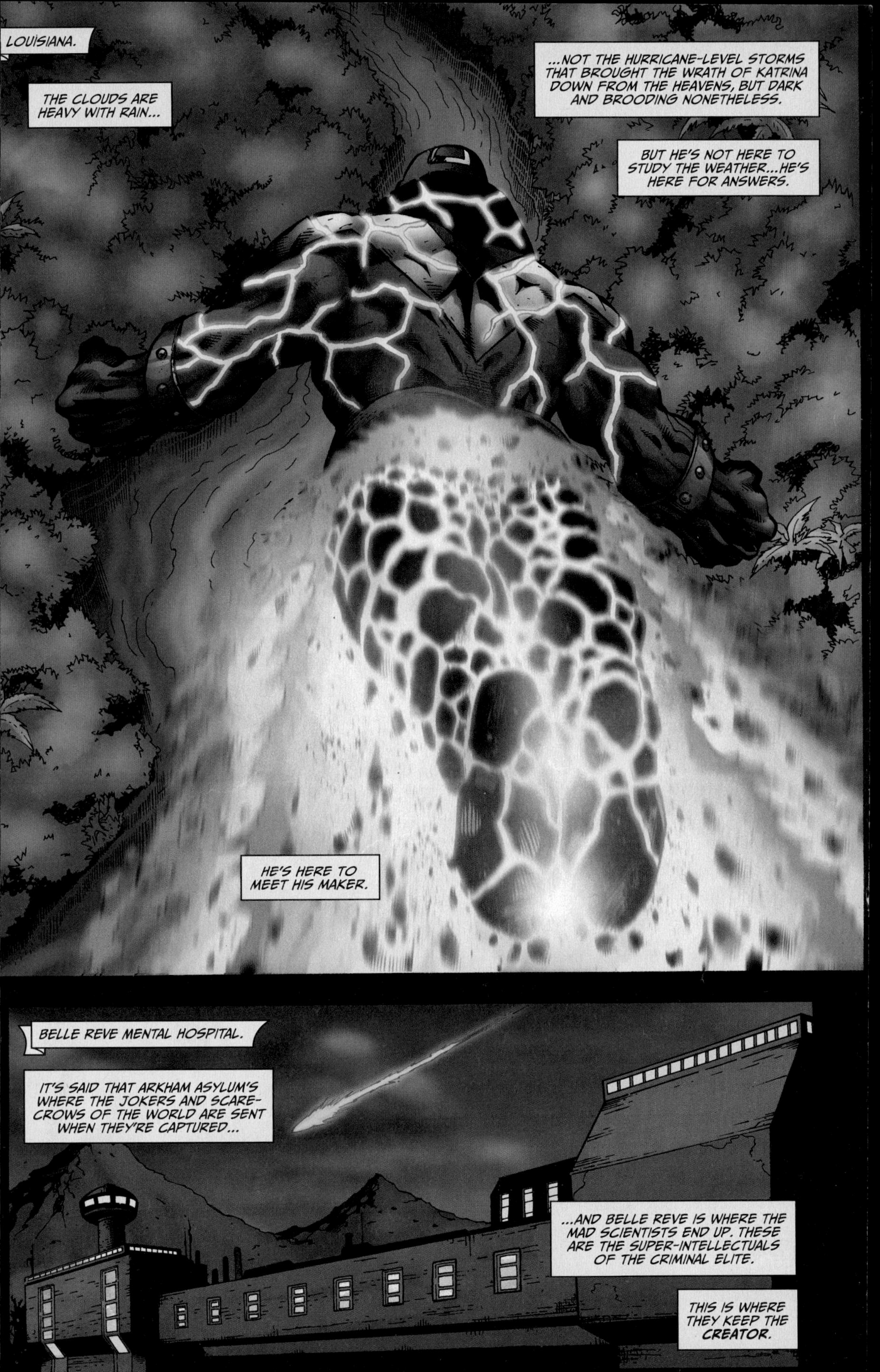
LOUISIANA.
THE CLOUDS ARE HEAVY WITH RAIN...
...NOT THE HURRICANE-LEVEL STORMS THAT BROUGHT THE WRATH OF KATRINA DOWN FROM THE HEAVENS, BUT DARK AND BROODING NONETHELESS.
BUT HE'S NOT HERE TO STUDY THE WEATHER...HE'S HERE FOR ANSWERS.
HE'S HERE TO MEET HIS MAKER.
BELLE REVE MENTAL HOSPITAL.
IT'S SAID THAT ARKHAM ASYLUM'S WHERE THE JOKERS AND SCARE-CROWS OF THE WORLD ARE SENT WHEN THEY'RE CAPTURED...
...AND BELLE REVE IS WHERE THE MAD SCIENTISTS END UP. THESE ARE THE SUPER-INTELLECTUALS OF THE CRIMINAL ELITE.
THIS IS WHERE THEY KEEP THE CREATOR.

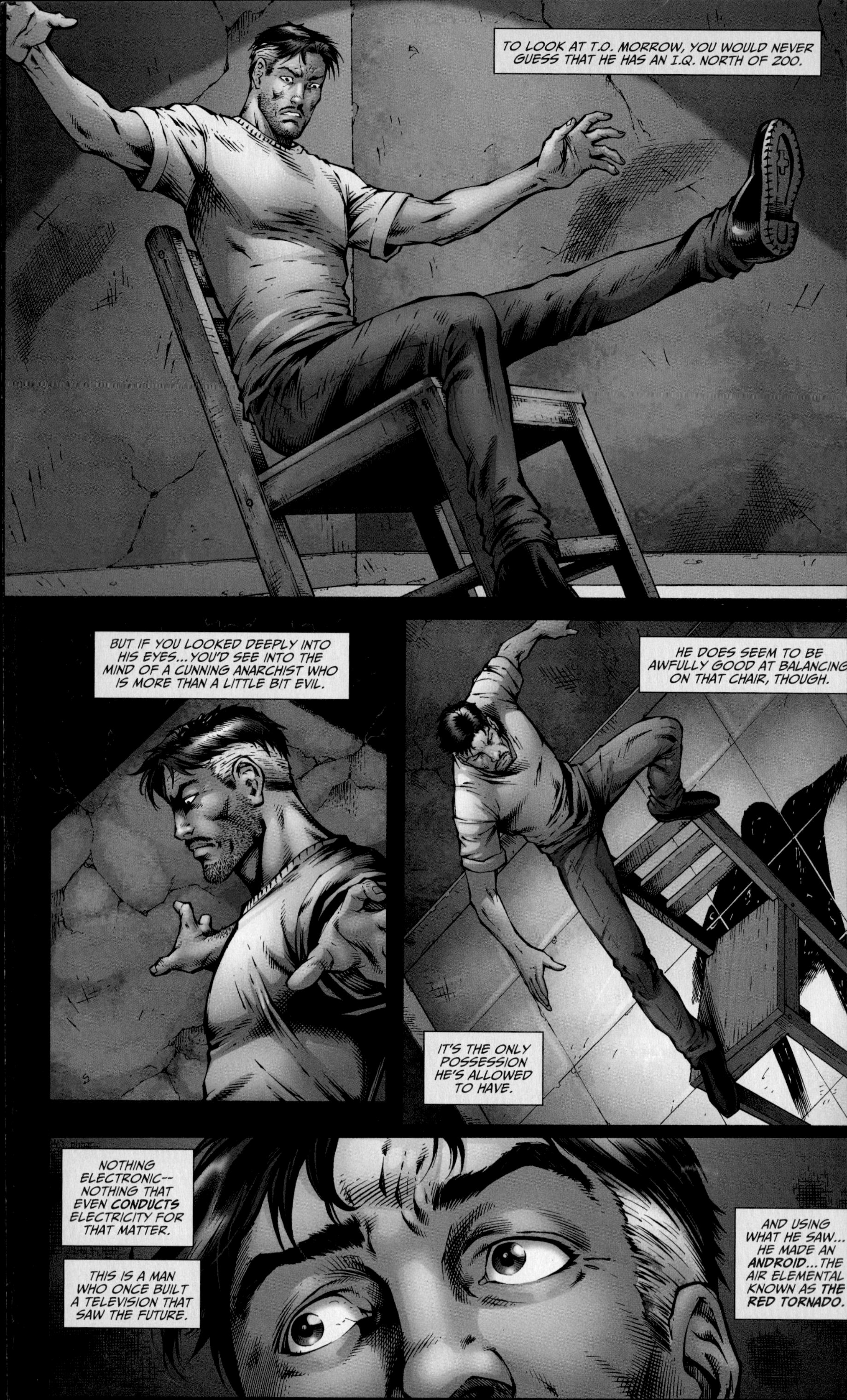
TO LOOK AT T.O. MORROW, YOU WOULD NEVER GUESS THAT HE HAS AN I.Q. NORTH OF ZOO.
BUT IF YOU LOOKED DEEPLY INTO HIS EYES...YOU'D SEE INTO THE MIND OF A CUNNING ANARCHIST WHO IS MORE THAN A LITTLE BIT EVIL.
HE DOES SEEM TO BE AWFULLY GOOD AT BALANCING ON THAT CHAIR, THOUGH.
IT'S THE ONLY POSSESSION HE'S ALLOWED TO HAVE.
NOTHING ELECTRONIC-- NOTHING THAT EVEN CONDUCTS ELECTRICITY FOR THAT MATTER.
THIS IS A MAN WHO ONCE BUILT A TELEVISION THAT SAW THE FUTURE.
AND USING WHAT HE SAW... HE MADE AN ANDROID...THE AIR ELEMENTAL KNOWN AS THE RED TORNADO.

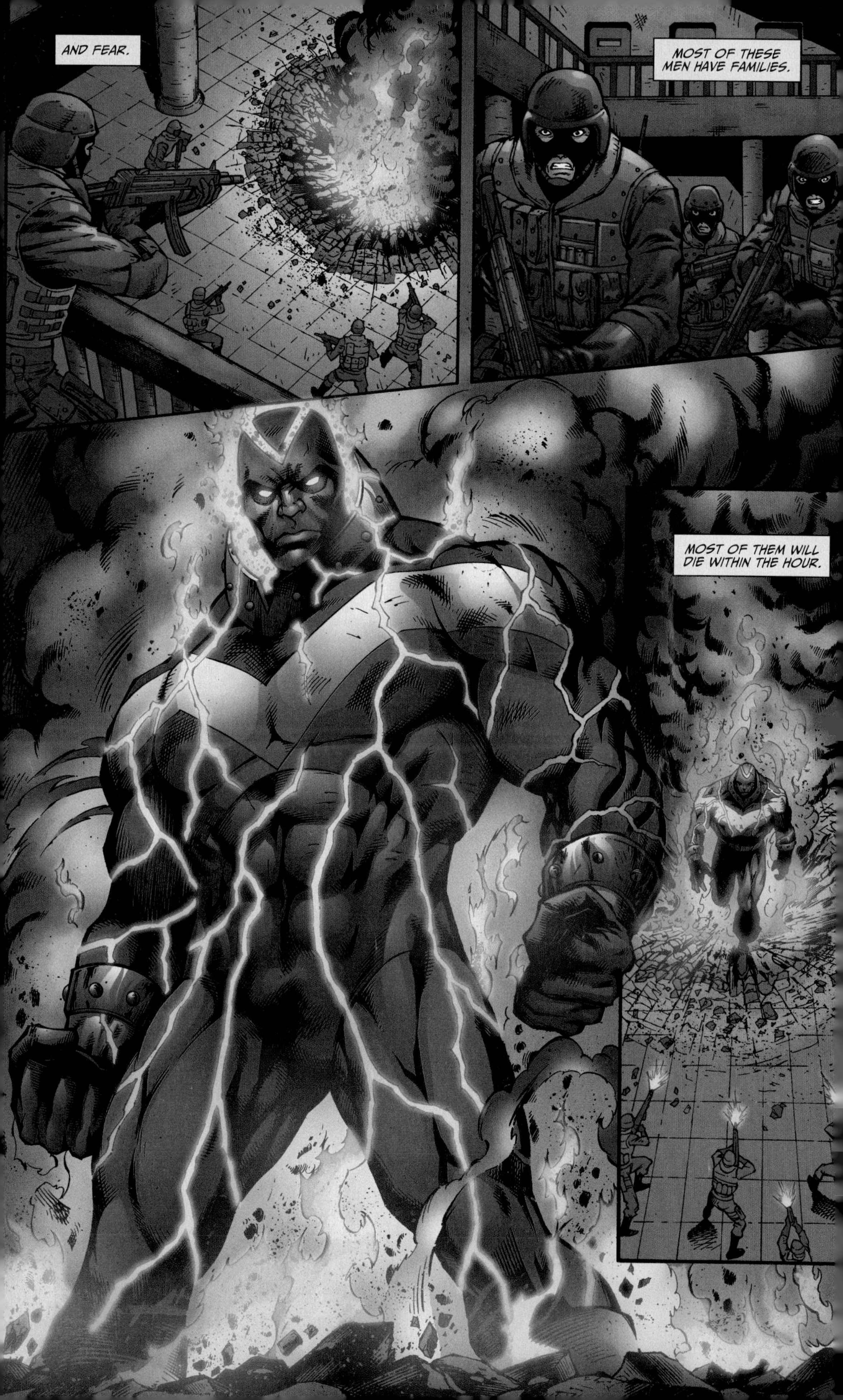
AND FEAR.
MOST OF THESE MEN HAVE FAMILIES.
MOST OF THEM WILL DIE WITHIN THE HOUR.

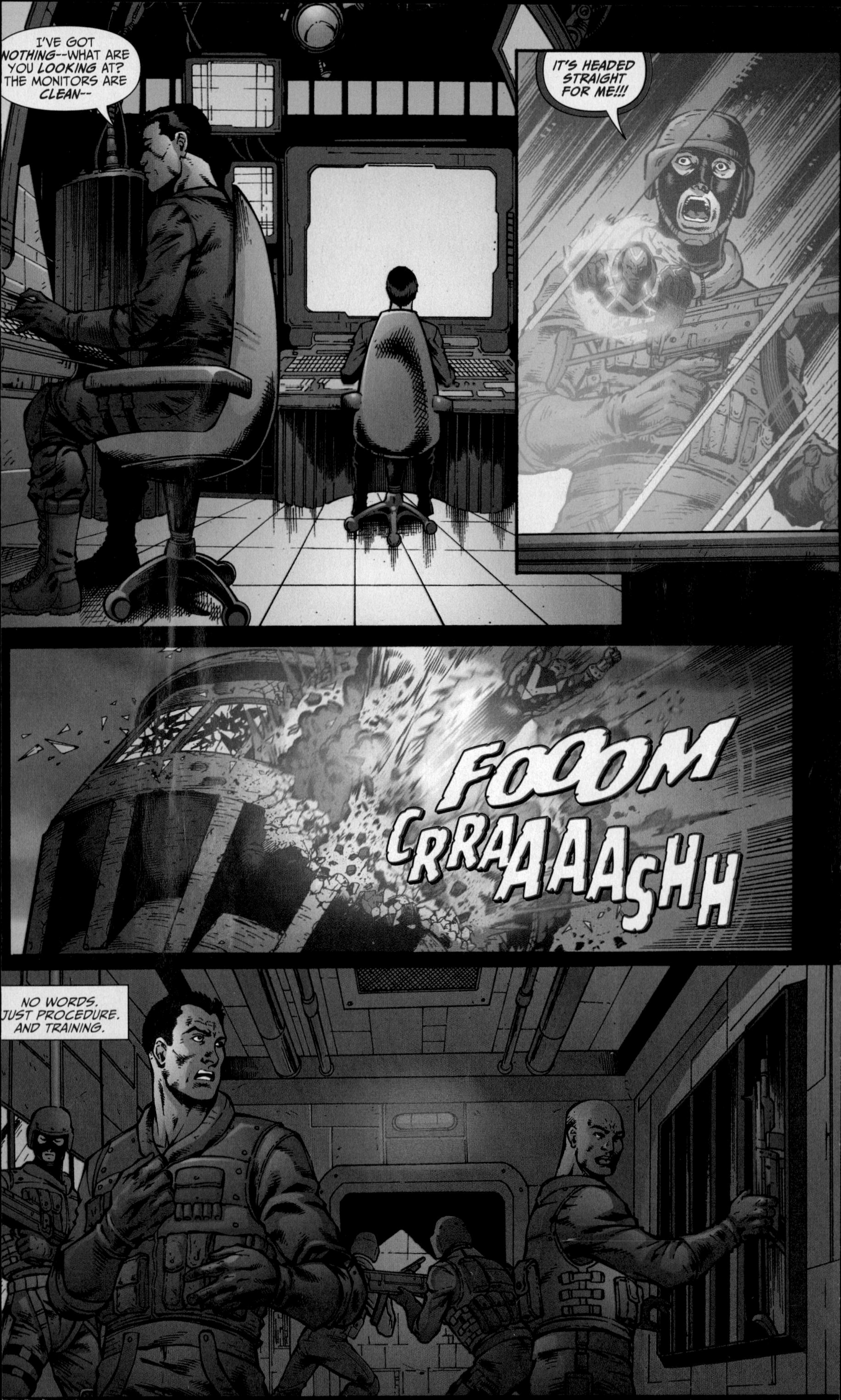
I'VE GOT NOTHING--WHAT ARE YOU LOOKING AT? THE MONITORS ARE CLEAN--
IT'S HEADED STRAIGHT FOR ME!!!
FOOOM
CRRAAAASHH
NO WORDS. JUST PROCEDURE. AND TRAINING.

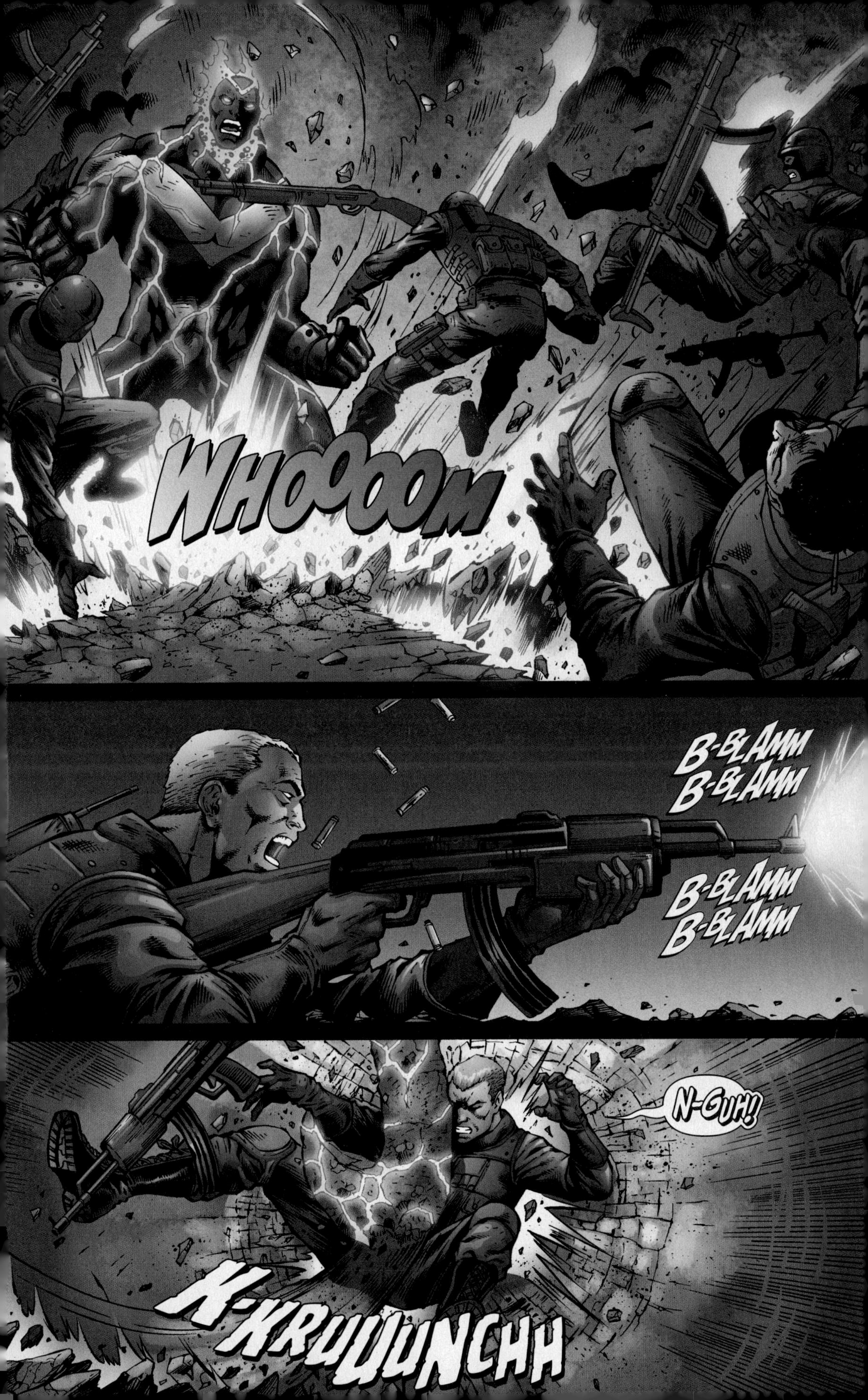
WHOOOOM
B-BLAMM
B-BLAMM
B-BLAMM
B-BLAMM
N-GUH!
K-KRUUUUNCHH

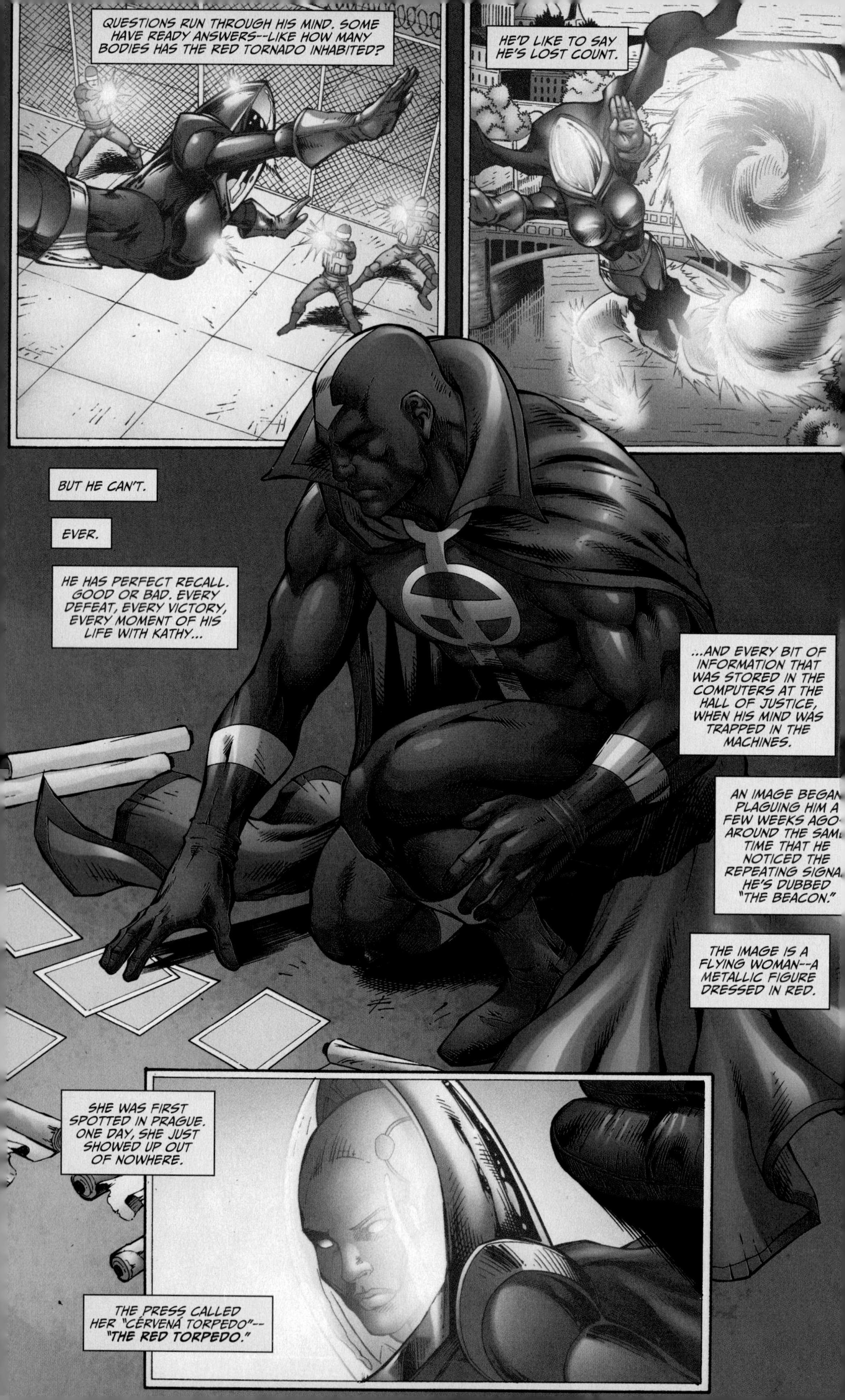
QUESTIONS RUN THROUGH HIS MIND. SOME HAVE READY ANSWERS--LIKE HOW MANY BODIES HAS THE RED TORNADO INHABITED?
HE'D LIKE TO SAY HE'S LOST COUNT.
BUT HE CAN'T.
EVER.
HE HAS PERFECT RECALL. GOOD OR BAD. EVERY DEFEAT, EVERY VICTORY, EVERY MOMENT OF HIS LIFE WITH KATHY...
...AND EVERY BIT OF INFORMATION THAT WAS STORED IN THE COMPUTERS AT THE HALL OF JUSTICE, WHEN HIS MIND WAS TRAPPED IN THE MACHINES.
AN IMAGE BEGAN PLAGUING HIM A FEW WEEKS AGO-- AROUND THE SAM TIME THAT HE NOTICED THE REPEATING SIGNA HE'S DUBBED "THE BEACON."
THE IMAGE IS A FLYING WOMAN--A METALLIC FIGURE DRESSED IN RED.
SHE WAS FIRST SPOTTED IN PRAGUE. ONE DAY, SHE JUST SHOWED UP OUT OF NOWHERE.
THE PRESS CALLED HER "ČERVENÁ TORPEDO"-- "THE RED TORPEDO."

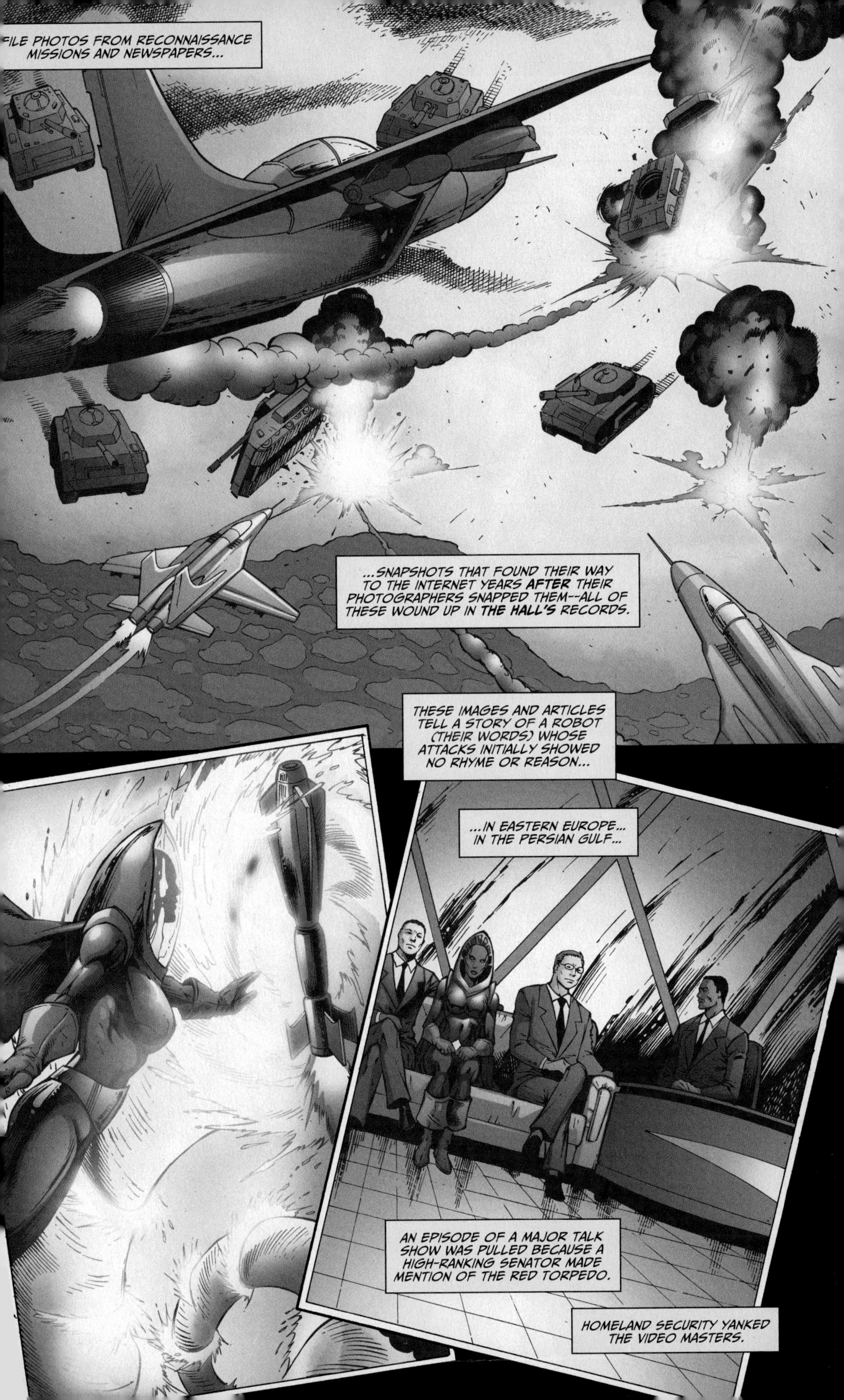
FILE PHOTOS FROM RECONNAISSANCE MISSIONS AND NEWSPAPERS...
...SNAPSHOTS THAT FOUND THEIR WAY TO THE INTERNET YEARS AFTER THEIR PHOTOGRAPHERS SNAPPED THEM--ALL OF THESE WOUND UP IN THE HALL'S RECORDS.
THESE IMAGES AND ARTICLES TELL A STORY OF A ROBOT (THEIR WORDS) WHOSE ATTACKS INITIALLY SHOWED NO RHYME OR REASON...
...IN EASTERN EUROPE... IN THE PERSIAN GULF...
AN EPISODE OF A MAJOR TALK SHOW WAS PULLED BECAUSE A HIGH-RANKING SENATOR MADE MENTION OF THE RED TORPEDO.
HOMELAND SECURITY YANKED THE VIDEO MASTERS.

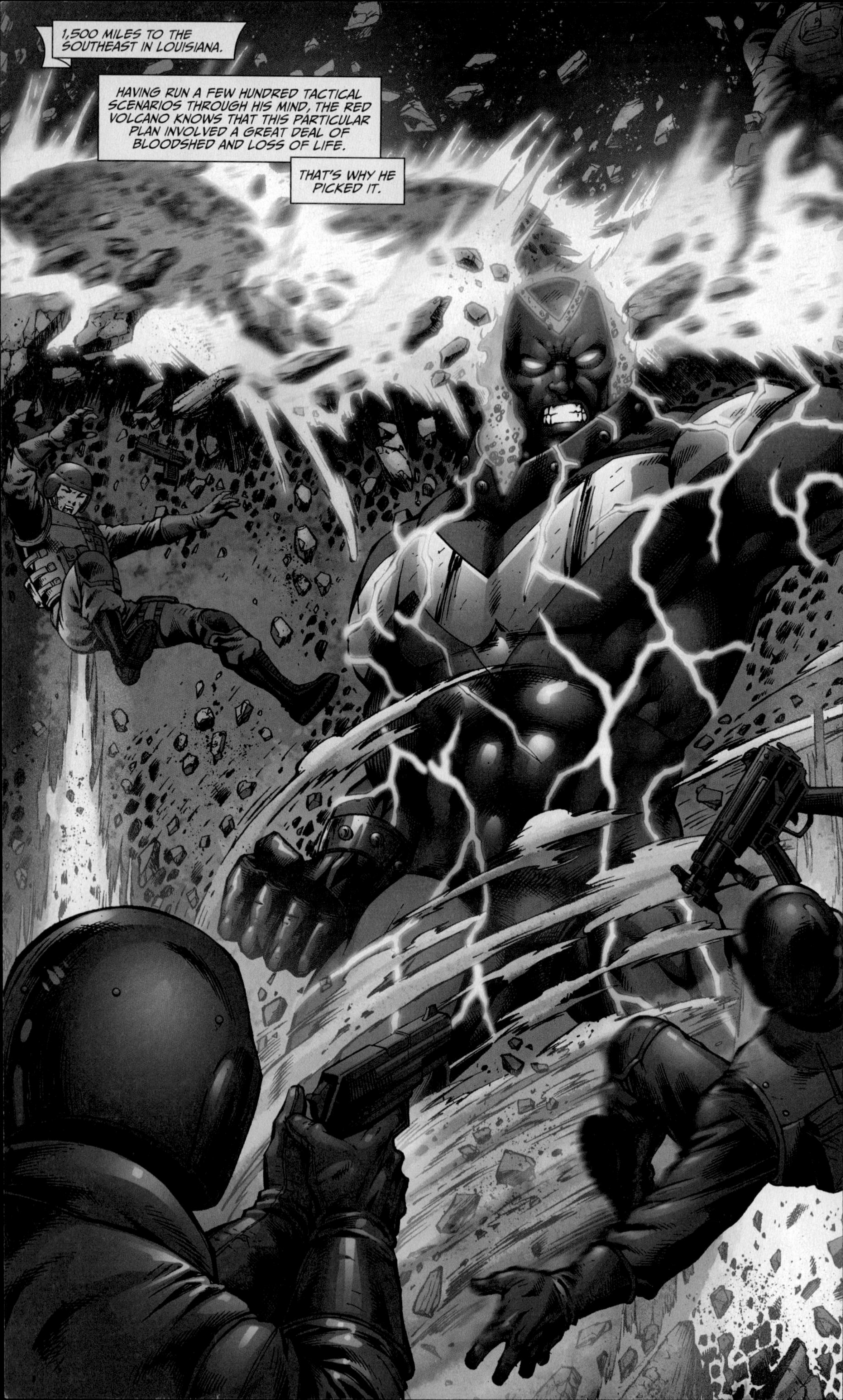
1,500 MILES TO THE SOUTHEAST IN LOUISIANA.
HAVING RUN A FEW HUNDRED TACTICAL SCENARIOS THROUGH HIS MIND, THE RED VOLCANO KNOWS THAT THIS PARTICULAR PLAN INVOLVED A GREAT DEAL OF BLOODSHED AND LOSS OF LIFE.
THAT'S WHY HE PICKED IT.

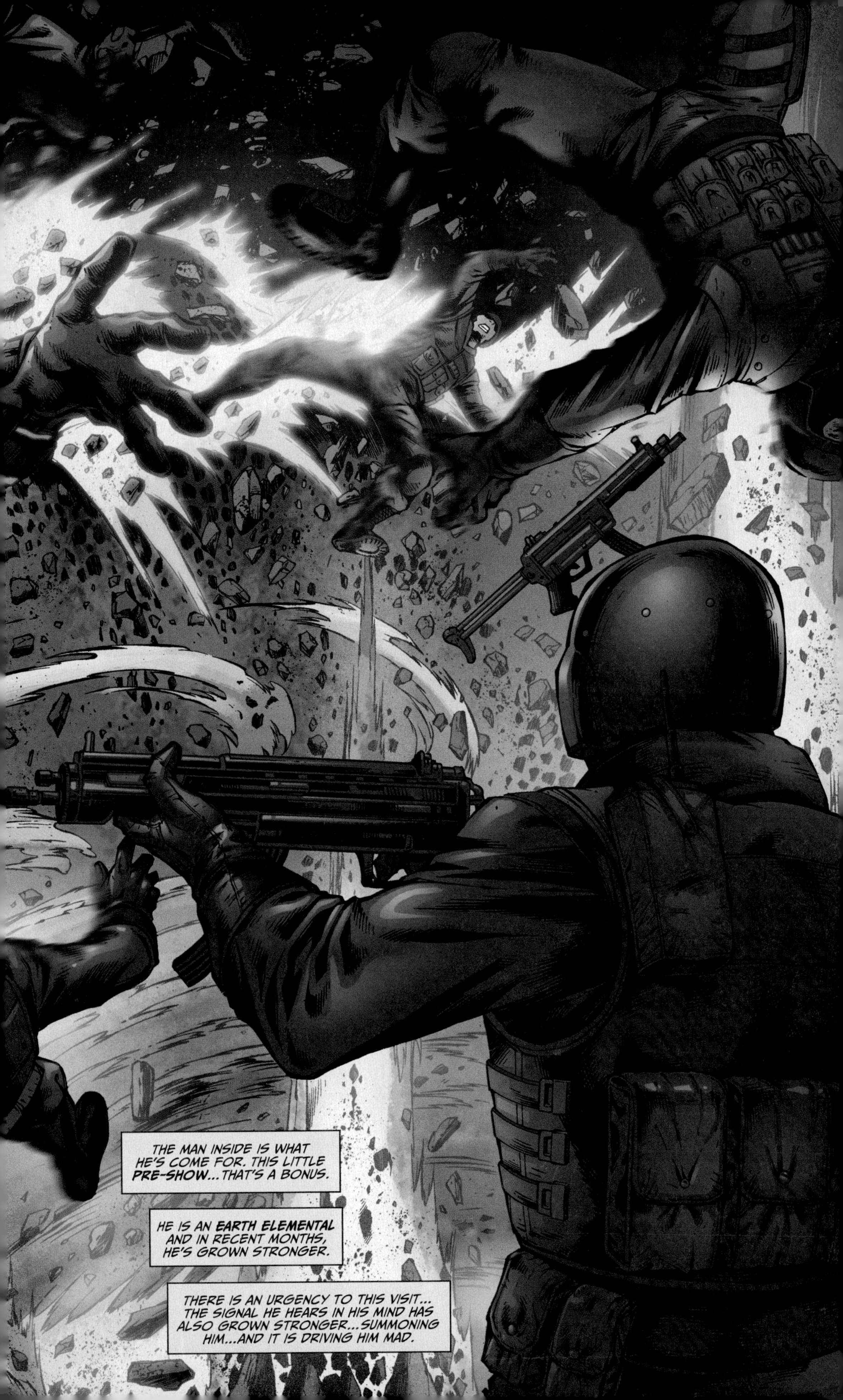
THE MAN INSIDE IS WHAT HE'S COME FOR. THIS LITTLE PRE-SHOW... THAT'S A BONUS.
HE IS AN EARTH ELEMENTAL AND IN RECENT MONTHS, HE'S GROWN STRONGER.
THERE IS AN URGENCY TO THIS VISIT... THE SIGNAL HE HEARS IN HIS MIND HAS ALSO GROWN STRONGER... SUMMONING HIM... AND IT IS DRIVING HIM MAD.

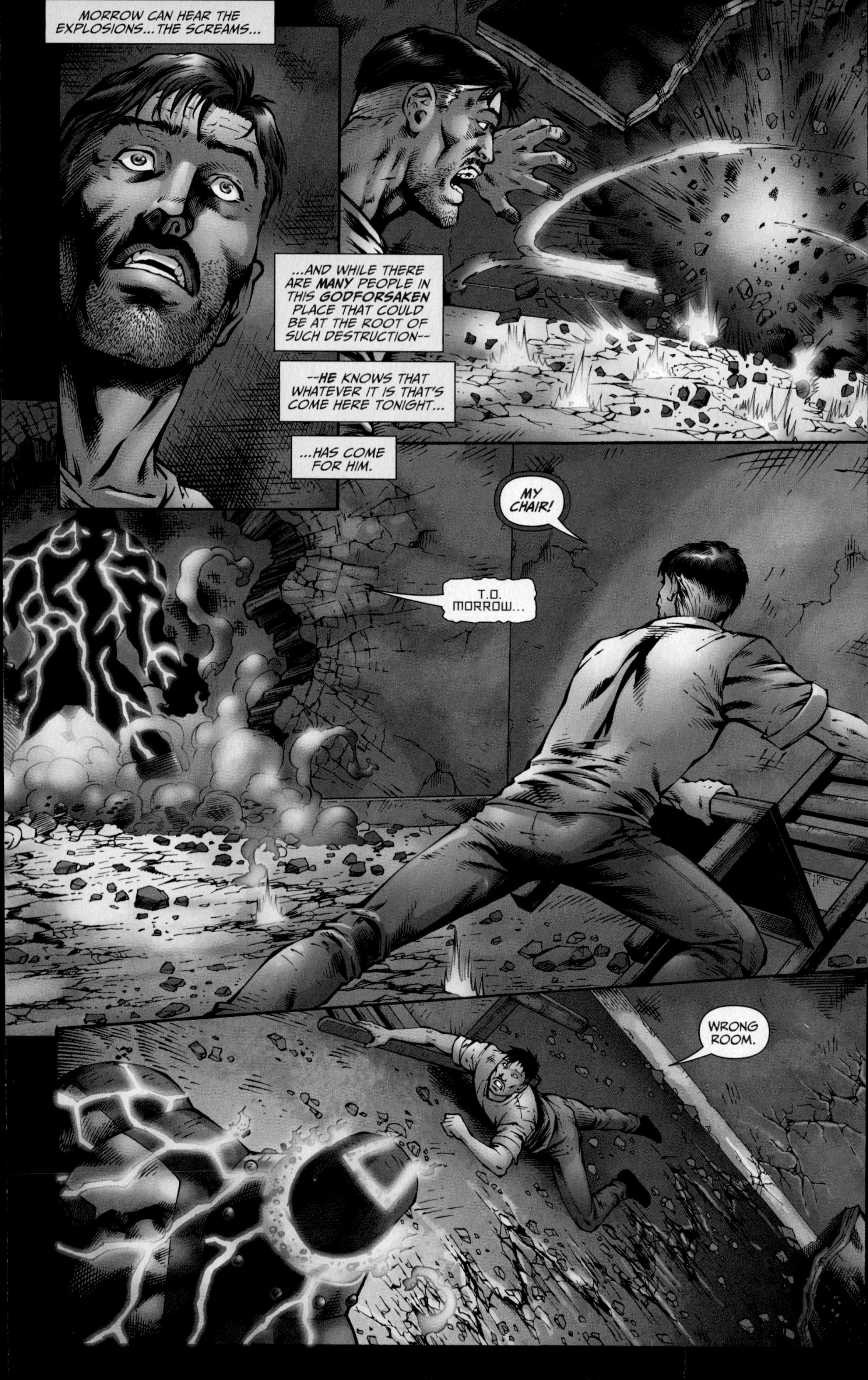
MORROW CAN HEAR THE EXPLOSIONS...THE SCREAMS...
...AND WHILE THERE ARE **MANY** PEOPLE IN THIS **GODFORSAKEN** PLACE THAT COULD BE AT THE ROOT OF SUCH DESTRUCTION--
--**HE** KNOWS THAT WHATEVER IT IS THAT'S COME HERE TONIGHT...
...HAS COME FOR HIM.
MY CHAIR!
T.O. MORROW...
WRONG ROOM.

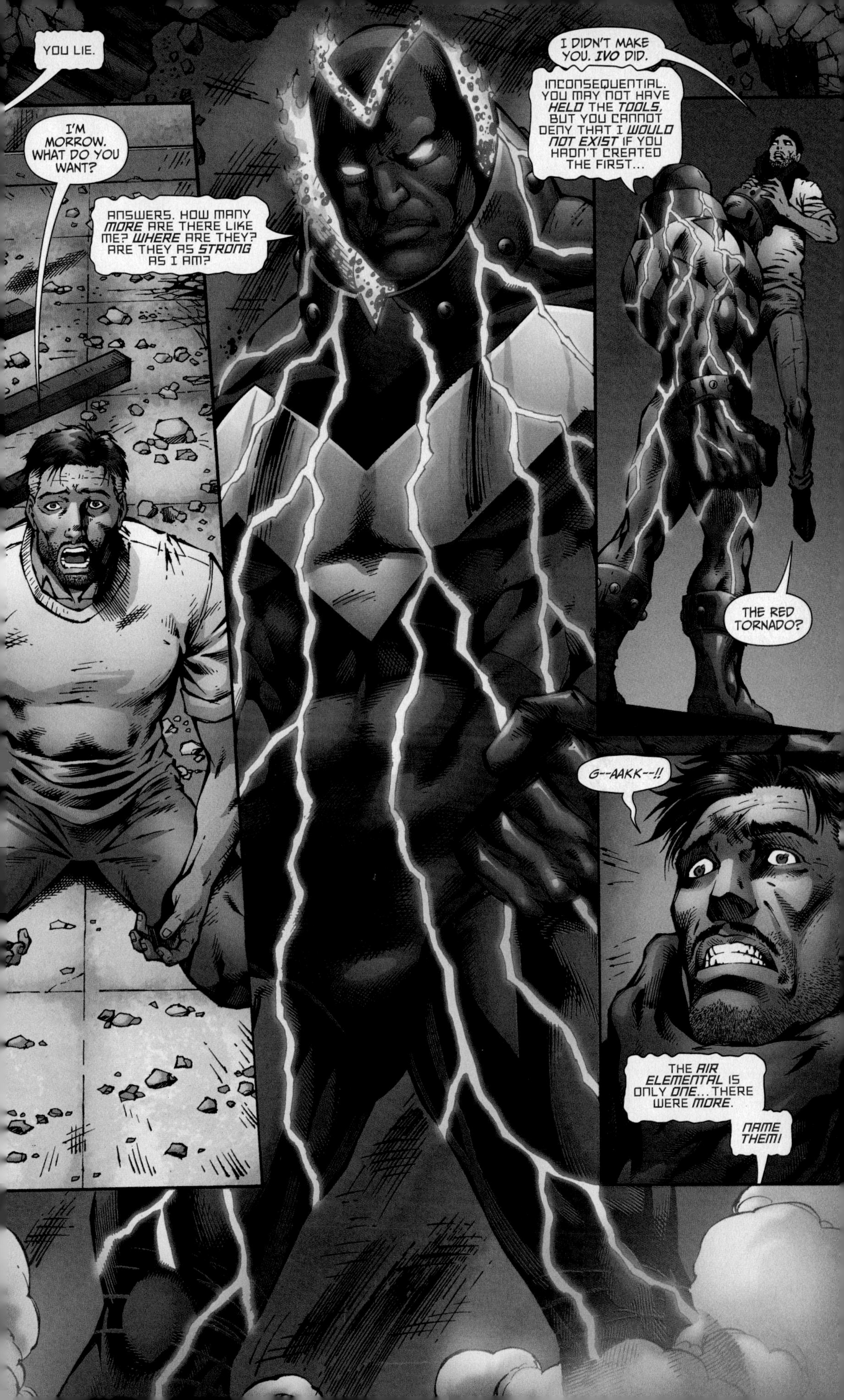
YOU LIE.
I'M MORROW. WHAT DO YOU WANT?
ANSWERS. HOW MANY MORE ARE THERE LIKE ME? WHERE ARE THEY? ARE THEY AS STRONG AS I AM?
I DIDN'T MAKE YOU. IVO DID.
INCONSEQUENTIAL. YOU MAY NOT HAVE HELD THE TOOLS, BUT YOU CANNOT DENY THAT I WOULD NOT EXIST IF YOU HADN'T CREATED THE FIRST...
THE RED TORNADO?
G--AAKK--!!
THE AIR ELEMENTAL IS ONLY ONE... THERE WERE MORE.
NAME THEM!

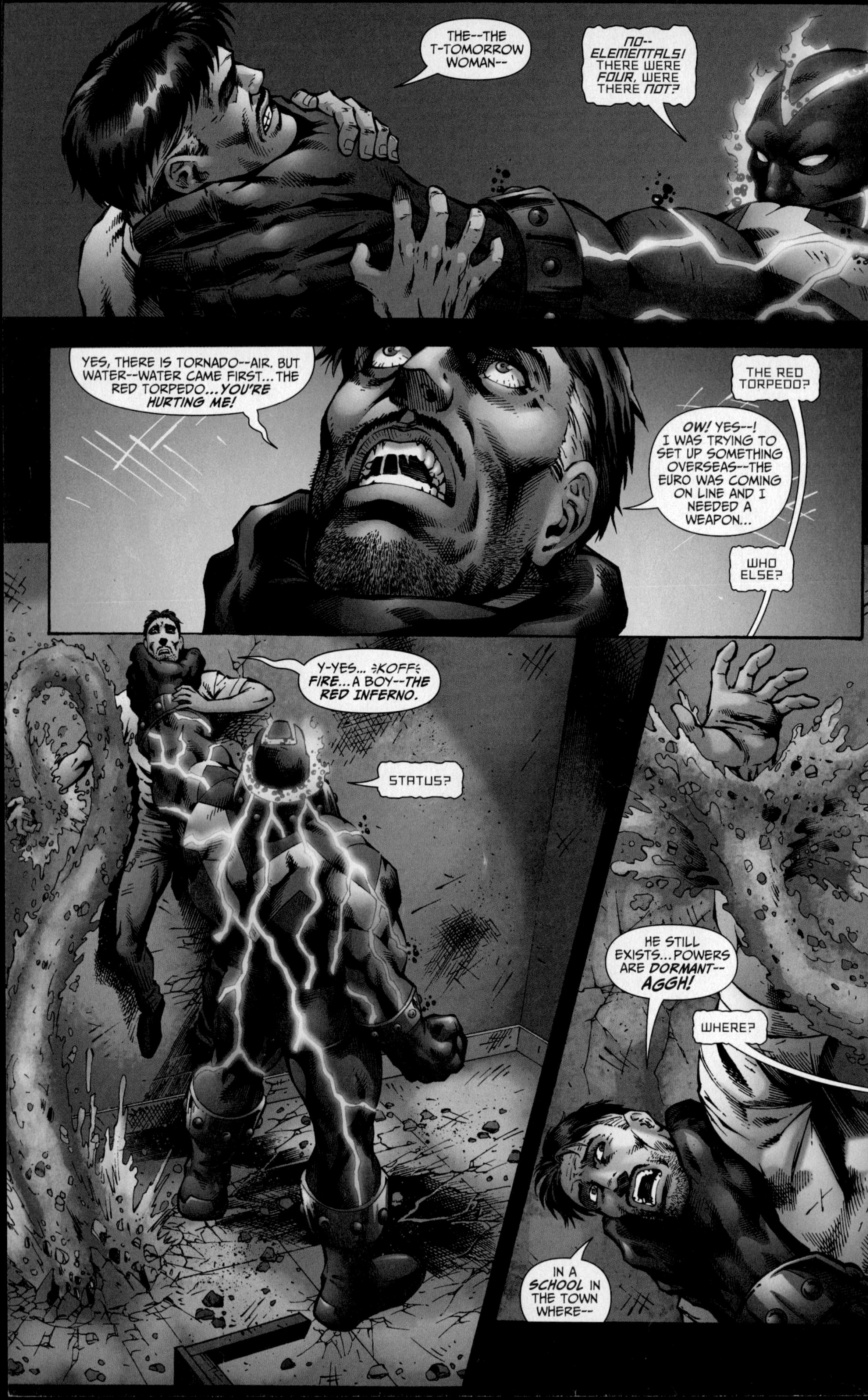
THE--THE T-TOMORROW WOMAN--
NO-- ELEMENTALS! THERE WERE FOUR, WERE THERE NOT?
YES, THERE IS TORNADO--AIR. BUT WATER--WATER CAME FIRST... THE RED TORPEDO... YOU'RE HURTING ME!
THE RED TORPEDO?
OW! YES--! I WAS TRYING TO SET UP SOMETHING OVERSEAS--THE EURO WAS COMING ON LINE AND I NEEDED A WEAPON...
WHO ELSE?
Y-YES... KOFF FIRE... A BOY--THE RED INFERNO.
STATUS?
HE STILL EXISTS... POWERS ARE DORMANT-- AGGH!
WHERE?
IN A SCHOOL IN THE TOWN WHERE--

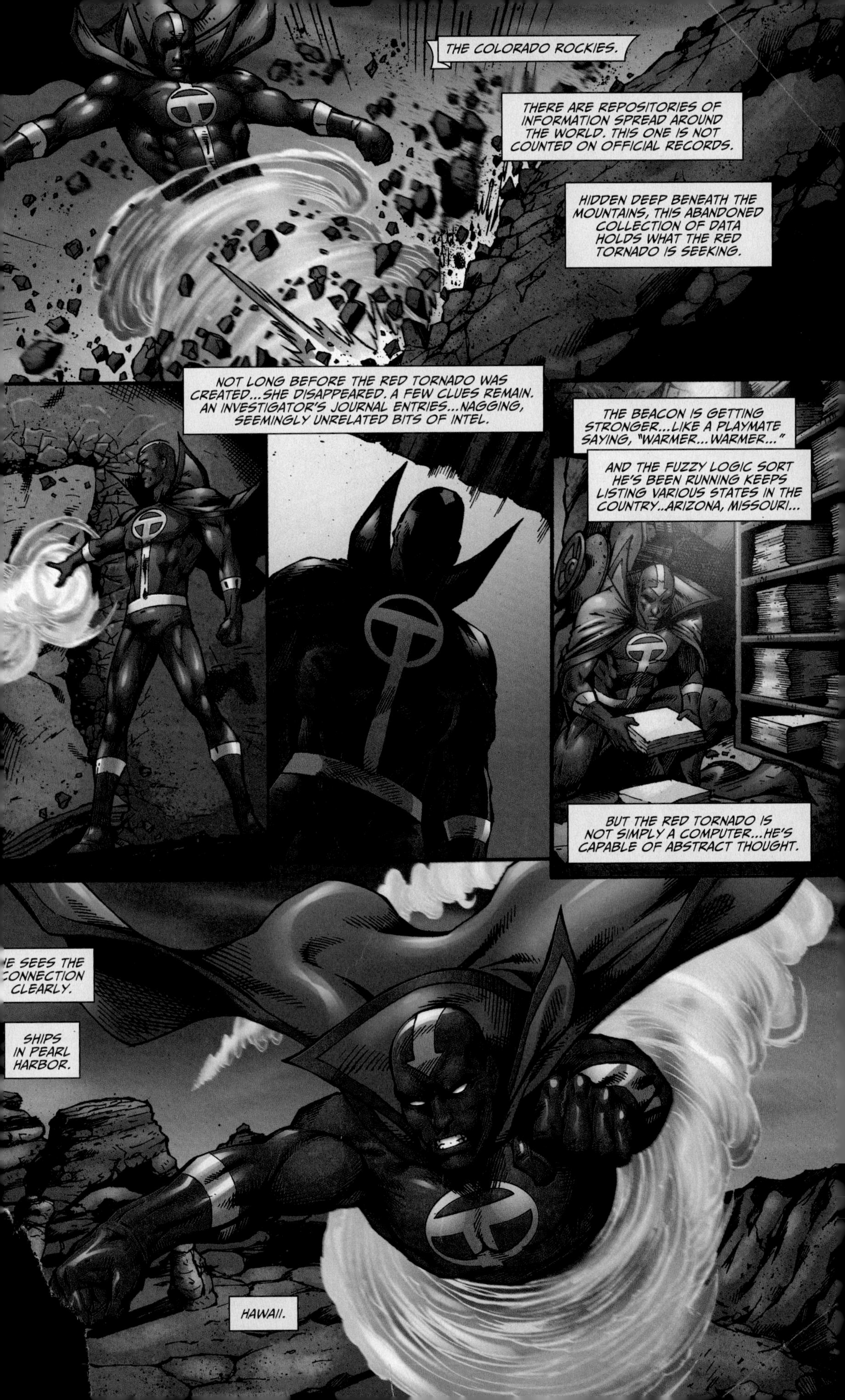
THE COLORADO ROCKIES.
THERE ARE REPOSITORIES OF INFORMATION SPREAD AROUND THE WORLD. THIS ONE IS NOT COUNTED ON OFFICIAL RECORDS.
HIDDEN DEEP BENEATH THE MOUNTAINS, THIS ABANDONED COLLECTION OF DATA HOLDS WHAT THE RED TORNADO IS SEEKING.
NOT LONG BEFORE THE RED TORNADO WAS CREATED...SHE DISAPPEARED. A FEW CLUES REMAIN. AN INVESTIGATOR'S JOURNAL ENTRIES...NAGGING, SEEMINGLY UNRELATED BITS OF INTEL.
THE BEACON IS GETTING STRONGER...LIKE A PLAYMATE SAYING, "WARMER...WARMER..."
AND THE FUZZY LOGIC SORT HE'S BEEN RUNNING KEEPS LISTING VARIOUS STATES IN THE COUNTRY..ARIZONA, MISSOURI...
BUT THE RED TORNADO IS NOT SIMPLY A COMPUTER...HE'S CAPABLE OF ABSTRACT THOUGHT.
E SEES THE CONNECTION CLEARLY.
SHIPS IN PEARL HARBOR.
HAWAII.

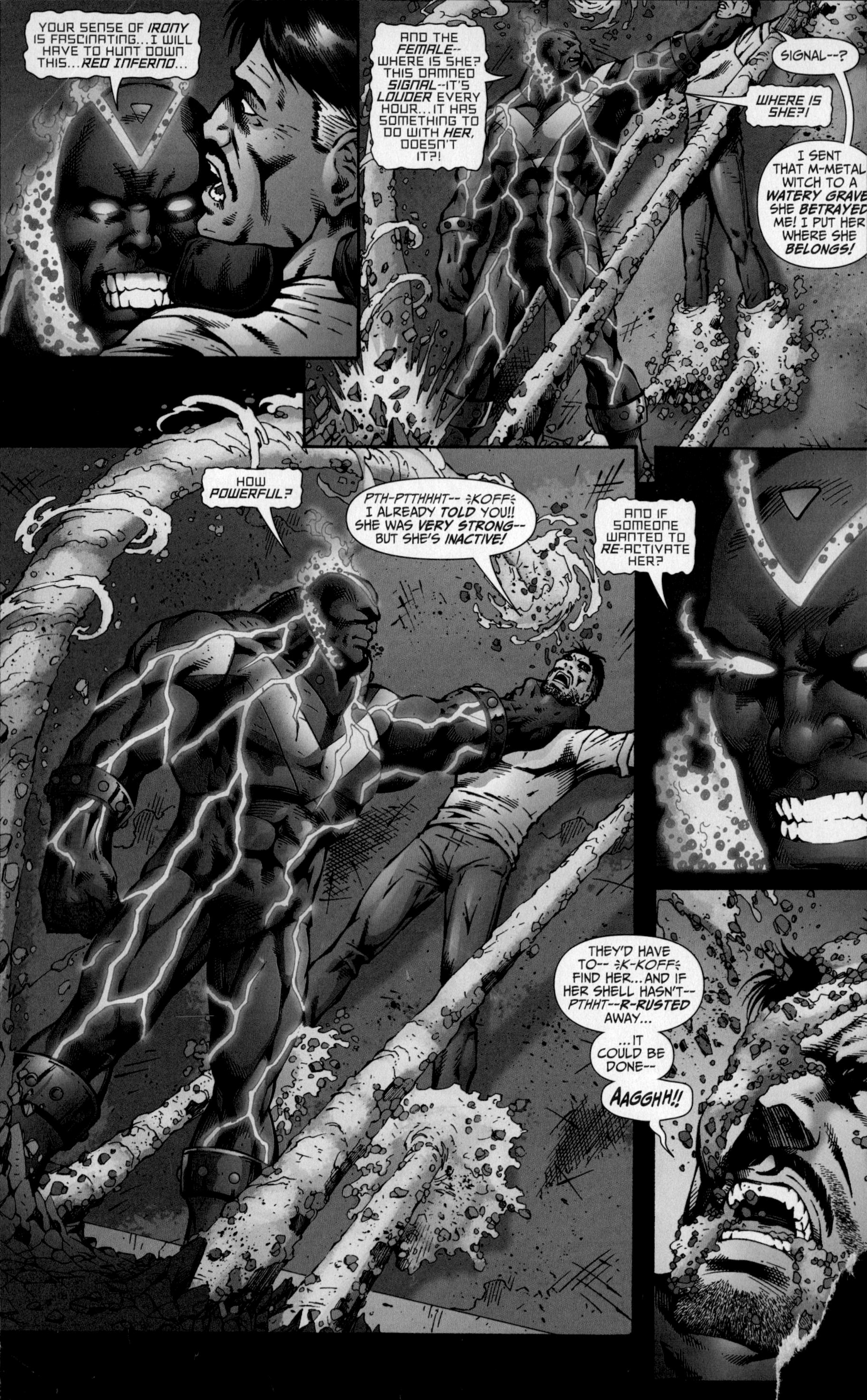
YOUR SENSE OF *IRONY* IS FASCINATING... I WILL HAVE TO HUNT DOWN THIS... *RED INFERNO*...
AND THE *FEMALE*-- WHERE IS SHE? THIS DAMNED *SIGNAL*--IT'S *LOUDER* EVERY HOUR... IT HAS SOMETHING TO DO WITH *HER*, DOESN'T IT?!
SIGNAL--?
*WHERE IS SHE?!*
I SENT THAT M-METAL WITCH TO A *WATERY GRAVE* SHE *BETRAYED* ME! I PUT HER WHERE SHE *BELONGS!*
HOW *POWERFUL?*
*PTH-PTTHHHT*-- *KOFF* I ALREADY *TOLD* YOU!! SHE WAS *VERY STRONG*-- BUT SHE'S *INACTIVE!*
AND IF SOMEONE WANTED TO *RE*-ACTIVATE HER?
THEY'D HAVE TO-- *K-KOFF* FIND HER... AND IF HER SHELL HASN'T-- *PTHHT*--*R-RUSTED* AWAY...
...IT COULD BE DONE--
AAGGHH!!

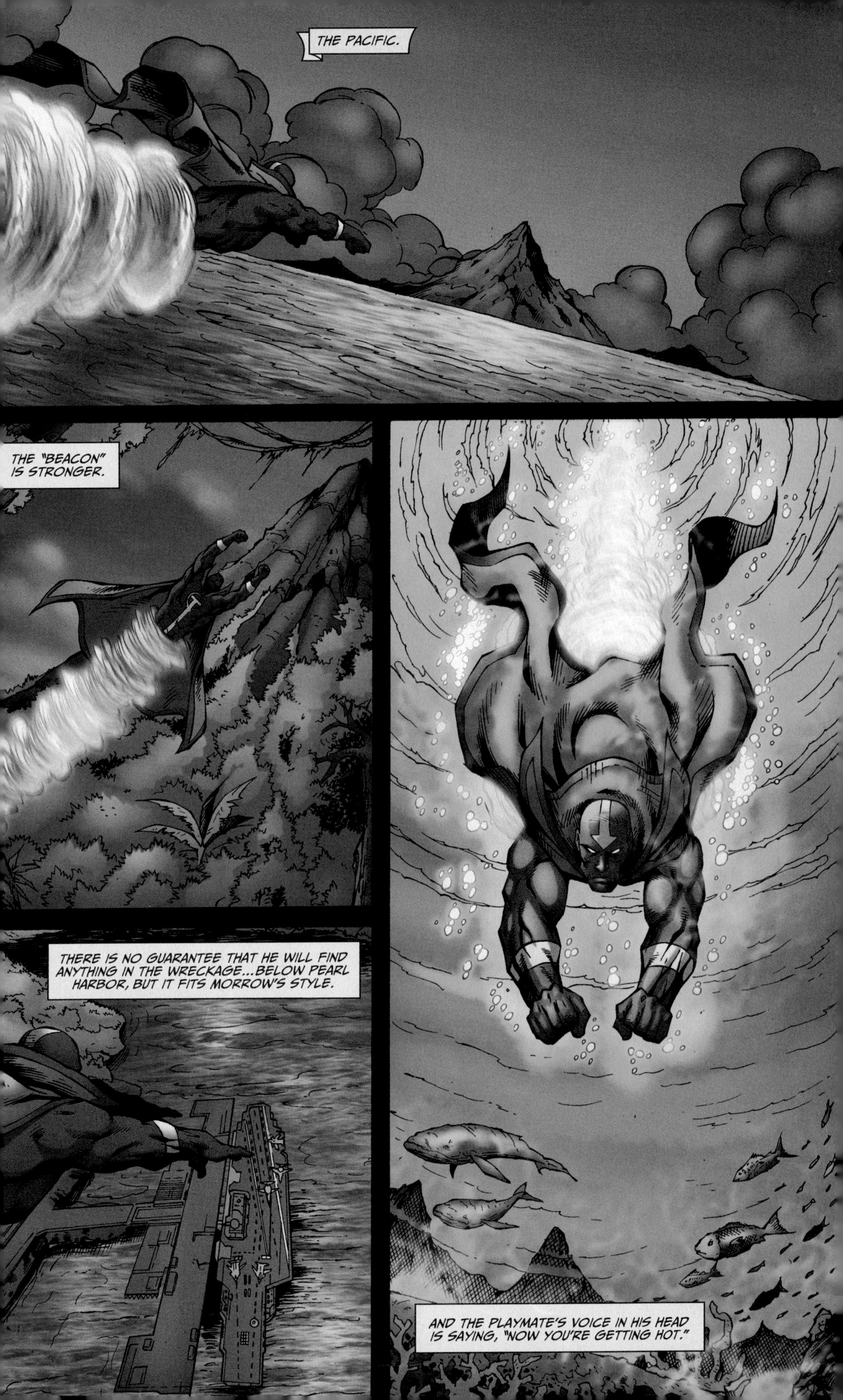
THE PACIFIC.
THE "BEACON" IS STRONGER.
THERE IS NO GUARANTEE THAT HE WILL FIND ANYTHING IN THE WRECKAGE...BELOW PEARL HARBOR, BUT IT FITS MORROW'S STYLE.
AND THE PLAYMATE'S VOICE IN HIS HEAD IS SAYING, "NOW YOU'RE GETTING HOT."

EVEN WITHOUT BEING *TRULY HUMAN*, THE RED TORNADO FEELS THE LOSS OF LIFE IN THIS PLACE...

THE FEELING OF *DEATH* IS ALMOST TANGIBLE.

IF SHE'S HERE AT ALL...

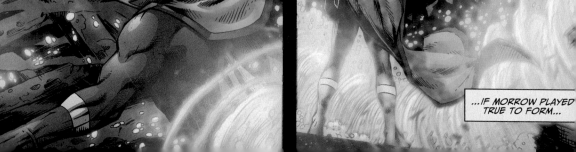

...IF MORROW PLAYED TRUE TO FORM...

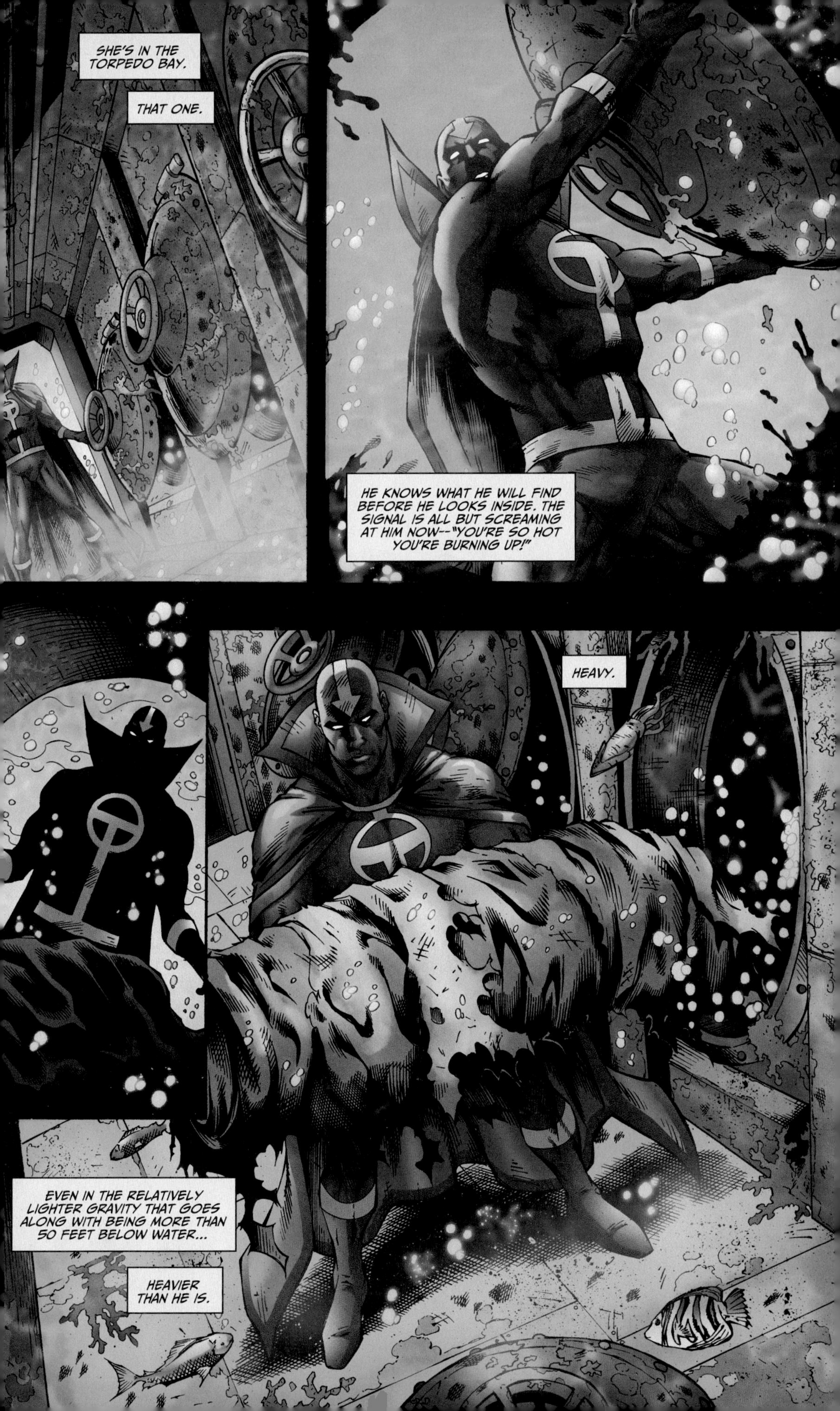

SHE'S IN THE TORPEDO BAY.
THAT ONE.
HE KNOWS WHAT HE WILL FIND BEFORE HE LOOKS INSIDE. THE SIGNAL IS ALL BUT SCREAMING AT HIM NOW--"YOU'RE SO HOT YOU'RE BURNING UP!"
HEAVY.
EVEN IN THE RELATIVELY LIGHTER GRAVITY THAT GOES ALONG WITH BEING MORE THAN 50 FEET BELOW WATER...
HEAVIER THAN HE IS.

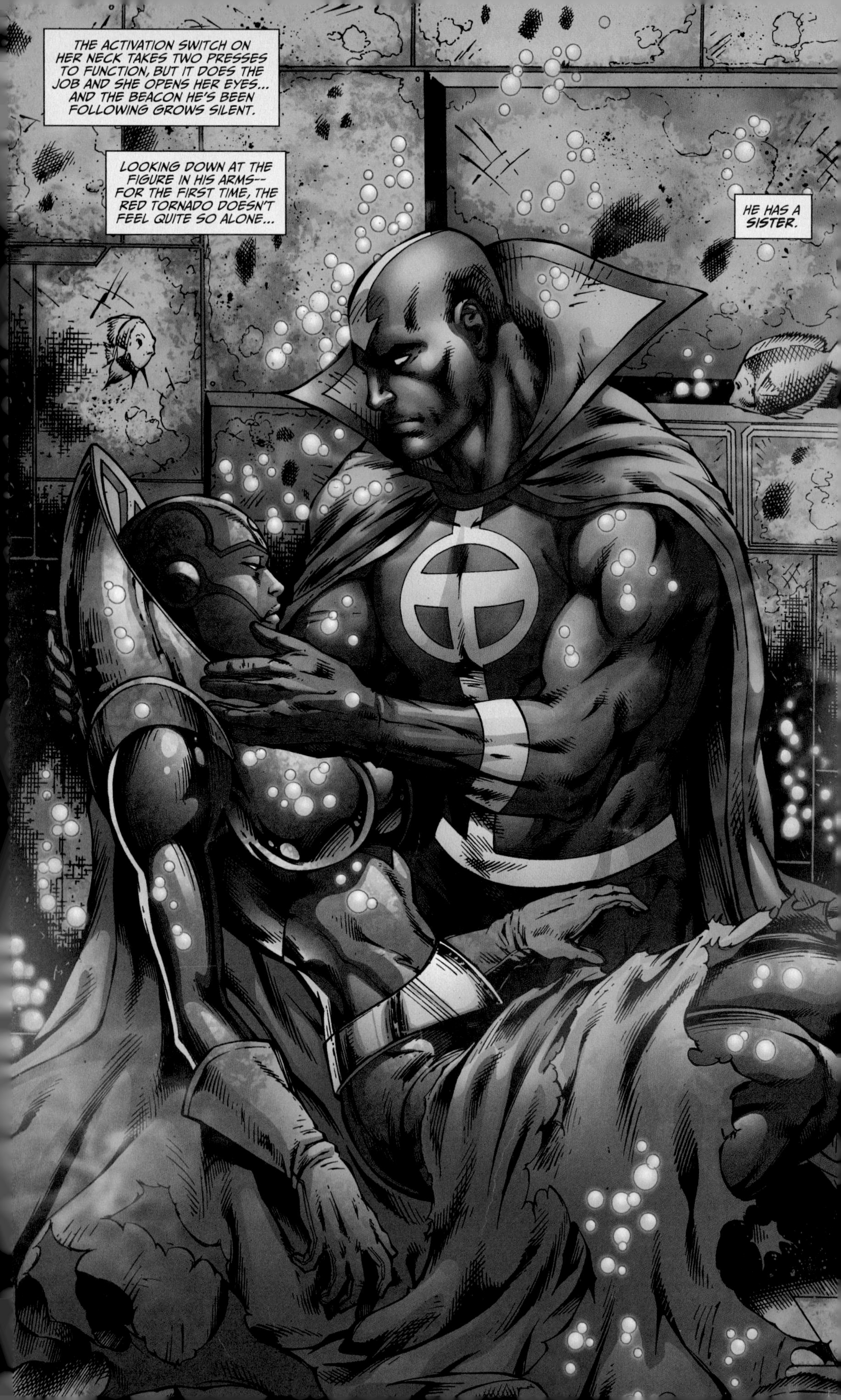
THE ACTIVATION SWITCH ON HER NECK TAKES TWO PRESSES TO FUNCTION, BUT IT DOES THE JOB AND SHE OPENS HER EYES... AND THE BEACON HE'S BEEN FOLLOWING GROWS SILENT.
LOOKING DOWN AT THE FIGURE IN HIS ARMS-- FOR THE FIRST TIME, THE RED TORNADO DOESN'T FEEL QUITE SO ALONE...
HE HAS A SISTER.

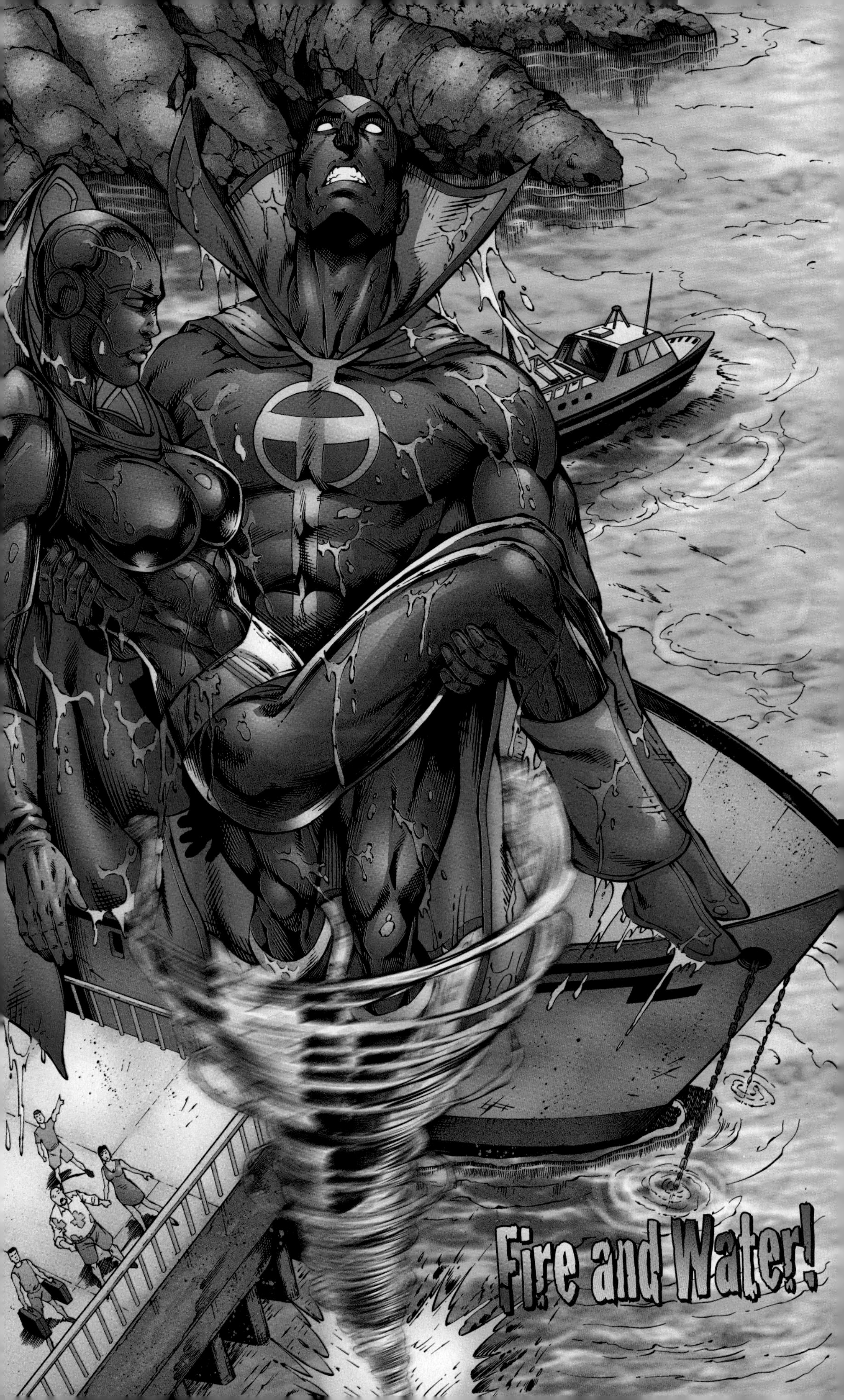
Fire and Water!

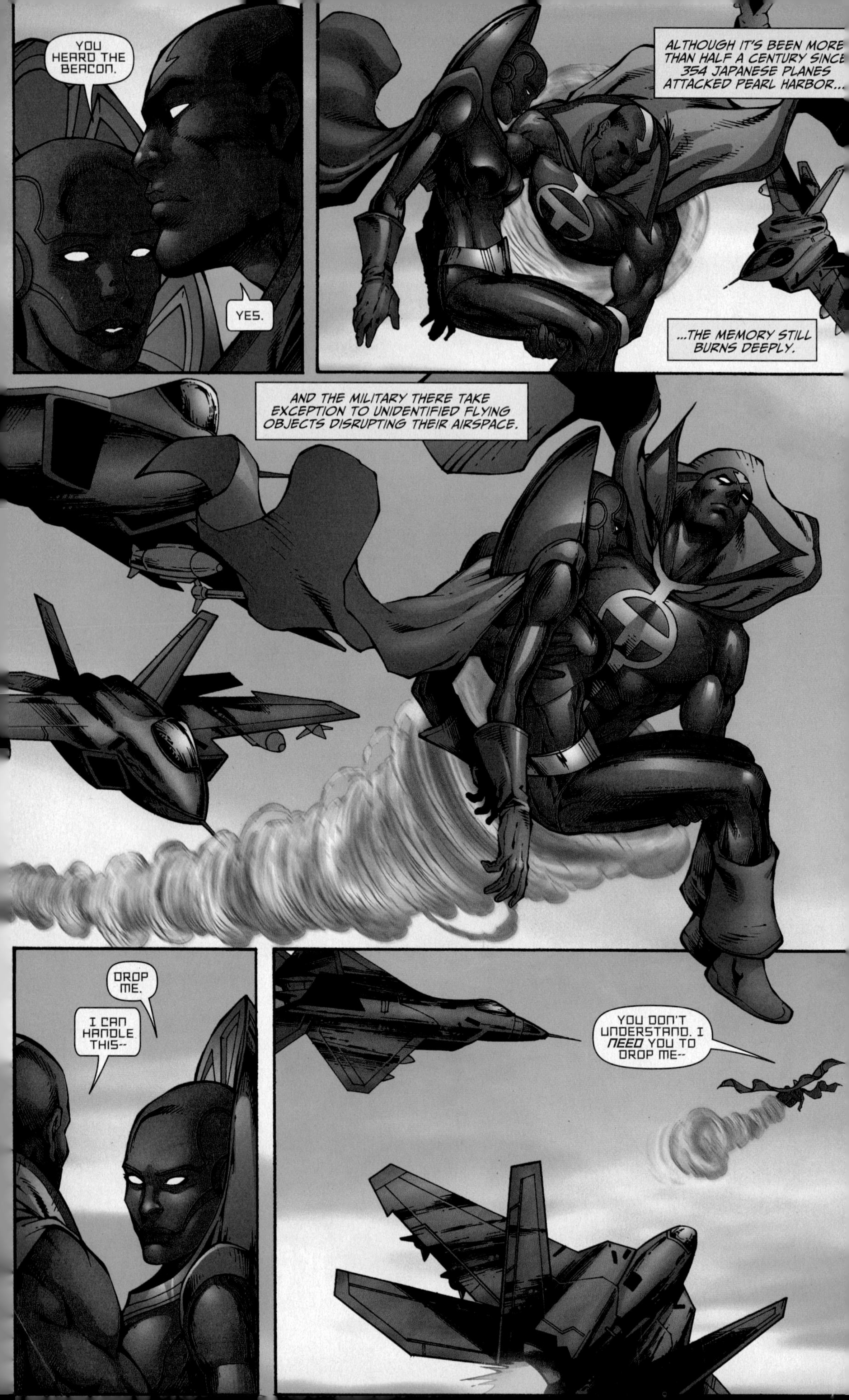
YOU HEARD THE BEACON.
YES.
ALTHOUGH IT'S BEEN MORE THAN HALF A CENTURY SINCE 354 JAPANESE PLANES ATTACKED PEARL HARBOR...
...THE MEMORY STILL BURNS DEEPLY.
AND THE MILITARY THERE TAKE EXCEPTION TO UNIDENTIFIED FLYING OBJECTS DISRUPTING THEIR AIRSPACE.
DROP ME.
I CAN HANDLE THIS--
YOU DON'T UNDERSTAND. I NEED YOU TO DROP ME--

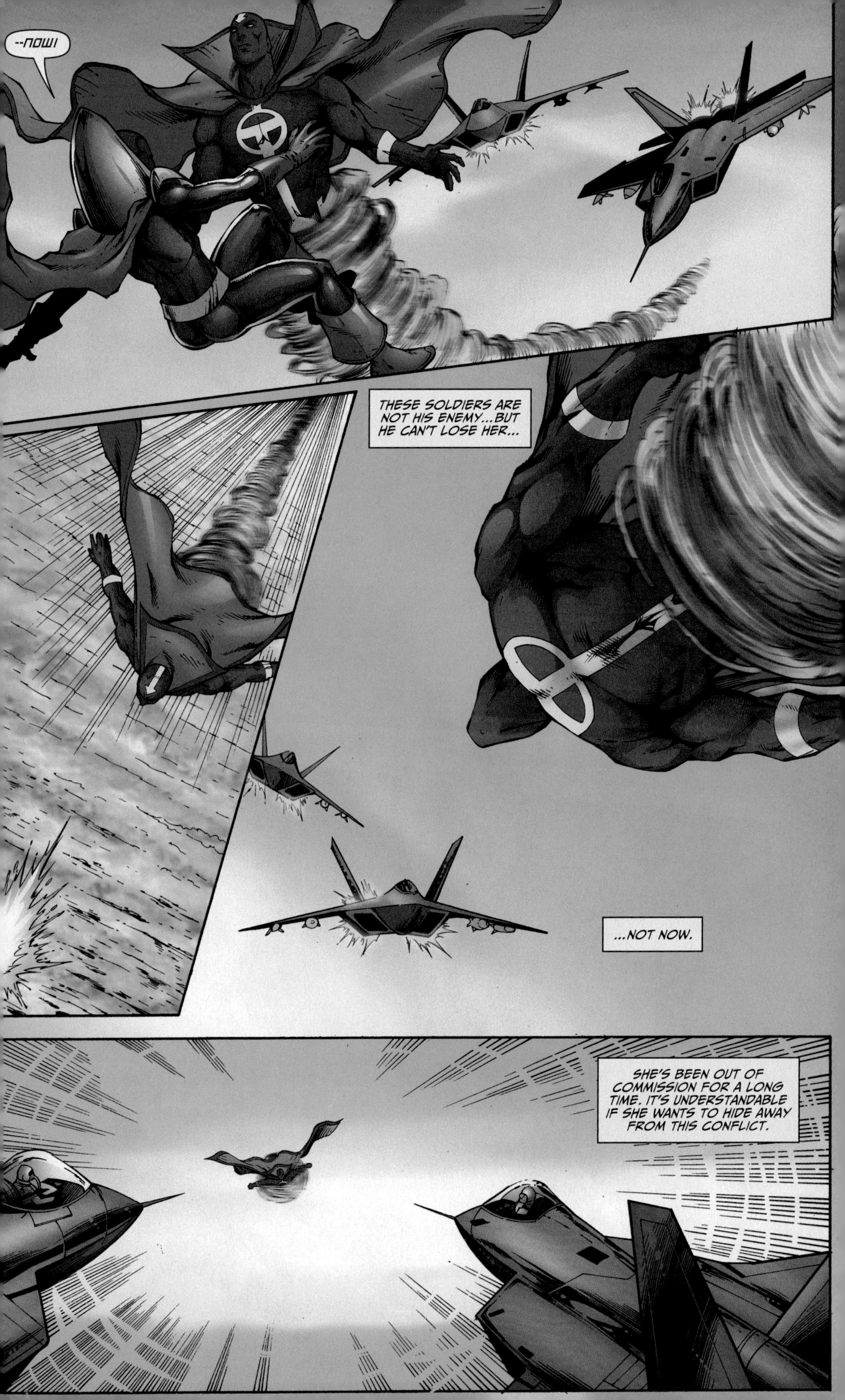
--NOW!
THESE SOLDIERS ARE NOT HIS ENEMY...BUT HE CAN'T LOSE HER...
...NOT NOW.
SHE'S BEEN OUT OF COMMISSION FOR A LONG TIME. IT'S UNDERSTANDABLE IF SHE WANTS TO HIDE AWAY FROM THIS CONFLICT.

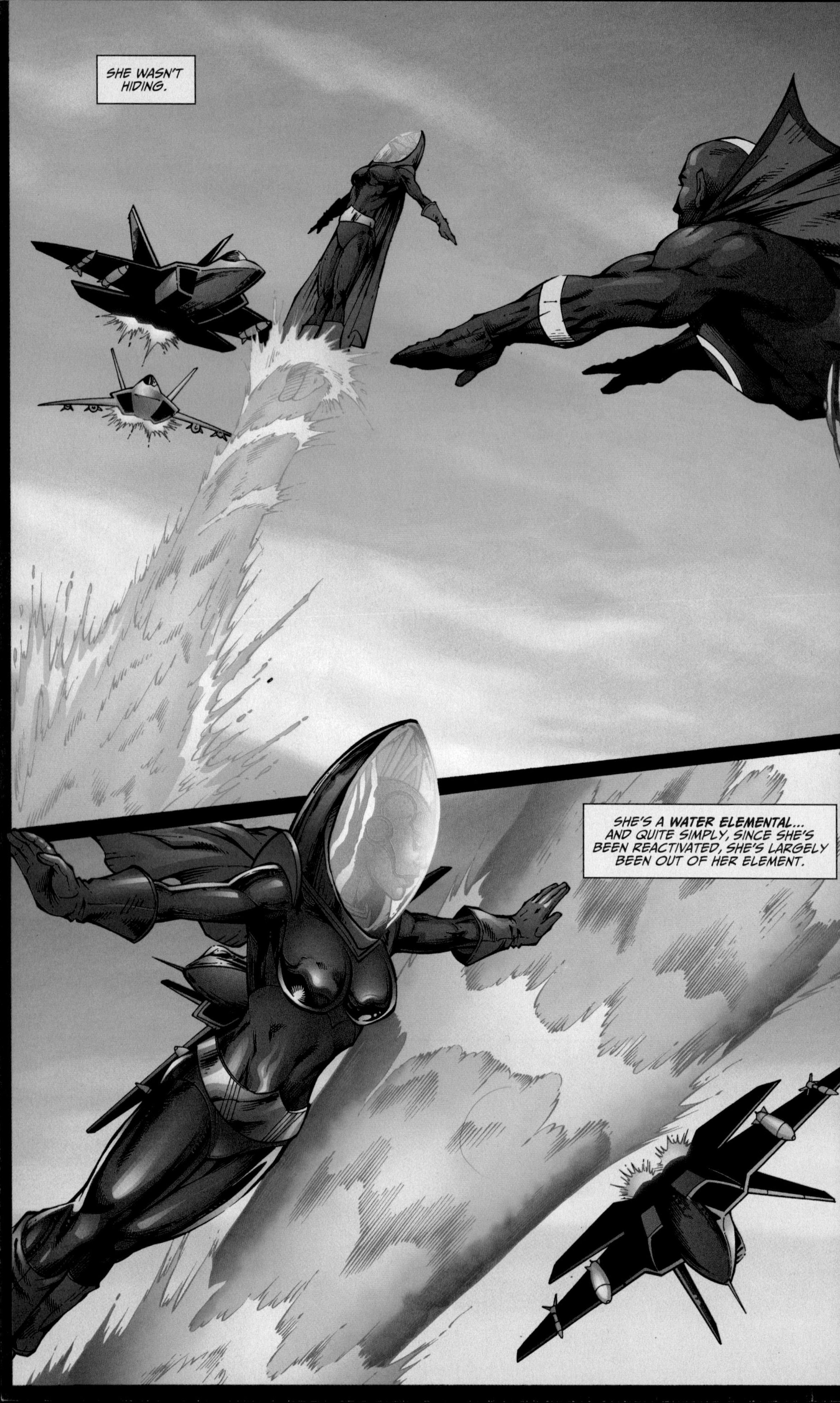
SHE WASN'T HIDING.
SHE'S A WATER ELEMENTAL... AND QUITE SIMPLY, SINCE SHE'S BEEN REACTIVATED, SHE'S LARGELY BEEN OUT OF HER ELEMENT.

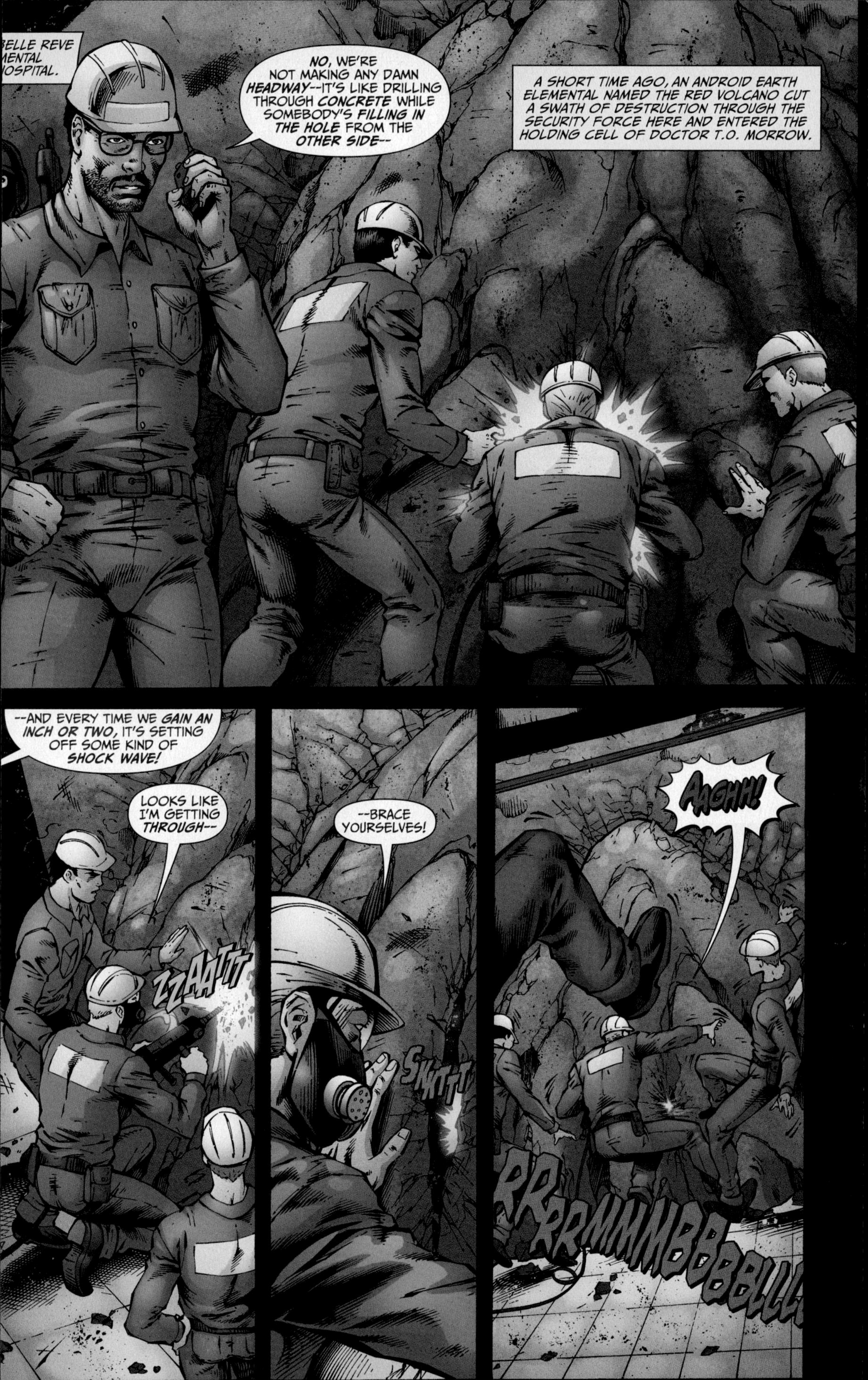
BELLE REVE
MENTAL
HOSPITAL.
NO, WE'RE NOT MAKING ANY DAMN HEADWAY--IT'S LIKE DRILLING THROUGH CONCRETE WHILE SOMEBODY'S FILLING IN THE HOLE FROM THE OTHER SIDE--
A SHORT TIME AGO, AN ANDROID EARTH ELEMENTAL NAMED THE RED VOLCANO CUT A SWATH OF DESTRUCTION THROUGH THE SECURITY FORCE HERE AND ENTERED THE HOLDING CELL OF DOCTOR T.O. MORROW.
--AND EVERY TIME WE GAIN AN INCH OR TWO, IT'S SETTING OFF SOME KIND OF SHOCK WAVE!
LOOKS LIKE I'M GETTING THROUGH--
ZZAATTT
--BRACE YOURSELVES!
SKATTT
AAGHH!
RRRRMMMBBBBLLL

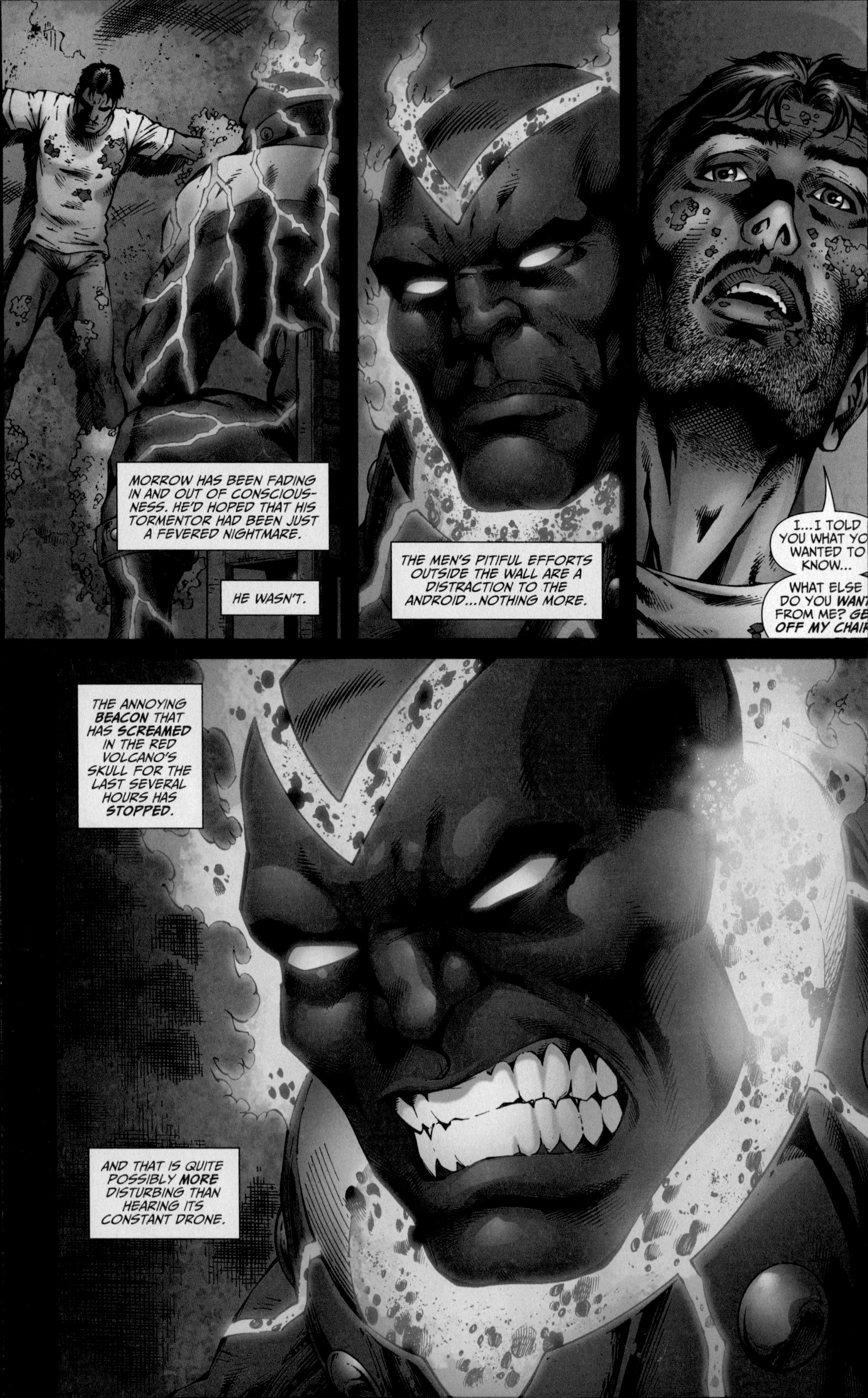
MORROW HAS BEEN FADING IN AND OUT OF CONSCIOUSNESS. HE'D HOPED THAT HIS TORMENTOR HAD BEEN JUST A FEVERED NIGHTMARE.
HE WASN'T.
THE MEN'S PITIFUL EFFORTS OUTSIDE THE WALL ARE A DISTRACTION TO THE ANDROID...NOTHING MORE.
I...I TOLD YOU WHAT YO WANTED TO KNOW...
WHAT ELSE DO YOU WANT FROM ME? GE OFF MY CHAIR
THE ANNOYING BEACON THAT HAS SCREAMED IN THE RED VOLCANO'S SKULL FOR THE LAST SEVERAL HOURS HAS STOPPED.
AND THAT IS QUITE POSSIBLY MORE DISTURBING THAN HEARING ITS CONSTANT DRONE.

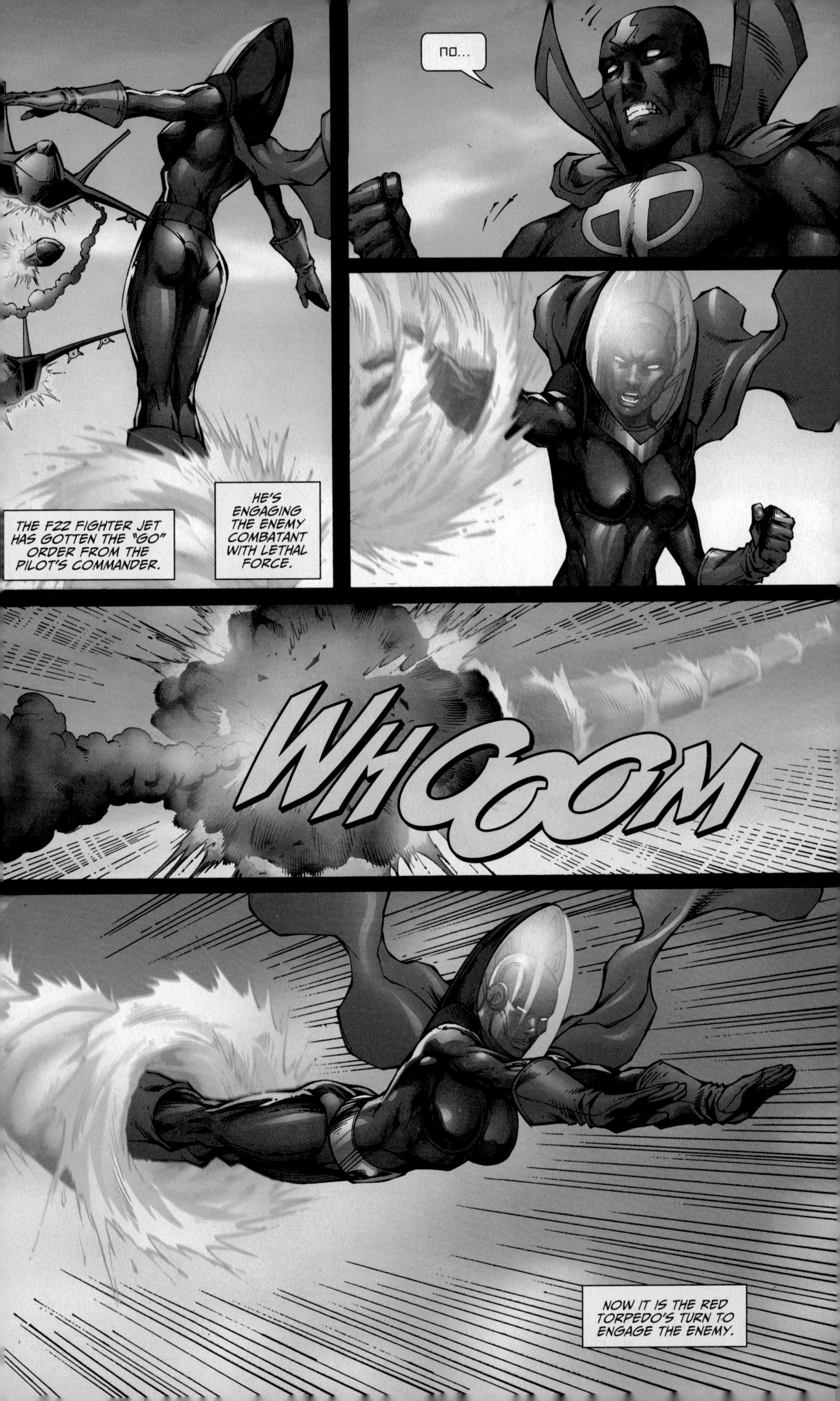
THE F22 FIGHTER JET HAS GOTTEN THE "GO" ORDER FROM THE PILOT'S COMMANDER.
HE'S ENGAGING THE ENEMY COMBATANT WITH LETHAL FORCE.
NO...
WHOOOOM
NOW IT IS THE RED TORPEDO'S TURN TO ENGAGE THE ENEMY.

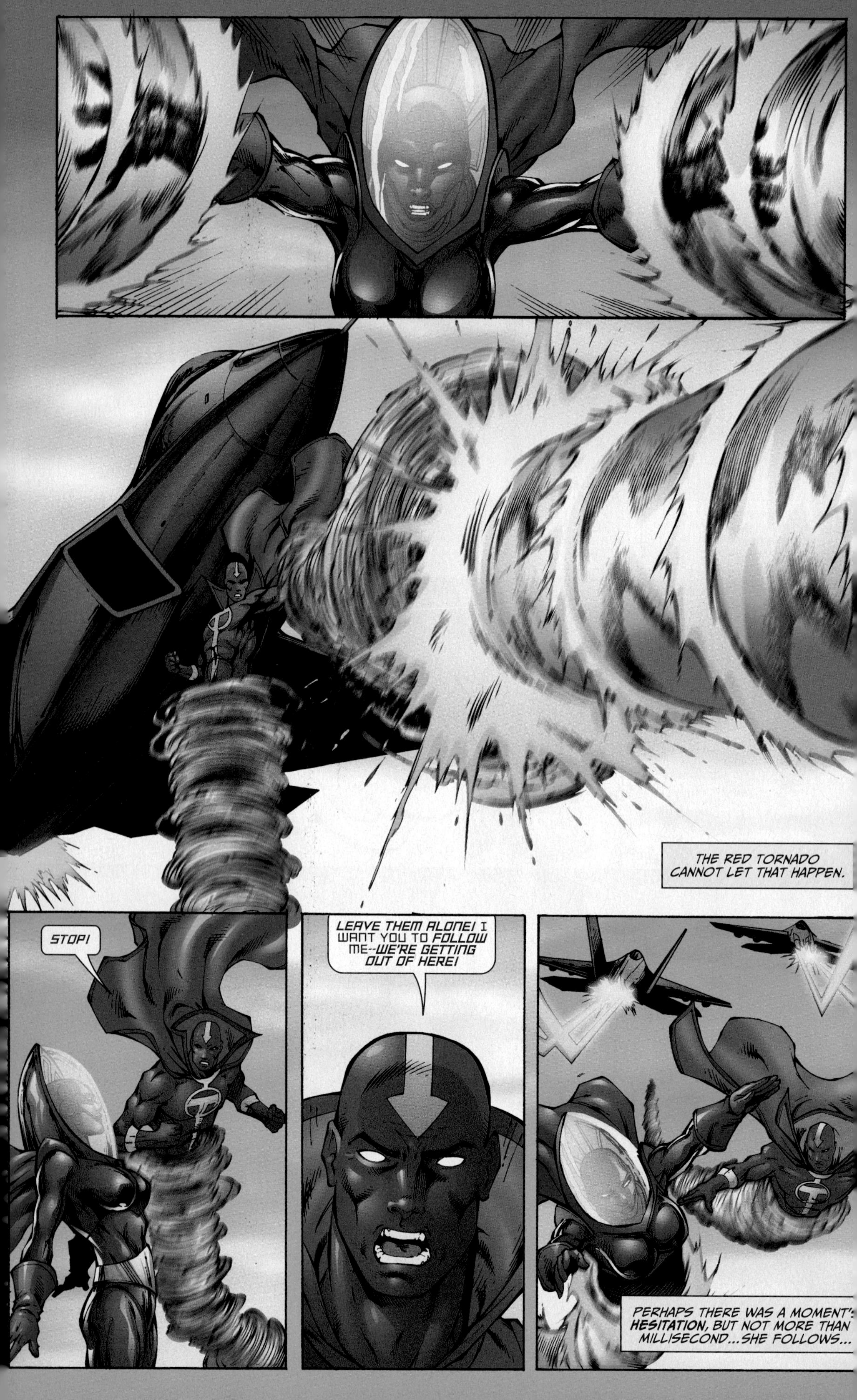
THE RED TORNADO CANNOT LET THAT HAPPEN.
STOP!
LEAVE THEM ALONE! I WANT YOU TO FOLLOW ME--WE'RE GETTING OUT OF HERE!
PERHAPS THERE WAS A MOMENT'S HESITATION, BUT NOT MORE THAN MILLISECOND...SHE FOLLOWS...

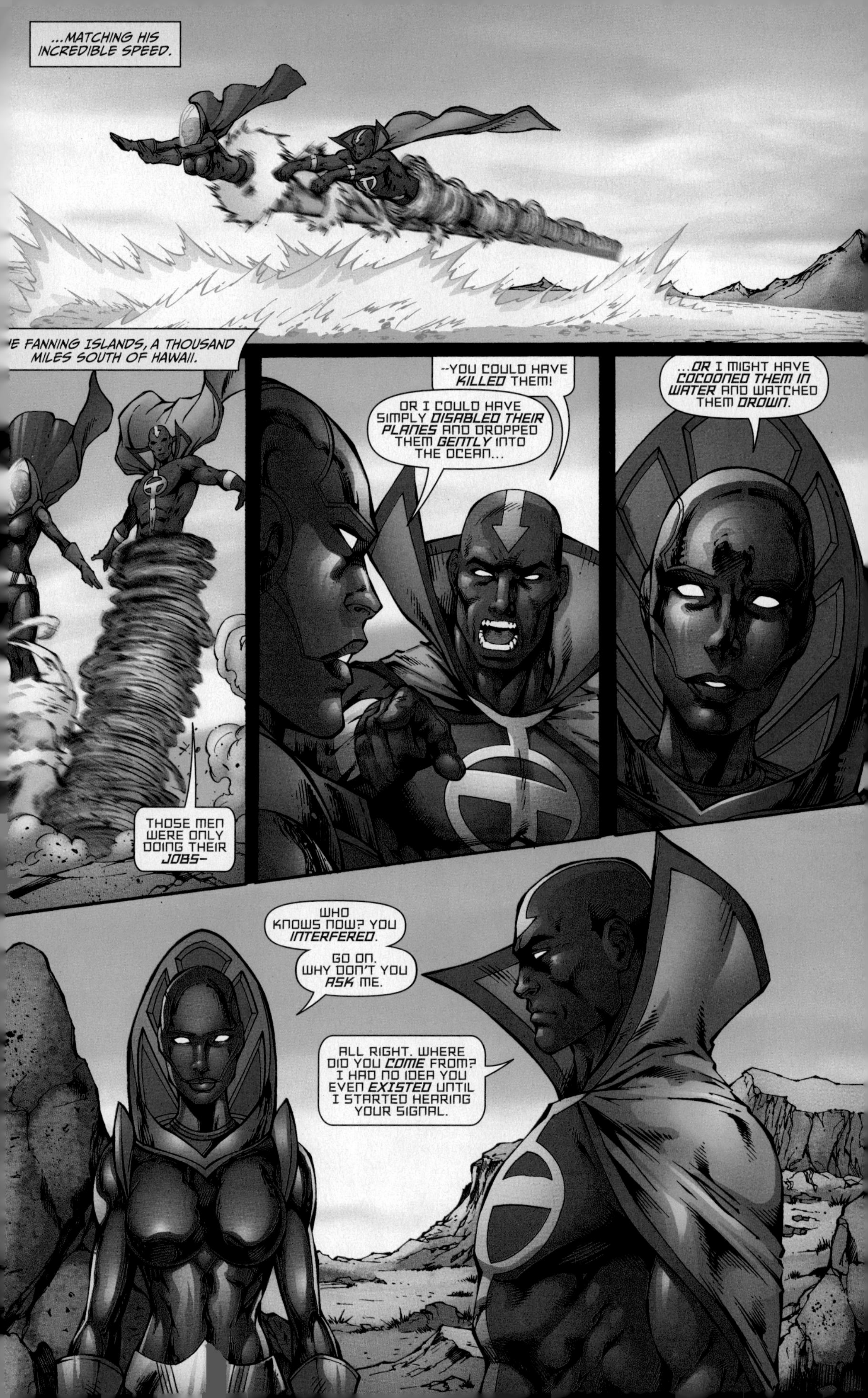
...MATCHING HIS INCREDIBLE SPEED.
E FANNING ISLANDS, A THOUSAND MILES SOUTH OF HAWAII.
THOSE MEN WERE ONLY DOING THEIR JOBS–
--YOU COULD HAVE KILLED THEM!
OR I COULD HAVE SIMPLY DISABLED THEIR PLANES AND DROPPED THEM GENTLY INTO THE OCEAN...
...OR I MIGHT HAVE COCOONED THEM IN WATER AND WATCHED THEM DROWN.
WHO KNOWS NOW? YOU INTERFERED.
GO ON. WHY DON'T YOU ASK ME.
ALL RIGHT. WHERE DID YOU COME FROM? I HAD NO IDEA YOU EVEN EXISTED UNTIL I STARTED HEARING YOUR SIGNAL.

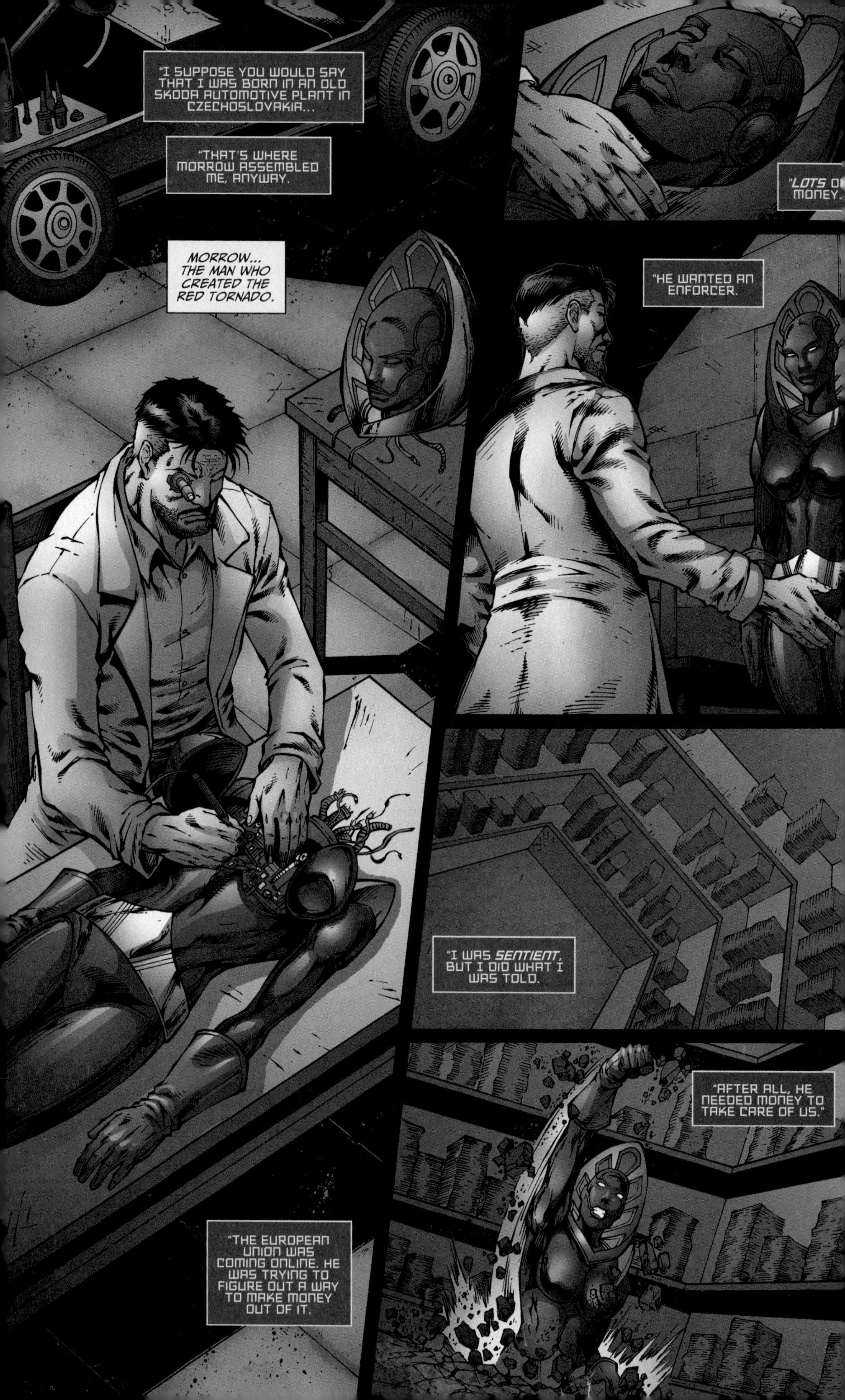
"I SUPPOSE YOU WOULD SAY THAT I WAS BORN IN AN OLD SKODA AUTOMOTIVE PLANT IN CZECHOSLOVAKIA...
"THAT'S WHERE MORROW ASSEMBLED ME, ANYWAY.
MORROW... THE MAN WHO CREATED THE RED TORNADO.
"THE EUROPEAN UNION WAS COMING ONLINE. HE WAS TRYING TO FIGURE OUT A WAY TO MAKE MONEY OUT OF IT.
"LOTS O
MONEY.
"HE WANTED AN ENFORCER.
"I WAS SENTIENT, BUT I DID WHAT I WAS TOLD.
"AFTER ALL, HE NEEDED MONEY TO TAKE CARE OF US."

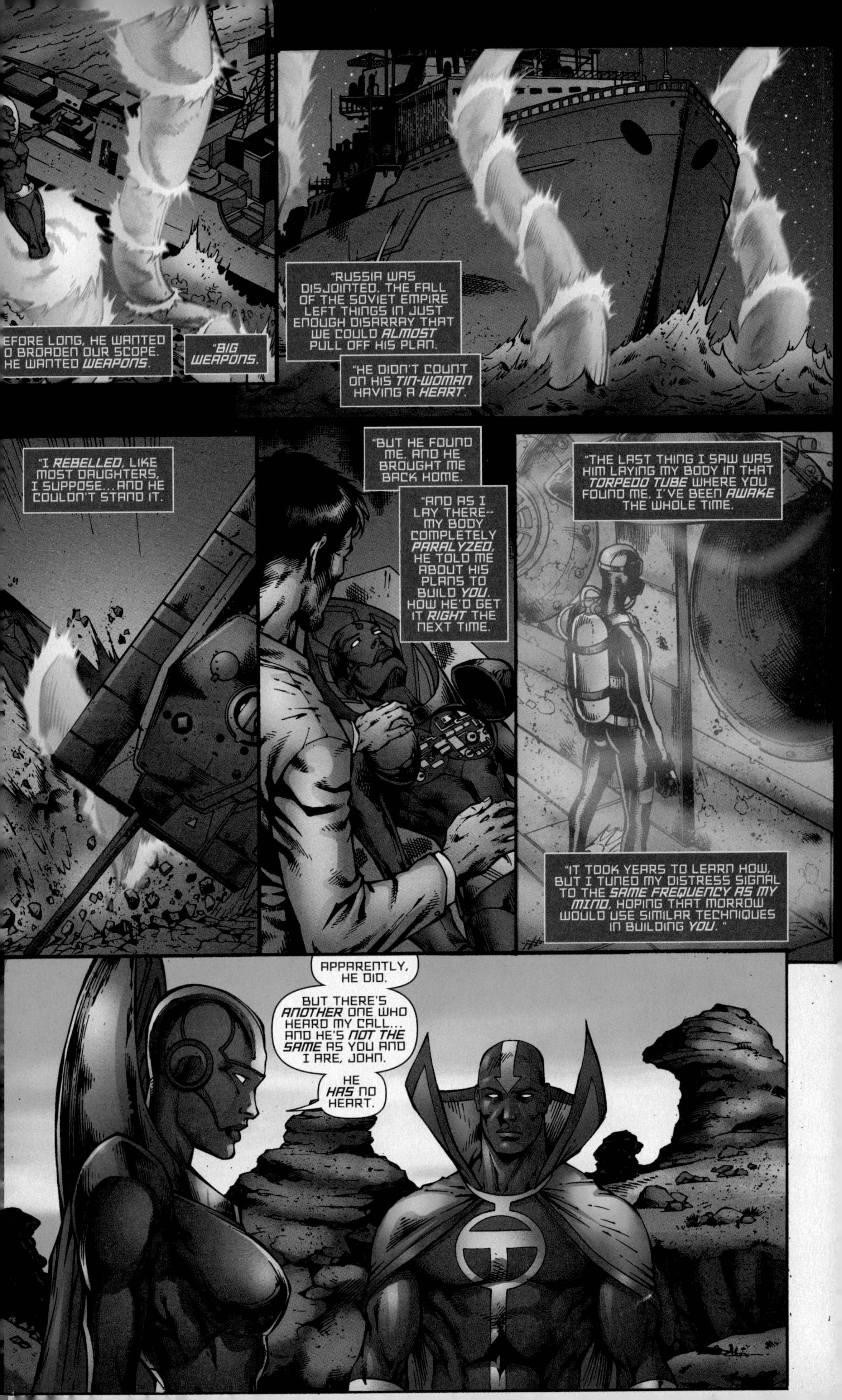

EFORE LONG, HE WANTED O BROADEN OUR SCOPE. HE WANTED WEAPONS.
"BIG WEAPONS.
"RUSSIA WAS DISJOINTED. THE FALL OF THE SOVIET EMPIRE LEFT THINGS IN JUST ENOUGH DISARRAY THAT WE COULD ALMOST PULL OFF HIS PLAN.
"HE DIDN'T COUNT ON HIS TIN-WOMAN HAVING A HEART.
"I REBELLED, LIKE MOST DAUGHTERS, I SUPPOSE... AND HE COULDN'T STAND IT.
"BUT HE FOUND ME. AND HE BROUGHT ME BACK HOME.
"AND AS I LAY THERE-- MY BODY COMPLETELY PARALYZED, HE TOLD ME ABOUT HIS PLANS TO BUILD YOU. HOW HE'D GET IT RIGHT THE NEXT TIME.
"THE LAST THING I SAW WAS HIM LAYING MY BODY IN THAT TORPEDO TUBE WHERE YOU FOUND ME. I'VE BEEN AWAKE THE WHOLE TIME.
"IT TOOK YEARS TO LEARN HOW, BUT I TUNED MY DISTRESS SIGNAL TO THE SAME FREQUENCY AS MY MIND, HOPING THAT MORROW WOULD USE SIMILAR TECHNIQUES IN BUILDING YOU."
APPARENTLY, HE DID.
BUT THERE'S ANOTHER ONE WHO HEARD MY CALL... AND HE'S NOT THE SAME AS YOU AND I ARE, JOHN.
HE HAS NO HEART.

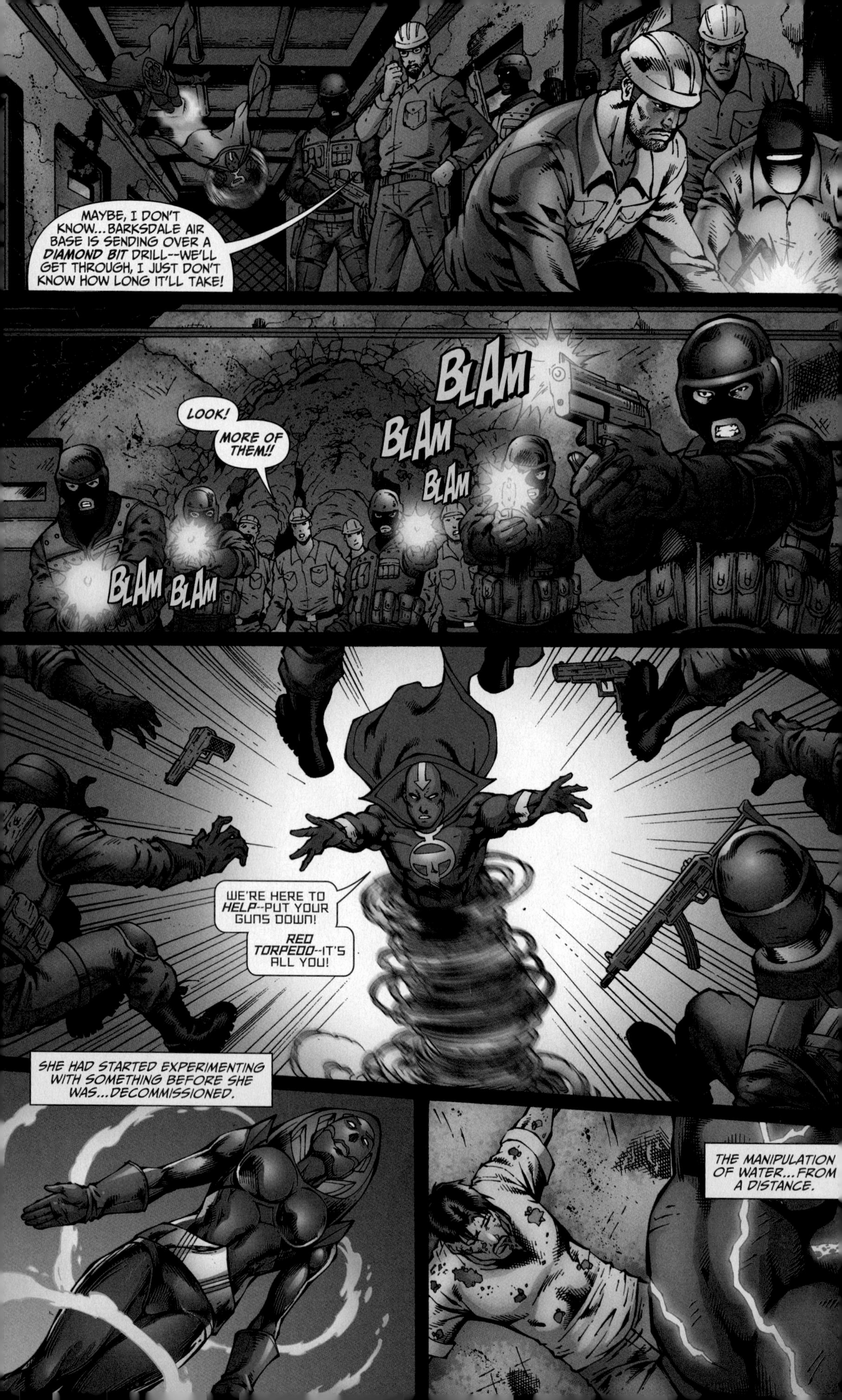
MAYBE, I DON'T KNOW...BARKSDALE AIR BASE IS SENDING OVER A DIAMOND BIT DRILL--WE'LL GET THROUGH, I JUST DON'T KNOW HOW LONG IT'LL TAKE!
LOOK!
MORE OF THEM!!
BLAM
BLAM
BLAM
BLAM BLAM
WE'RE HERE TO HELP--PUT YOUR GUNS DOWN!
RED TORPEDO--IT'S ALL YOU!
SHE HAD STARTED EXPERIMENTING WITH SOMETHING BEFORE SHE WAS...DECOMMISSIONED.
THE MANIPULATION OF WATER...FROM A DISTANCE.

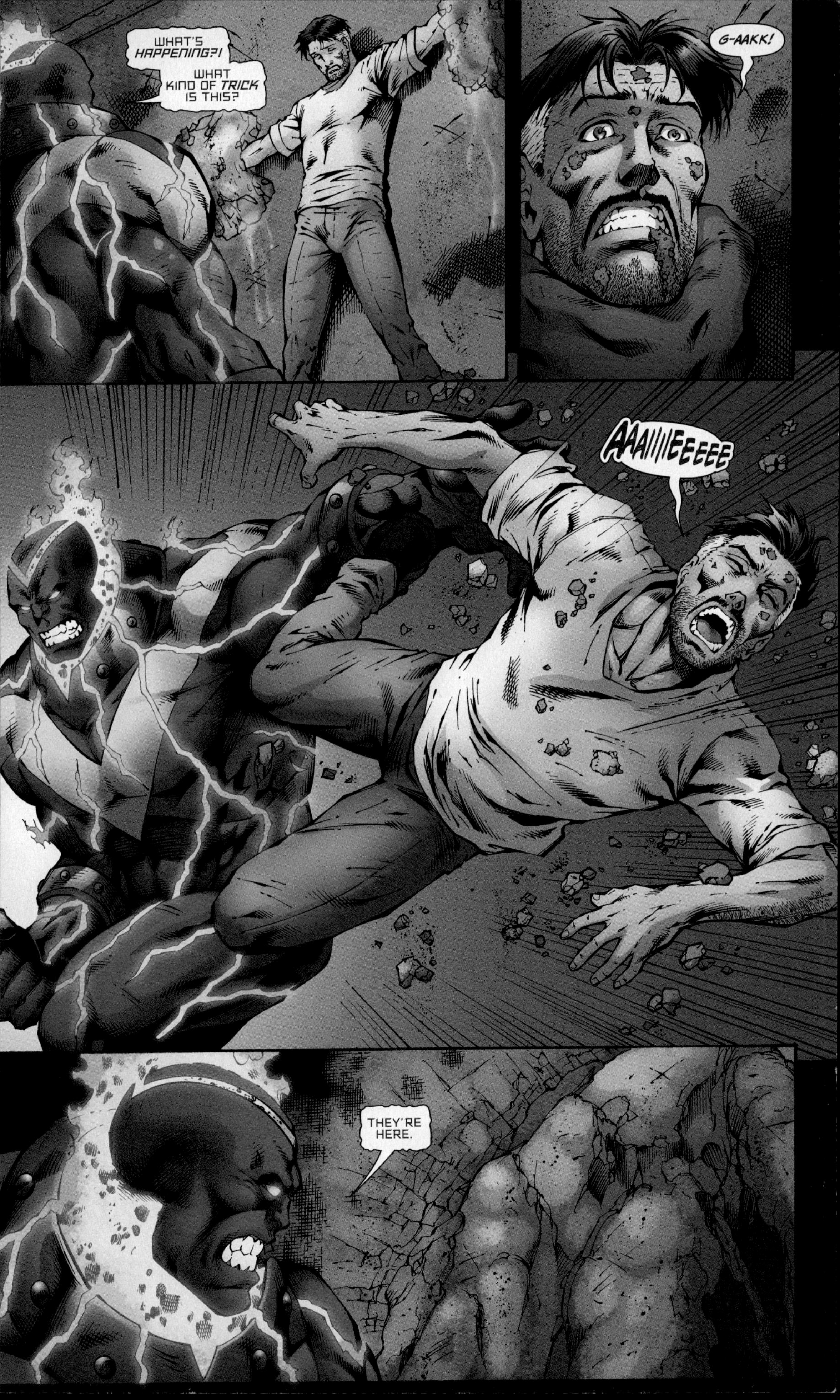
WHAT'S HAPPENING?! WHAT KIND OF TRICK IS THIS?
G-AAKK!
AAAIIIIEEEEE
THEY'RE HERE.

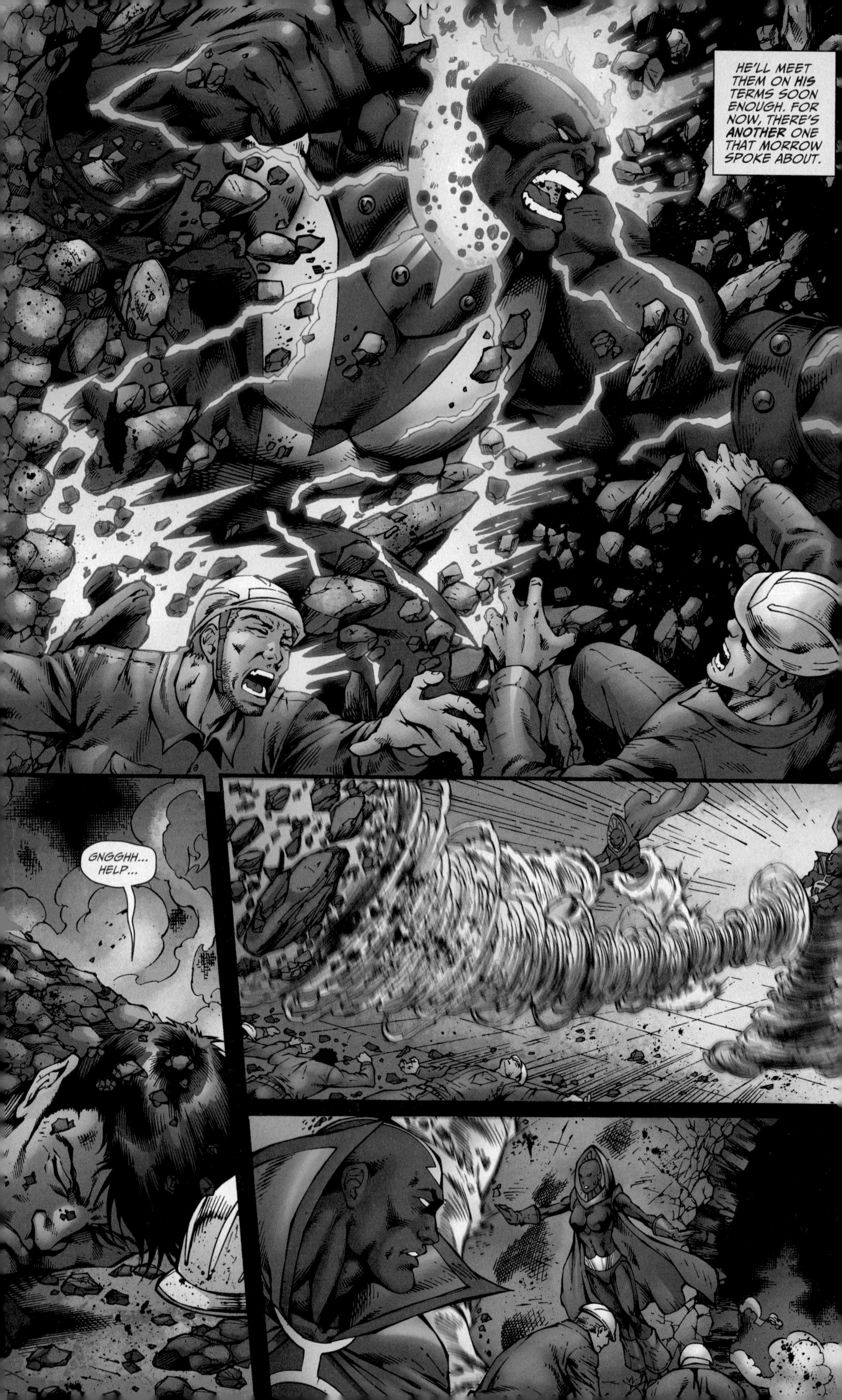
HE'LL MEET THEM ON HIS TERMS SOON ENOUGH. FOR NOW, THERE'S ANOTHER ONE THAT MORROW SPOKE ABOUT.
GNGGHH... HELP...

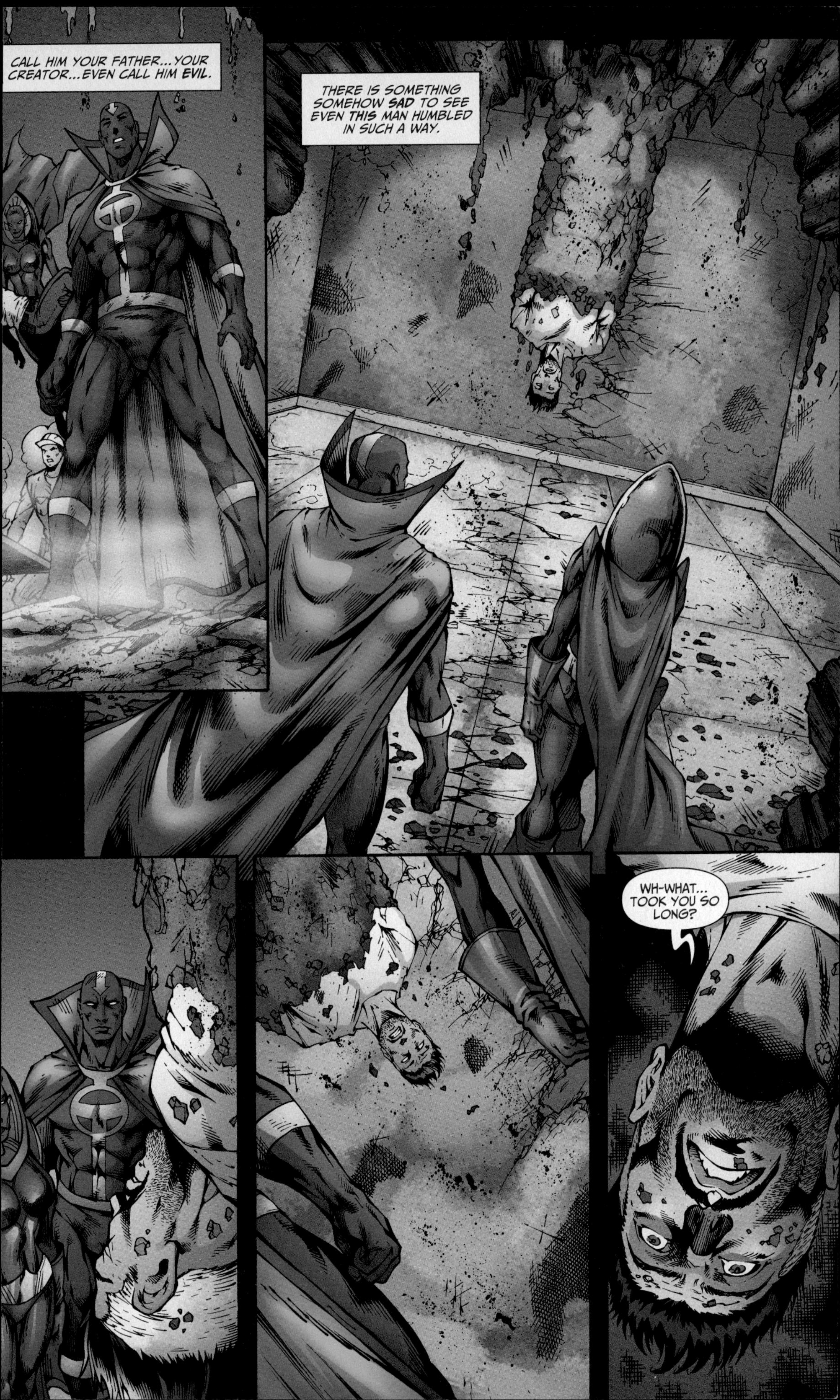
CALL HIM YOUR FATHER... YOUR CREATOR... EVEN CALL HIM EVIL.
THERE IS SOMETHING SOMEHOW SAD TO SEE EVEN THIS MAN HUMBLED IN SUCH A WAY.
WH-WHAT... TOOK YOU SO LONG?

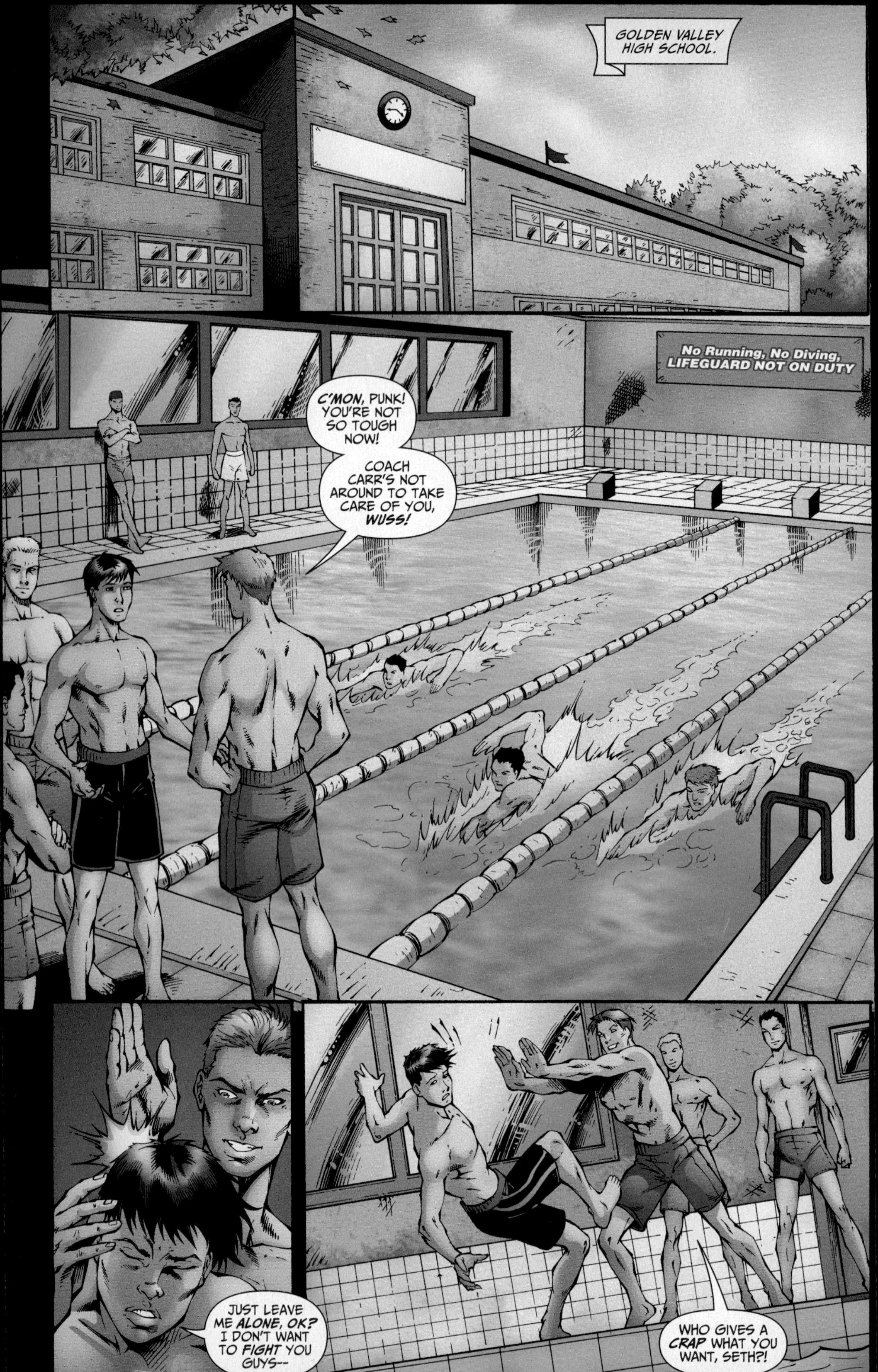
GOLDEN VALLEY HIGH SCHOOL.
No Running, No Diving, LIFEGUARD NOT ON DUTY
C'MON, PUNK! YOU'RE NOT SO TOUGH NOW!
COACH CARR'S NOT AROUND TO TAKE CARE OF YOU, WUSS!
JUST LEAVE ME ALONE, OK? I DON'T WANT TO FIGHT YOU GUYS--
WHO GIVES A CRAP WHAT YOU WANT, SETH?!

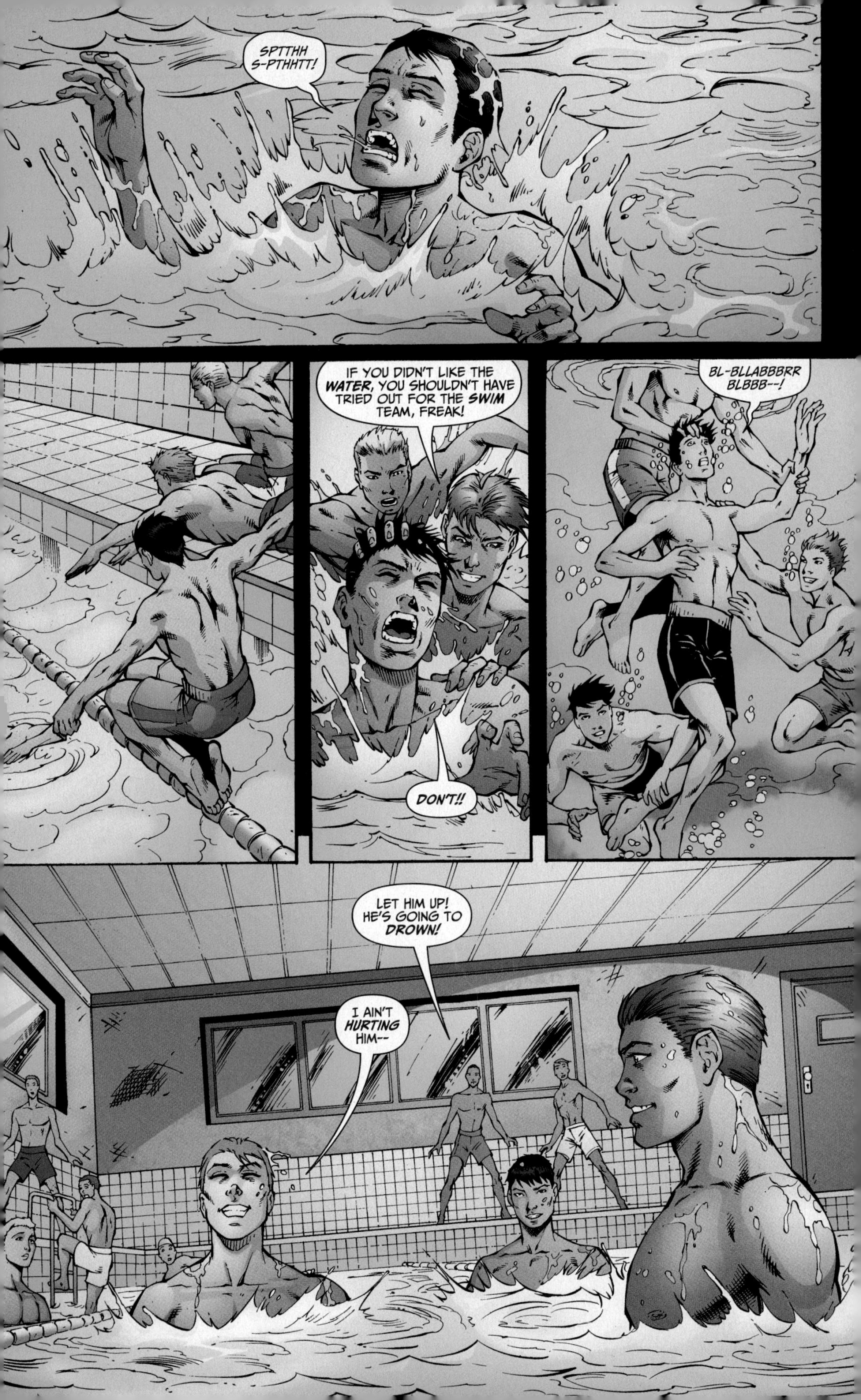
SPTTHH S-PTHHTT!
IF YOU DIDN'T LIKE THE WATER, YOU SHOULDN'T HAVE TRIED OUT FOR THE SWIM TEAM, FREAK!
DON'T!!
BL-BLLABBBRR BLBBB--!
LET HIM UP! HE'S GOING TO DROWN!
I AIN'T HURTING HIM--

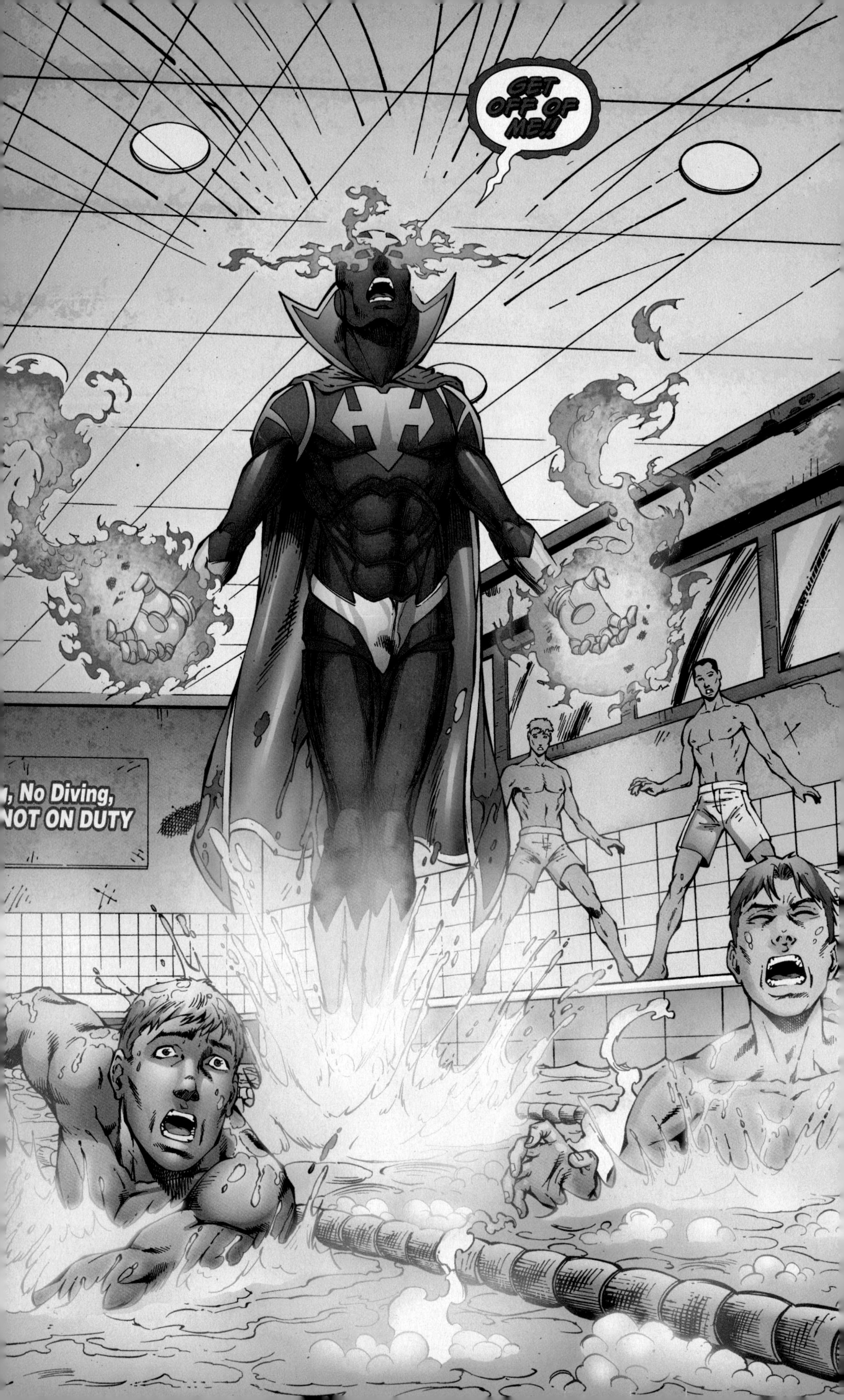
GET OFF OF ME!!
, No Diving,
NOT ON DUTY

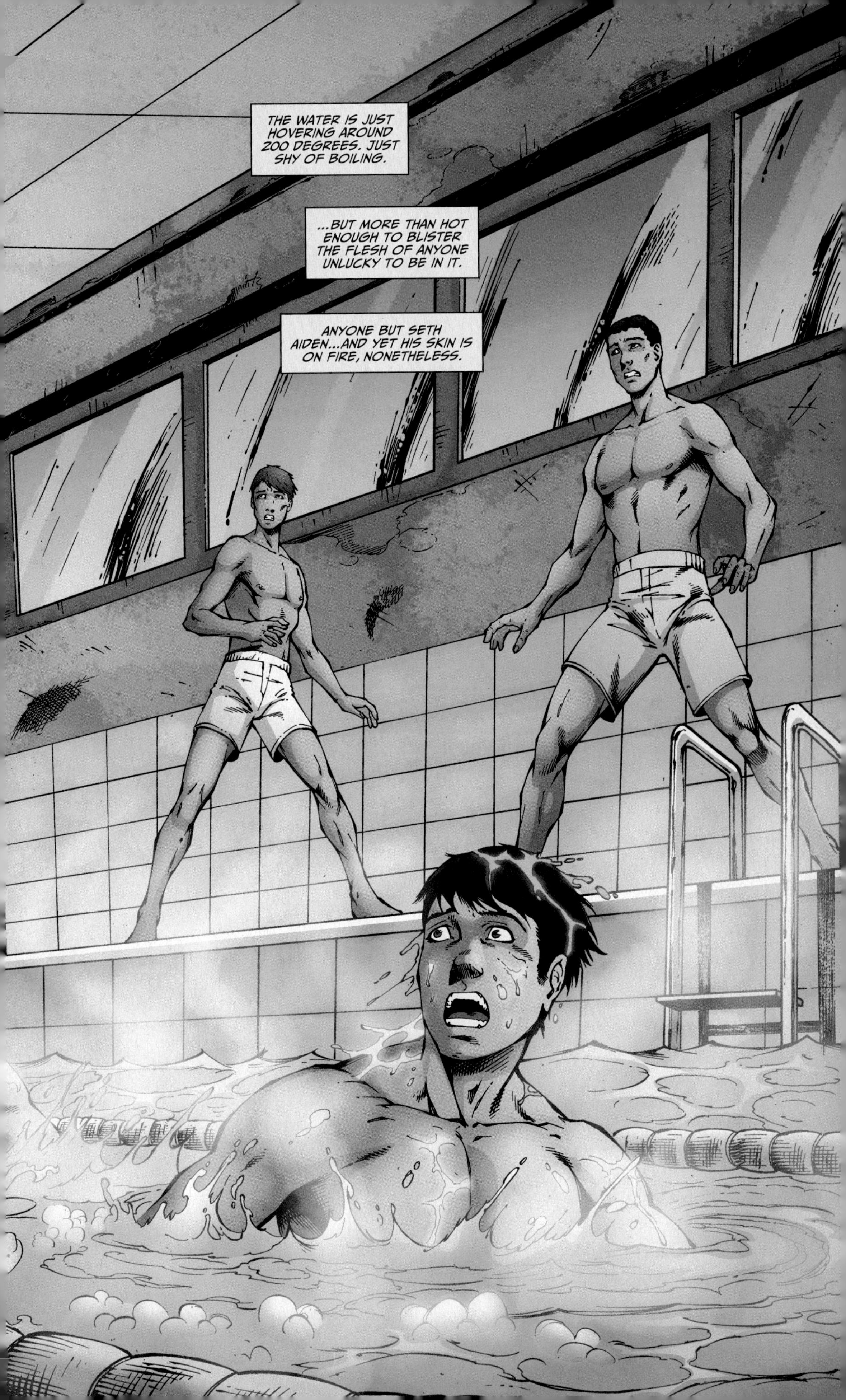
THE WATER IS JUST HOVERING AROUND 200 DEGREES. JUST SHY OF BOILING.
...BUT MORE THAN HOT ENOUGH TO BLISTER THE FLESH OF ANYONE UNLUCKY TO BE IN IT.
ANYONE BUT SETH AIDEN...AND YET HIS SKIN IS ON FIRE, NONETHELESS.

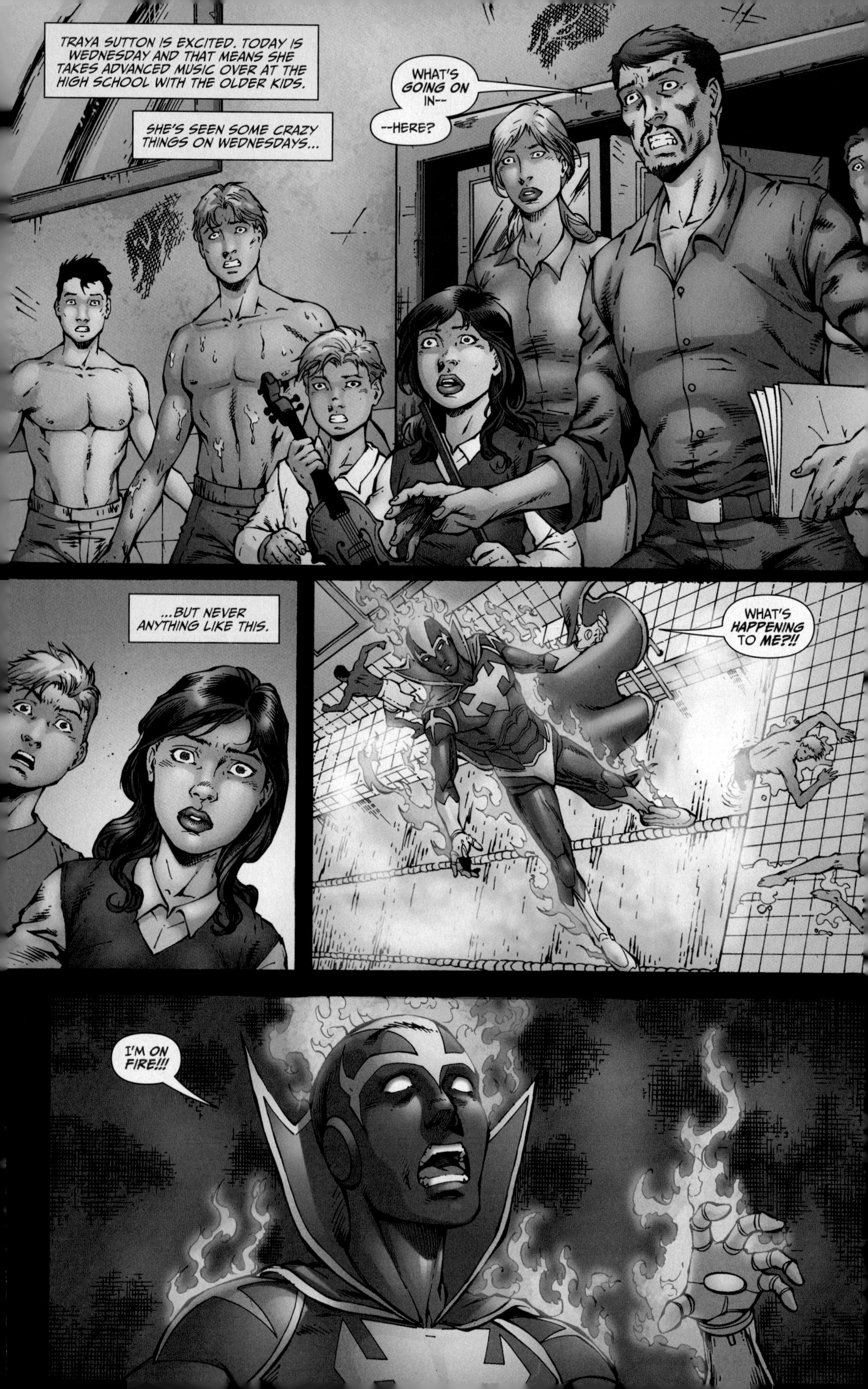
TRAYA SUTTON IS EXCITED. TODAY IS WEDNESDAY AND THAT MEANS SHE TAKES ADVANCED MUSIC OVER AT THE HIGH SCHOOL WITH THE OLDER KIDS.
SHE'S SEEN SOME CRAZY THINGS ON WEDNESDAYS...
WHAT'S GOING ON IN--
--HERE?
...BUT NEVER ANYTHING LIKE THIS.
WHAT'S HAPPENING TO ME?!!
I'M ON FIRE!!!

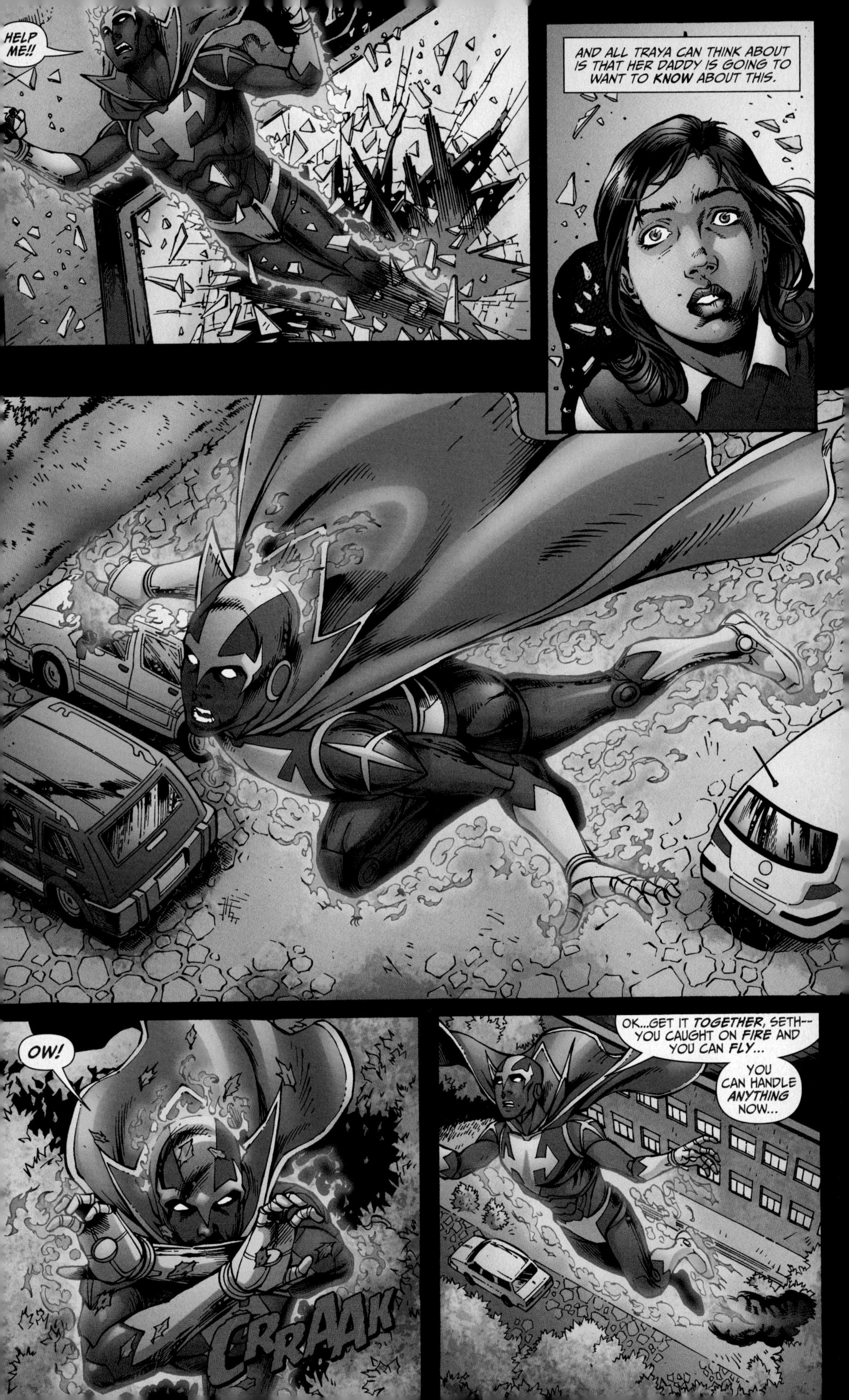
HELP ME!!
AND ALL TRAYA CAN THINK ABOUT IS THAT HER DADDY IS GOING TO WANT TO KNOW ABOUT THIS.
OW!
CRRAAK
OK...GET IT TOGETHER, SETH-- YOU CAUGHT ON FIRE AND YOU CAN FLY...
YOU CAN HANDLE ANYTHING NOW...

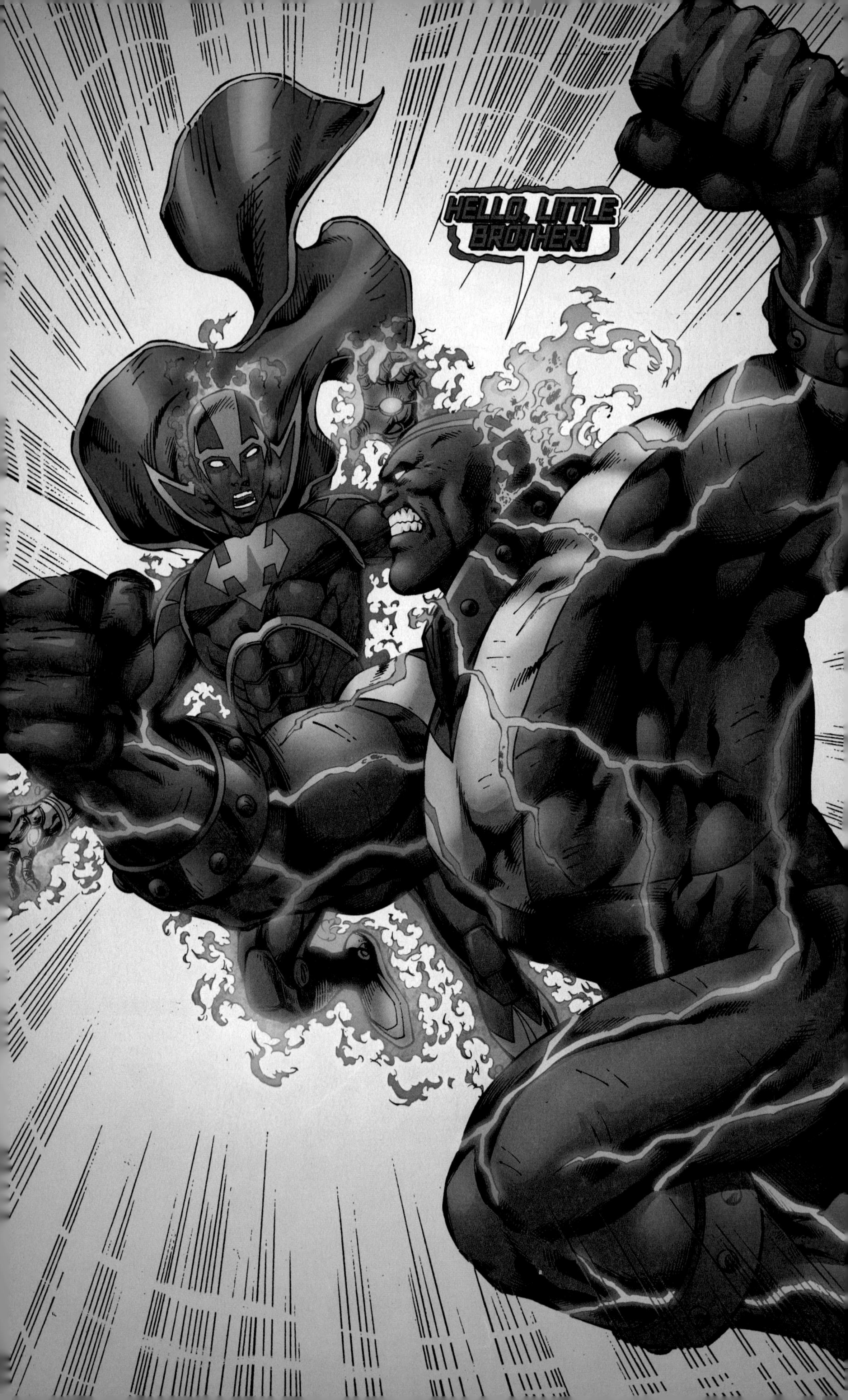
HELLO, LITTLE BROTHER!

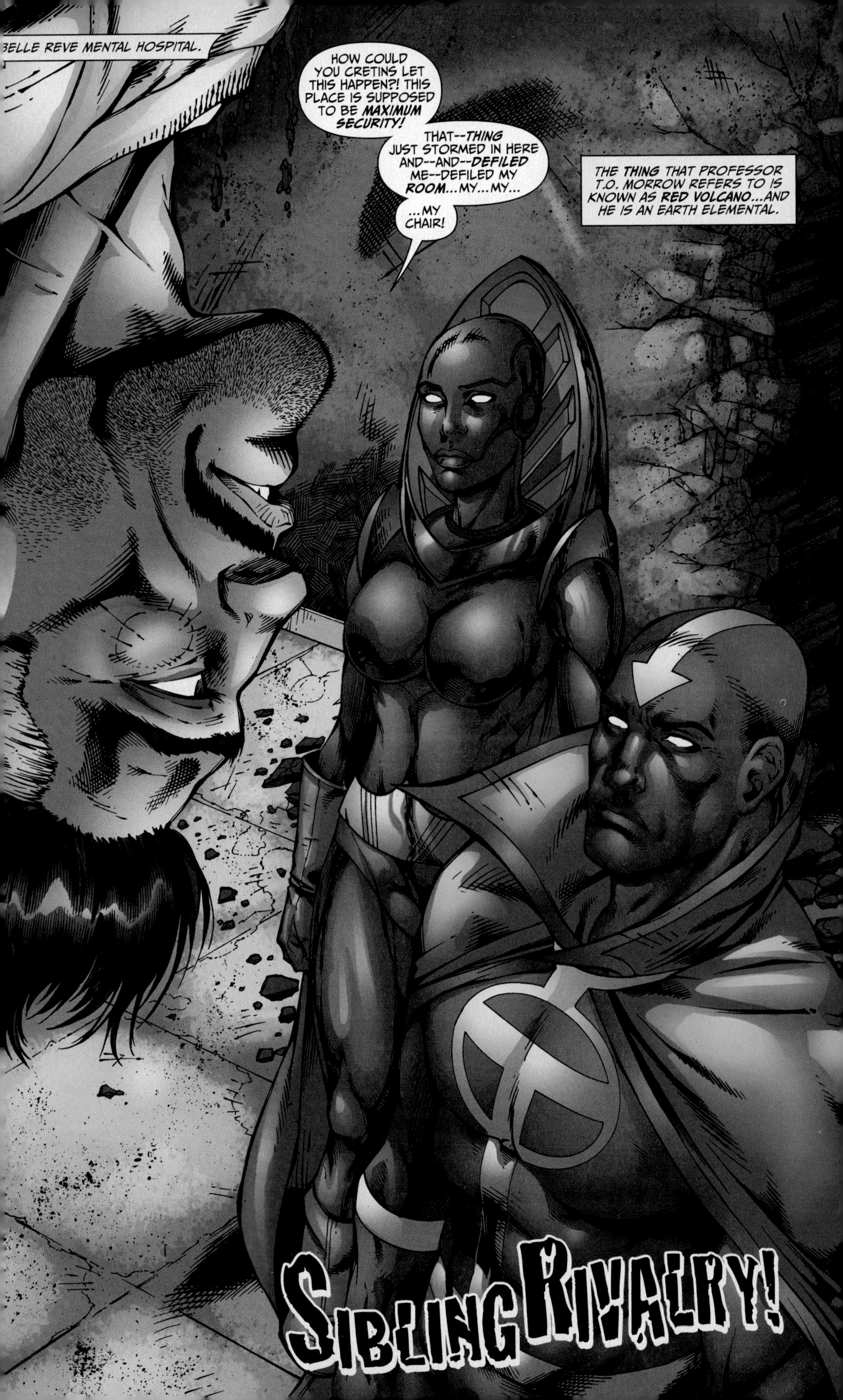

BELLE REVE MENTAL HOSPITAL.
HOW COULD YOU CRETINS LET THIS HAPPEN?! THIS PLACE IS SUPPOSED TO BE MAXIMUM SECURITY!
THAT--THING JUST STORMED IN HERE AND--AND--DEFILED ME--DEFILED MY ROOM...MY...MY...
...MY CHAIR!
THE THING THAT PROFESSOR T.O. MORROW REFERS TO IS KNOWN AS RED VOLCANO...AND HE IS AN EARTH ELEMENTAL.
SIBLING RIVALRY!

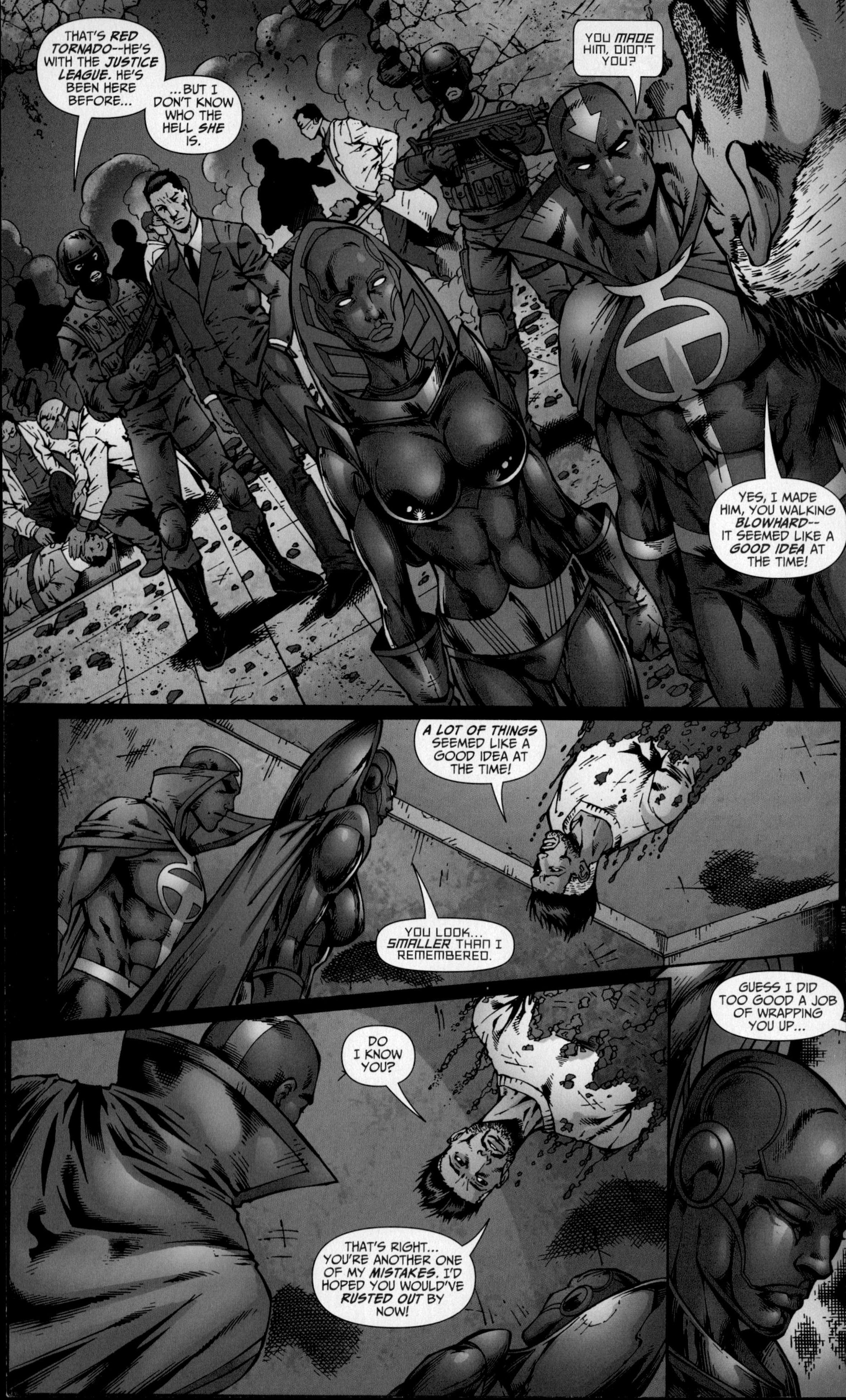
THAT'S RED TORNADO--HE'S WITH THE JUSTICE LEAGUE. HE'S BEEN HERE BEFORE...
...BUT I DON'T KNOW WHO THE HELL SHE IS.
YOU MADE HIM, DIDN'T YOU?
YES, I MADE HIM, YOU WALKING BLOWHARD-- IT SEEMED LIKE A GOOD IDEA AT THE TIME!
A LOT OF THINGS SEEMED LIKE A GOOD IDEA AT THE TIME!
YOU LOOK... SMALLER THAN I REMEMBERED.
DO I KNOW YOU?
THAT'S RIGHT... YOU'RE ANOTHER ONE OF MY MISTAKES. I'D HOPED YOU WOULD'VE RUSTED OUT BY NOW!
GUESS I DID TOO GOOD A JOB OF WRAPPING YOU UP...

WHAT'S HAPPENING?!

NGNNNGH-- MY HEAD IS POUNDING!

SNIFF... SPPTHH I'M BLEEDING!

Y HEAD!! NNNAAHHH!

...AND RIGHT NOW SHE'S ENJOYING TORMENTING HER CREATOR AS SHE SUCKS THE MOISTURE FROM HIS BODY.

YOU'RE THE GENIUS, T.O. MORROW...WHAT PERCENTAGE OF THE HUMAN BODY IS MADE UP...

...OF WATER?

NNNGGHH!!

AAAGHHH!

TORPEDO...

THE RED TORPEDO IS A WATER ELEMENTAL...

STOP IT!

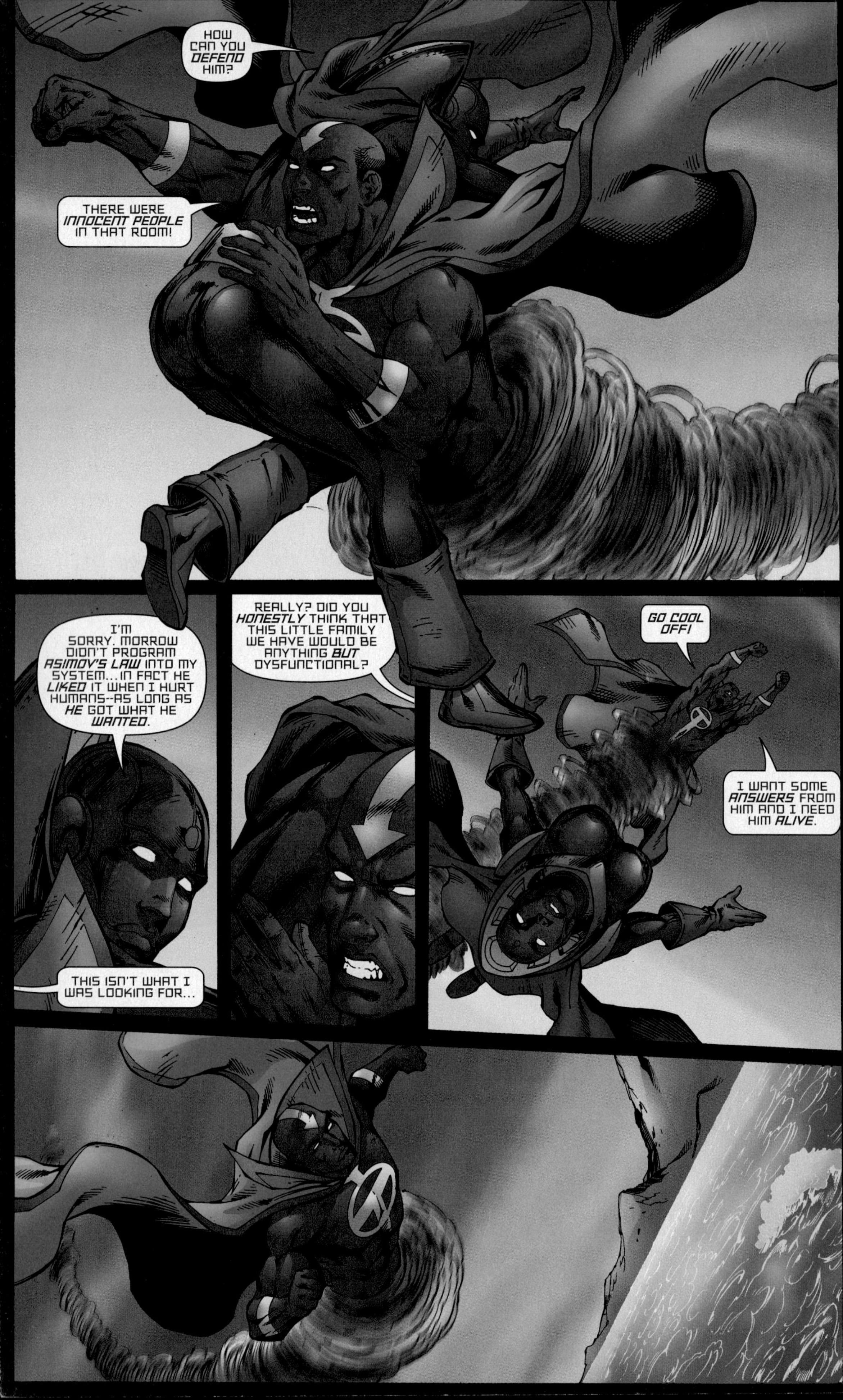

HOW CAN YOU DEFEND HIM?
THERE WERE INNOCENT PEOPLE IN THAT ROOM!
I'M SORRY. MORROW DIDN'T PROGRAM ASIMOV'S LAW INTO MY SYSTEM... IN FACT HE LIKED IT WHEN I HURT HUMANS--AS LONG AS HE GOT WHAT HE WANTED.
THIS ISN'T WHAT I WAS LOOKING FOR...
REALLY? DID YOU HONESTLY THINK THAT THIS LITTLE FAMILY WE HAVE WOULD BE ANYTHING BUT DYSFUNCTIONAL?
GO COOL OFF!
I WANT SOME ANSWERS FROM HIM AND I NEED HIM ALIVE.

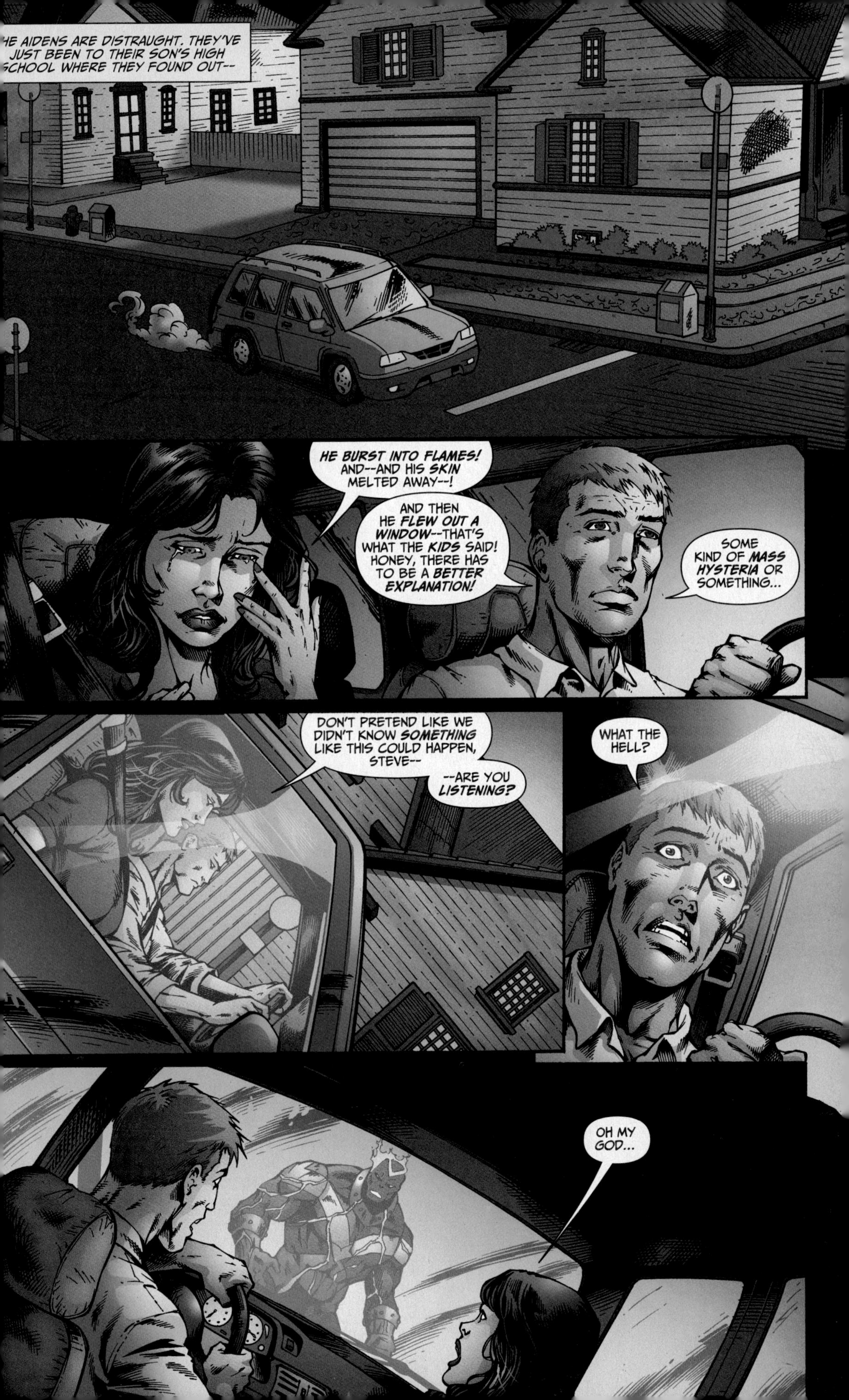
HE AIDENS ARE DISTRAUGHT. THEY'VE JUST BEEN TO THEIR SON'S HIGH SCHOOL WHERE THEY FOUND OUT--
HE BURST INTO FLAMES! AND--AND HIS SKIN MELTED AWAY--!
AND THEN HE FLEW OUT A WINDOW--THAT'S WHAT THE KIDS SAID! HONEY, THERE HAS TO BE A BETTER EXPLANATION!
SOME KIND OF MASS HYSTERIA OR SOMETHING...
DON'T PRETEND LIKE WE DIDN'T KNOW SOMETHING LIKE THIS COULD HAPPEN, STEVE--
--ARE YOU LISTENING?
WHAT THE HELL?
OH MY GOD...

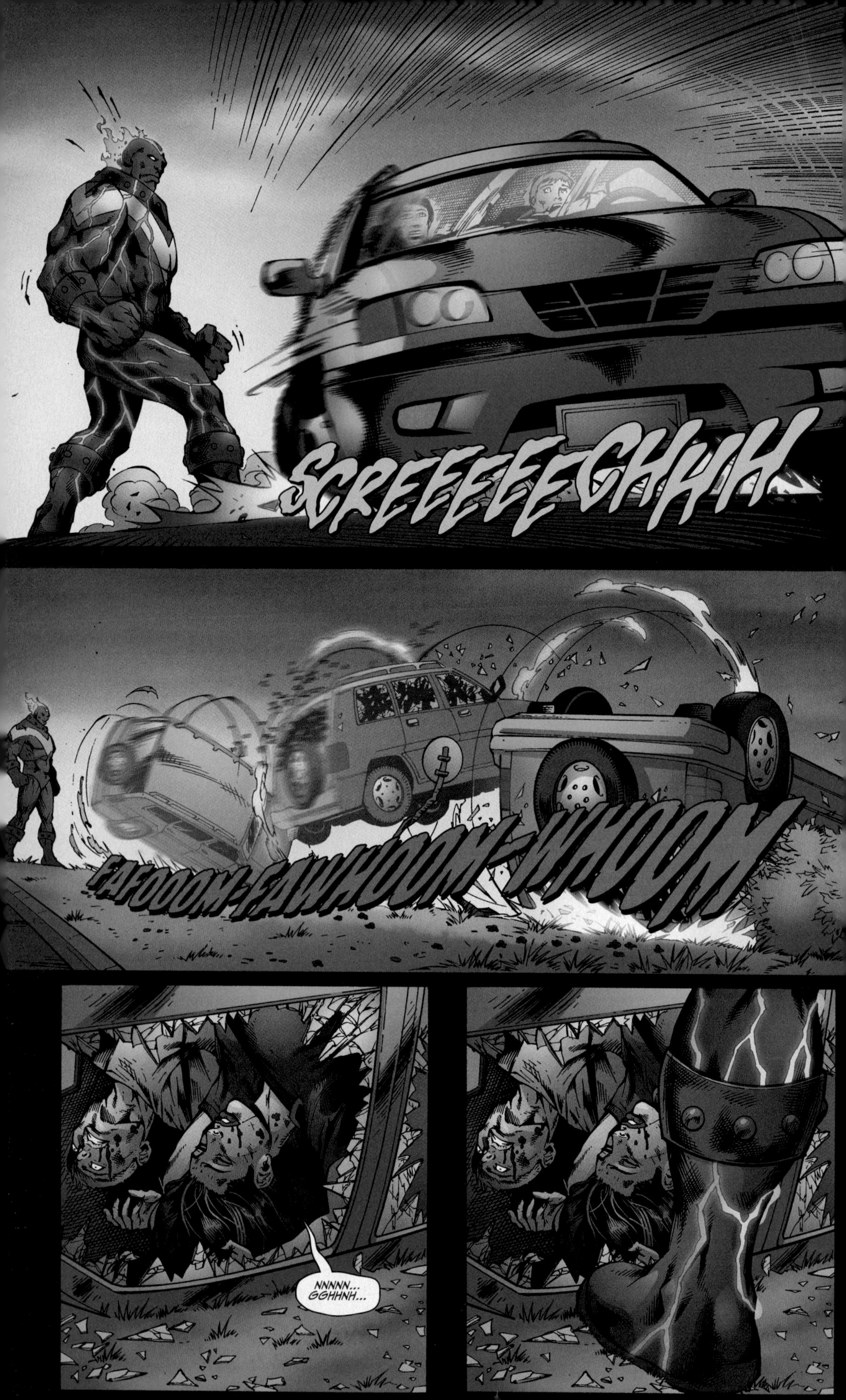
SCREEEEEECHHH
FAFOOOM-FAWHOOM-WHOOM
NNNNN... GGHHNH...

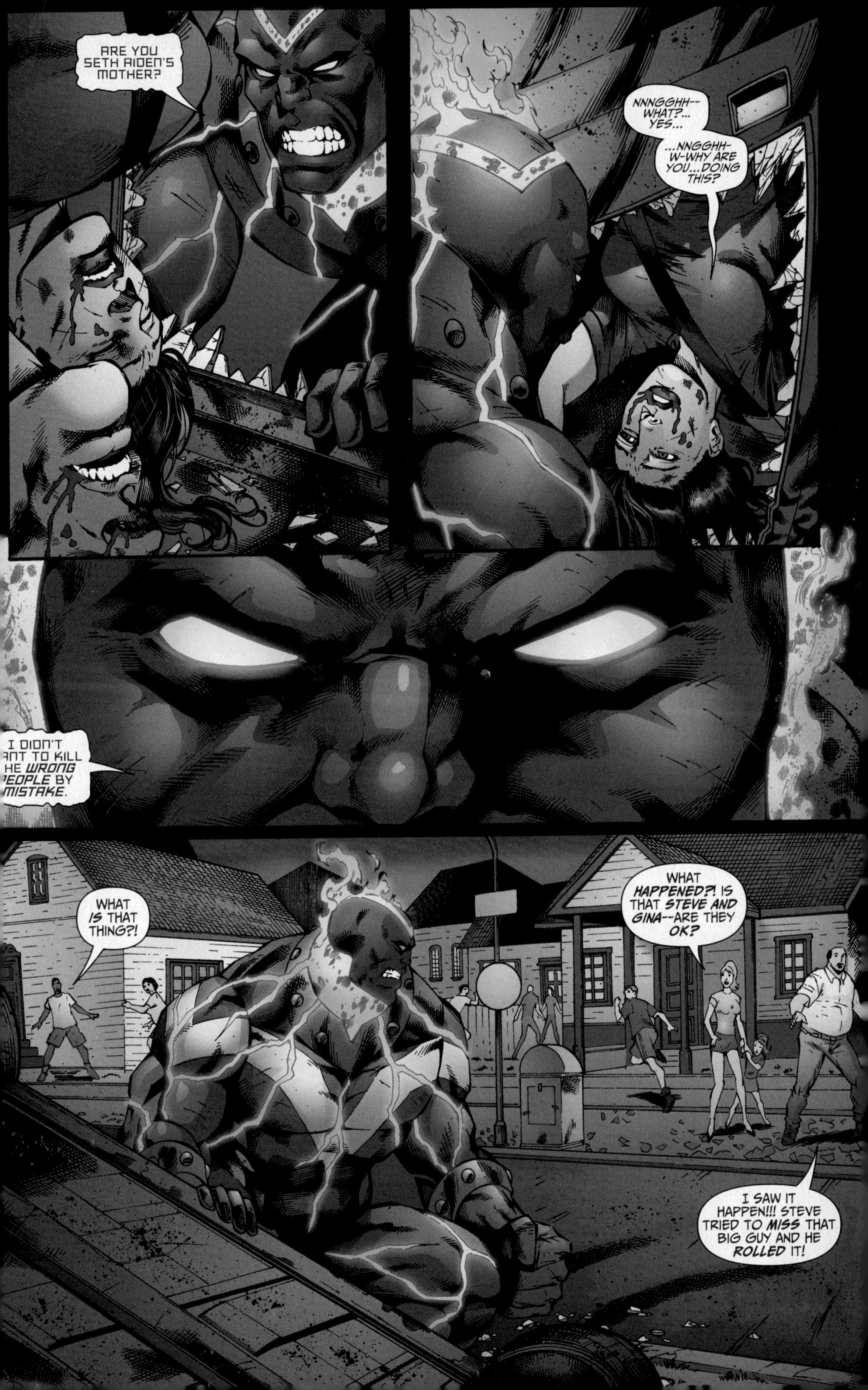
ARE YOU SETH RIDEN'S MOTHER?
NNNGGHH-- WHAT?... YES...
...NNGGHH-- W-WHY ARE YOU...DOING THIS?
I DIDN'T ANT TO KILL HE WRONG EOPLE BY MISTAKE.
WHAT IS THAT THING?!
WHAT HAPPENED?! IS THAT STEVE AND GINA--ARE THEY OK?
I SAW IT HAPPEN!!! STEVE TRIED TO MISS THAT BIG GUY AND HE ROLLED IT!

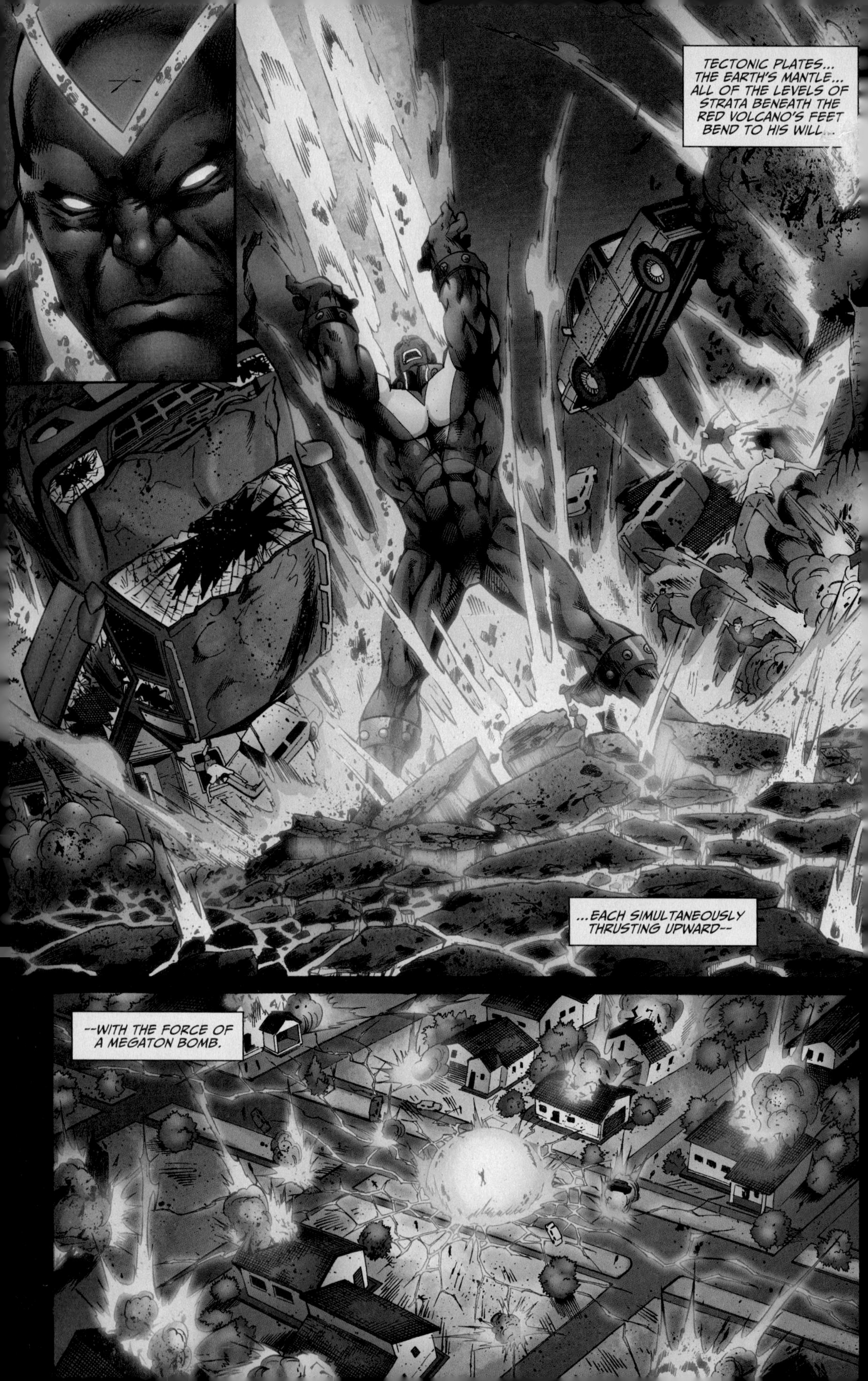
TECTONIC PLATES... THE EARTH'S MANTLE... ALL OF THE LEVELS OF STRATA BENEATH THE RED VOLCANO'S FEET BEND TO HIS WILL...
...EACH SIMULTANEOUSLY THRUSTING UPWARD--
--WITH THE FORCE OF A MEGATON BOMB.

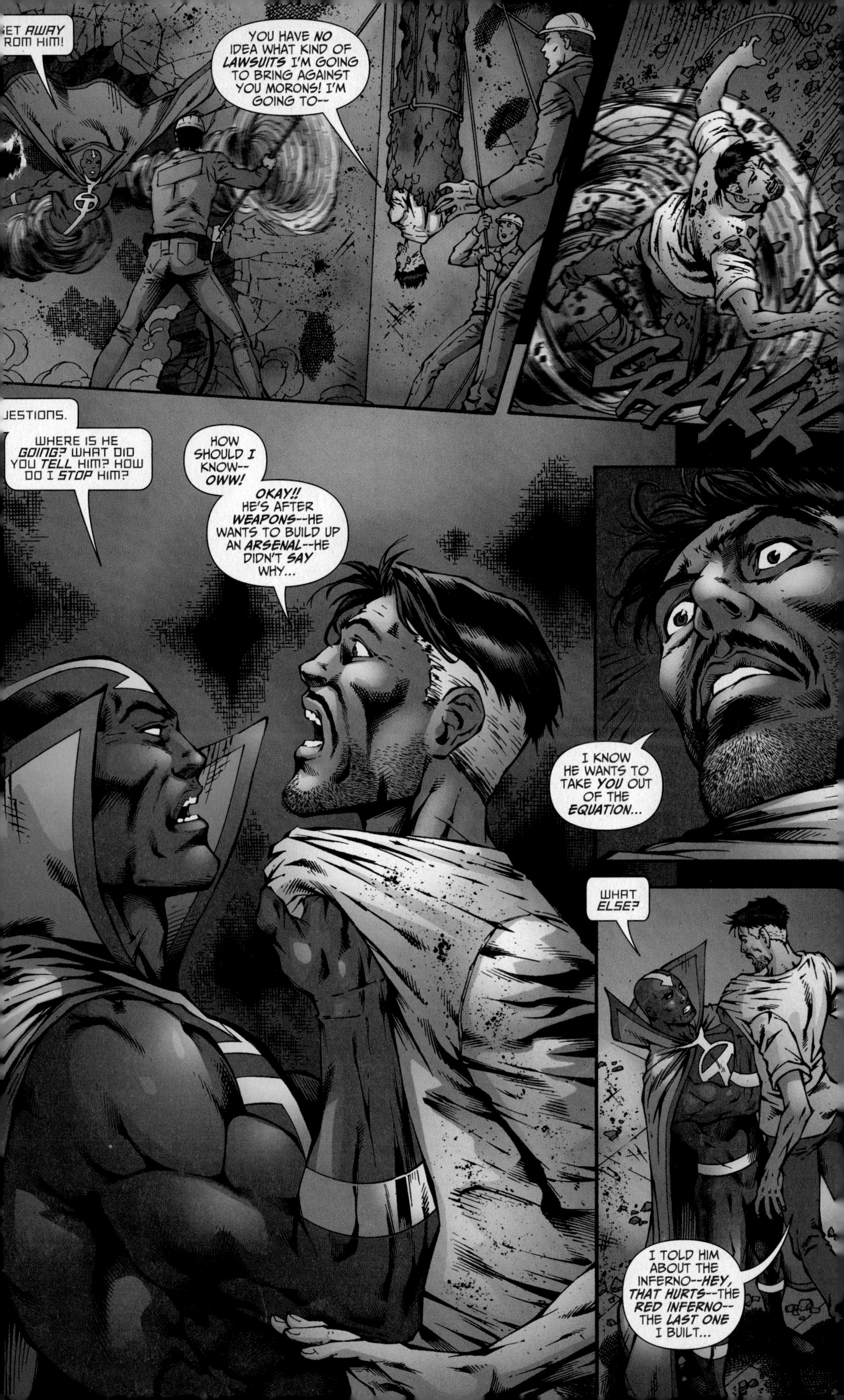

ET AWAY
ROM HIM!
YOU HAVE NO IDEA WHAT KIND OF LAWSUITS I'M GOING TO BRING AGAINST YOU MORONS! I'M GOING TO--
GRAKK
JESTIONS.
WHERE IS HE GOING? WHAT DID YOU TELL HIM? HOW DO I STOP HIM?
HOW SHOULD I KNOW-- OWW!
OKAY!! HE'S AFTER WEAPONS--HE WANTS TO BUILD UP AN ARSENAL--HE DIDN'T SAY WHY...
I KNOW HE WANTS TO TAKE YOU OUT OF THE EQUATION...
WHAT ELSE?
I TOLD HIM ABOUT THE INFERNO--HEY, THAT HURTS--THE RED INFERNO--THE LAST ONE I BUILT...

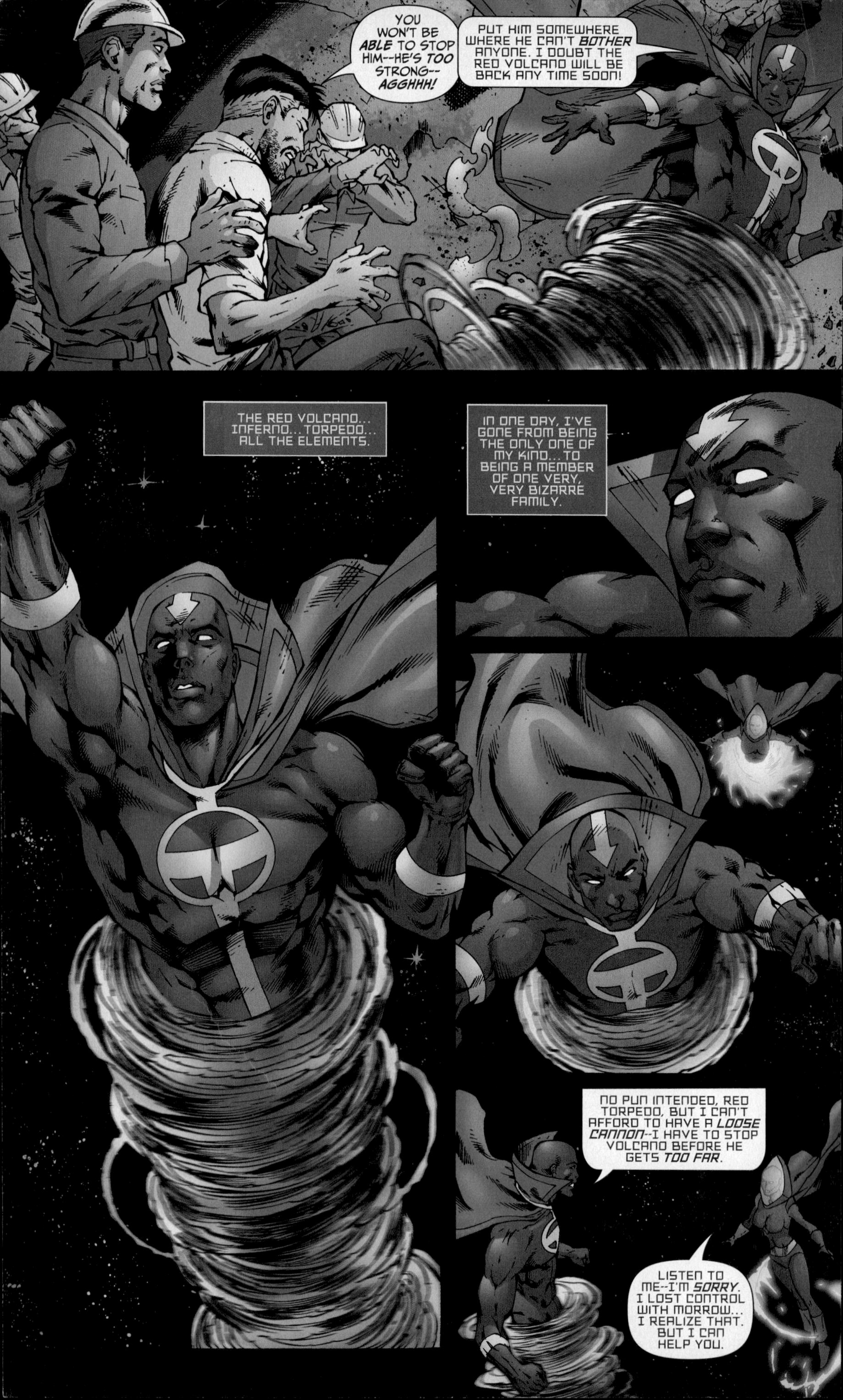
YOU WON'T BE ABLE TO STOP HIM--HE'S TOO STRONG-- AGGHHH!
PUT HIM SOMEWHERE WHERE HE CAN'T BOTHER ANYONE. I DOUBT THE RED VOLCANO WILL BE BACK ANY TIME SOON!
THE RED VOLCANO... INFERNO...TORPEDO... ALL THE ELEMENTS.
IN ONE DAY, I'VE GONE FROM BEING THE ONLY ONE OF MY KIND...TO BEING A MEMBER OF ONE VERY, VERY BIZARRE FAMILY.
NO PUN INTENDED, RED TORPEDO, BUT I CAN'T AFFORD TO HAVE A LOOSE CANNON--I HAVE TO STOP VOLCANO BEFORE HE GETS TOO FAR.
LISTEN TO ME--I'M SORRY. I LOST CONTROL WITH MORROW... I REALIZE THAT. BUT I CAN HELP YOU.

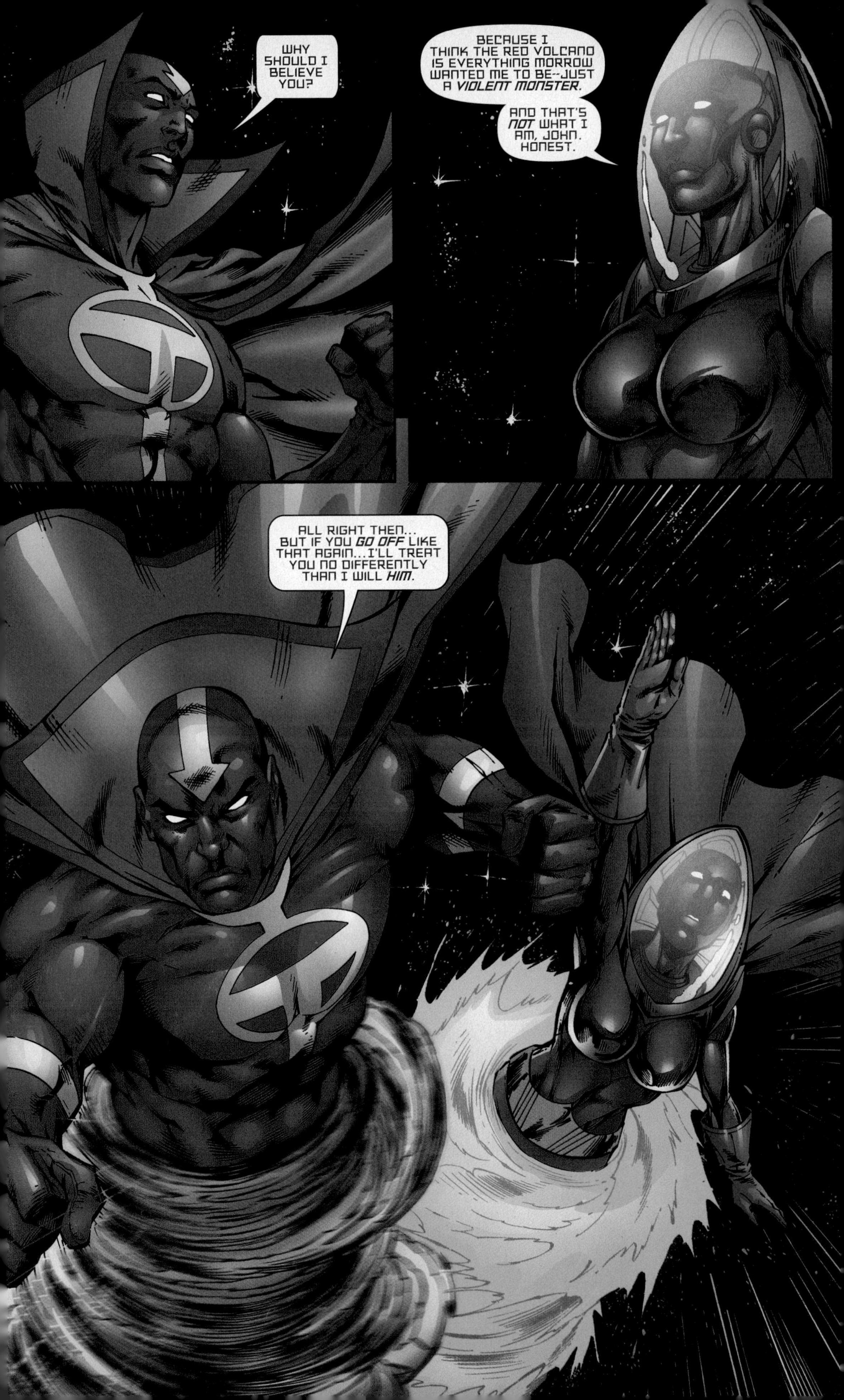

WHY SHOULD I BELIEVE YOU?
BECAUSE I THINK THE RED VOLCANO IS EVERYTHING MORROW WANTED ME TO BE--JUST A *VIOLENT MONSTER*.
AND THAT'S *NOT* WHAT I AM, JOHN. HONEST.
ALL RIGHT THEN... BUT IF YOU *GO OFF* LIKE THAT AGAIN...I'LL TREAT YOU NO DIFFERENTLY THAN I WILL *HIM*.

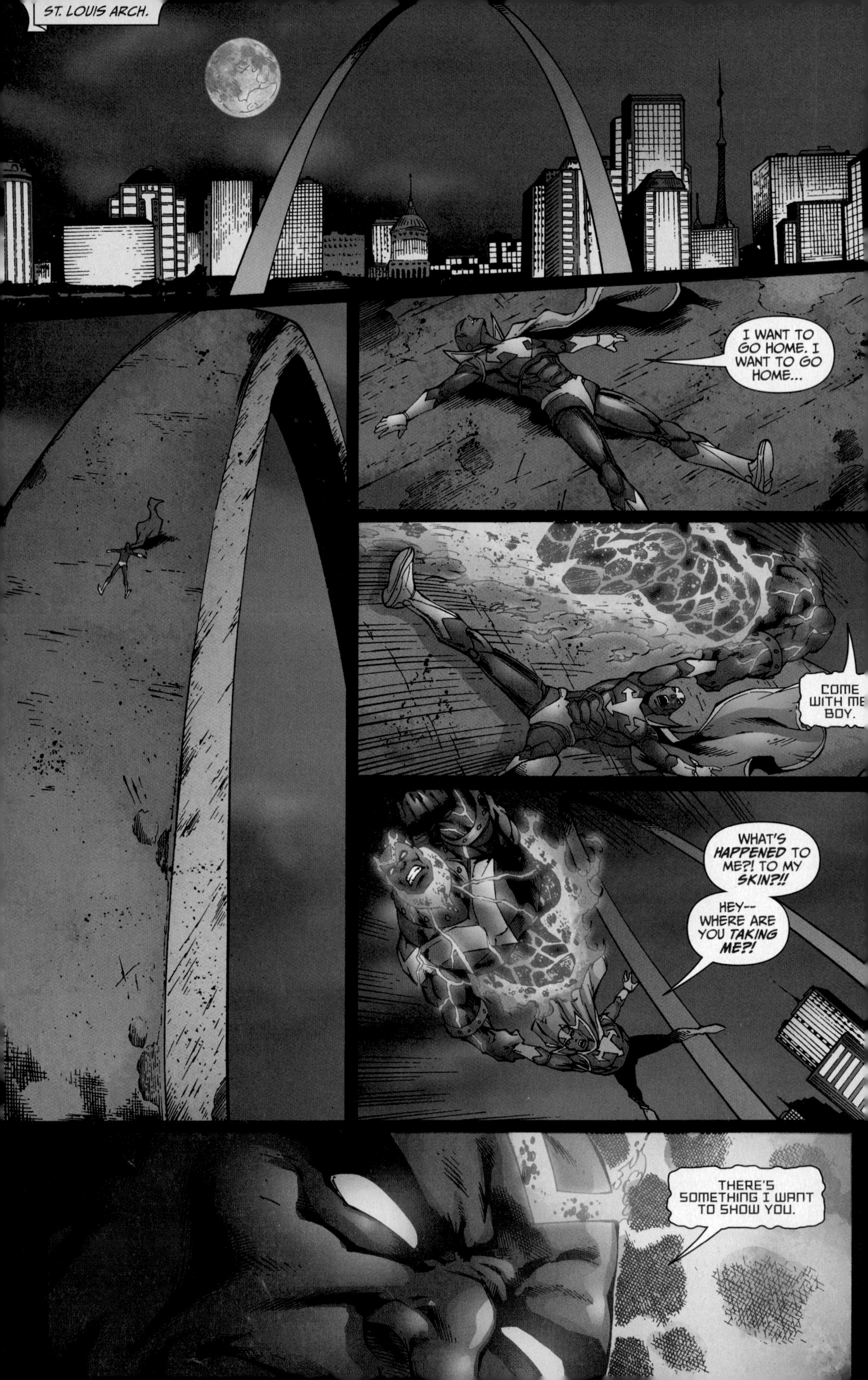
ST. LOUIS ARCH.
I WANT TO GO HOME. I WANT TO GO HOME...
COME WITH ME BOY.
WHAT'S *HAPPENED* TO ME?! TO MY *SKIN?!!*
HEY-- WHERE ARE YOU *TAKING ME?!*
THERE'S SOMETHING I WANT TO SHOW YOU.

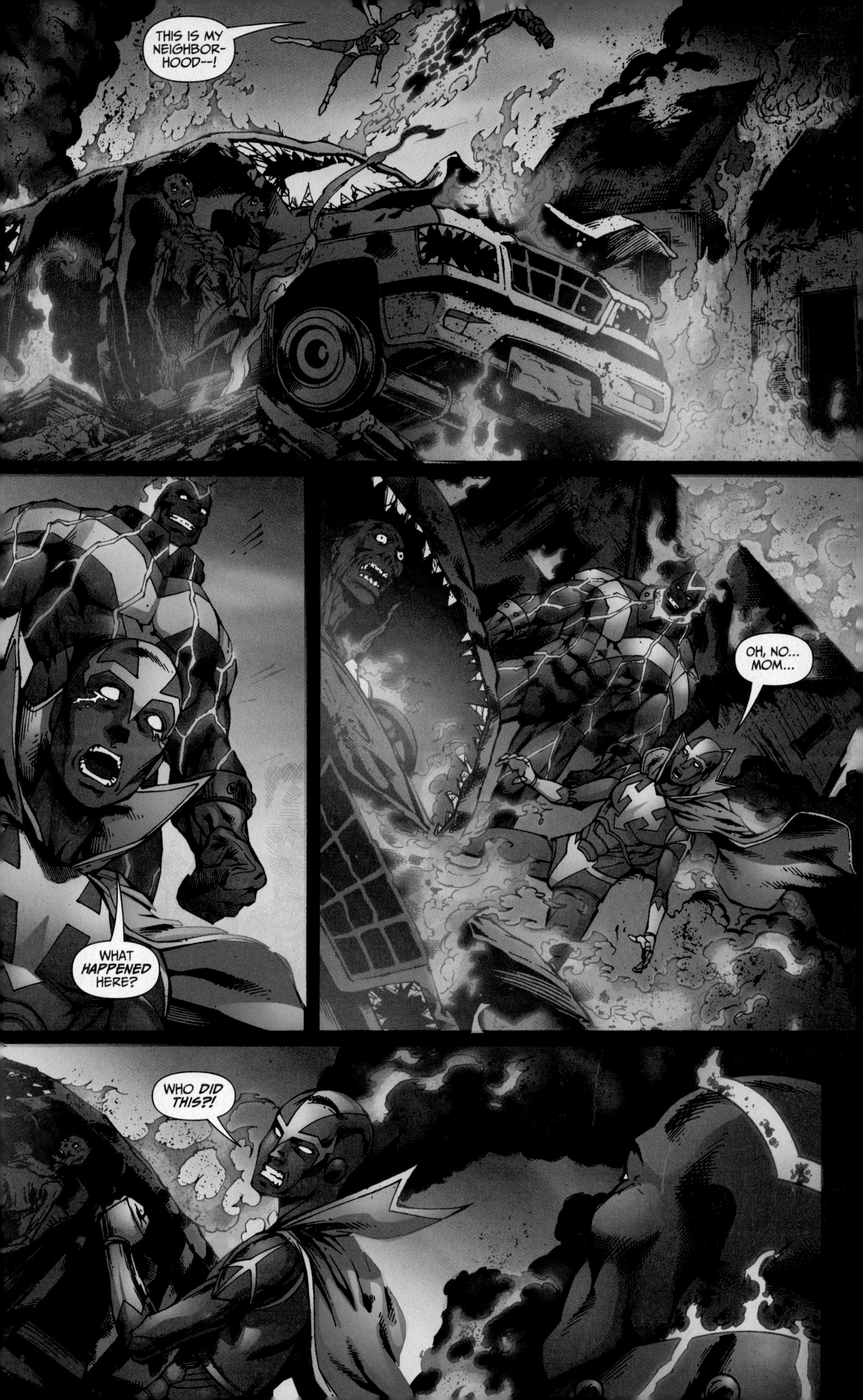
THIS IS MY NEIGHBOR-HOOD--!
WHAT HAPPENED HERE?
OH, NO... MOM...
WHO DID THIS?!

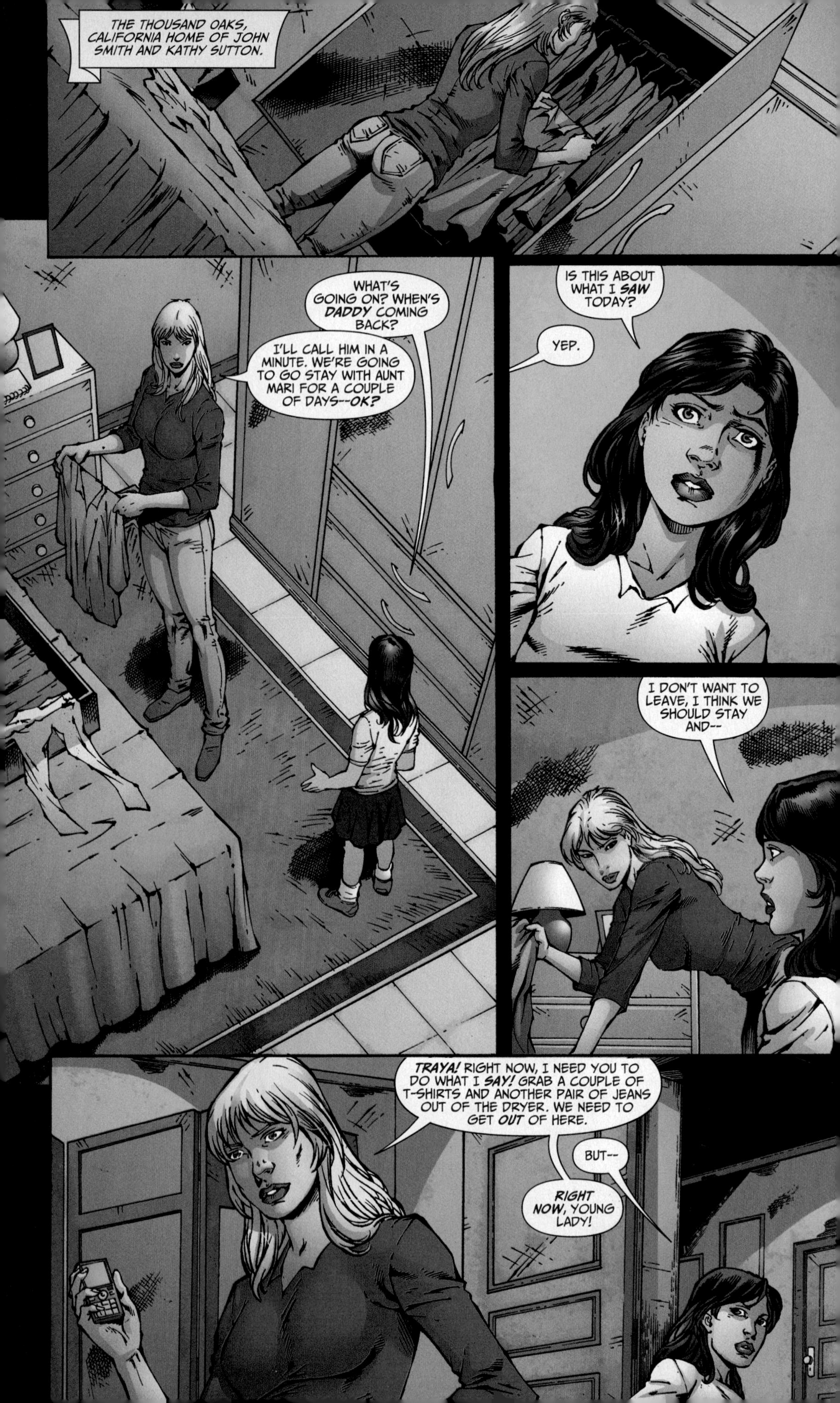
THE THOUSAND OAKS, CALIFORNIA HOME OF JOHN SMITH AND KATHY SUTTON.
WHAT'S GOING ON? WHEN'S DADDY COMING BACK?
I'LL CALL HIM IN A MINUTE. WE'RE GOING TO GO STAY WITH AUNT MARI FOR A COUPLE OF DAYS--OK?
IS THIS ABOUT WHAT I SAW TODAY?
YEP.
I DON'T WANT TO LEAVE, I THINK WE SHOULD STAY AND--
TRAYA! RIGHT NOW, I NEED YOU TO DO WHAT I SAY! GRAB A COUPLE OF T-SHIRTS AND ANOTHER PAIR OF JEANS OUT OF THE DRYER. WE NEED TO GET OUT OF HERE.
BUT--
RIGHT NOW, YOUNG LADY!

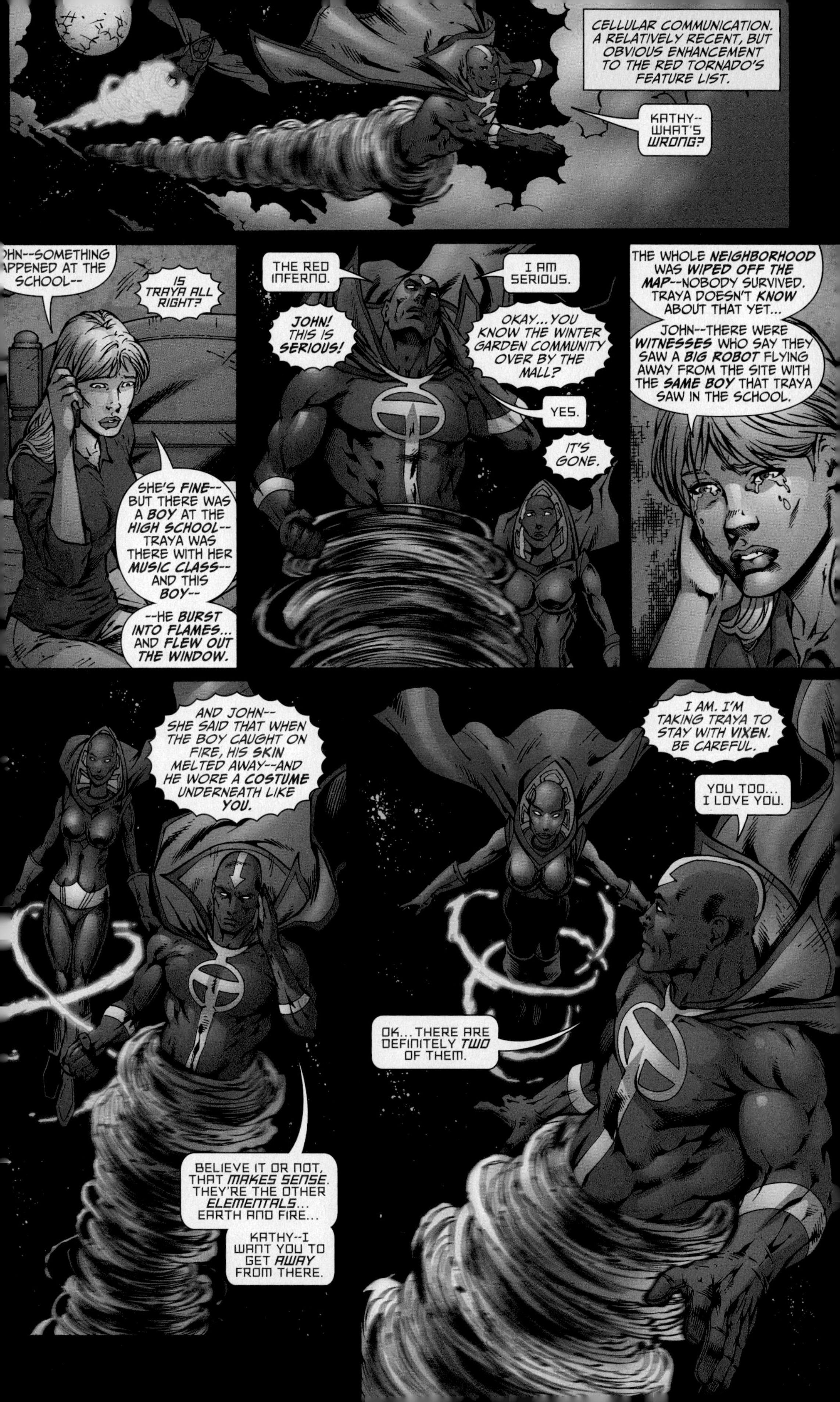

CELLULAR COMMUNICATION. A RELATIVELY RECENT, BUT OBVIOUS ENHANCEMENT TO THE RED TORNADO'S FEATURE LIST.
KATHY-- WHAT'S WRONG?
JOHN--SOMETHING HAPPENED AT THE SCHOOL--
IS TRAYA ALL RIGHT?
SHE'S FINE-- BUT THERE WAS A BOY AT THE HIGH SCHOOL-- TRAYA WAS THERE WITH HER MUSIC CLASS-- AND THIS BOY--
--HE BURST INTO FLAMES... AND FLEW OUT THE WINDOW.
THE RED INFERNO.
JOHN! THIS IS SERIOUS!
I AM SERIOUS.
OKAY...YOU KNOW THE WINTER GARDEN COMMUNITY OVER BY THE MALL?
YES.
IT'S GONE.
THE WHOLE NEIGHBORHOOD WAS WIPED OFF THE MAP--NOBODY SURVIVED. TRAYA DOESN'T KNOW ABOUT THAT YET...
JOHN--THERE WERE WITNESSES WHO SAY THEY SAW A BIG ROBOT FLYING AWAY FROM THE SITE WITH THE SAME BOY THAT TRAYA SAW IN THE SCHOOL.
AND JOHN-- SHE SAID THAT WHEN THE BOY CAUGHT ON FIRE, HIS SKIN MELTED AWAY--AND HE WORE A COSTUME UNDERNEATH LIKE YOU.
BELIEVE IT OR NOT, THAT MAKES SENSE. THEY'RE THE OTHER ELEMENTALS... EARTH AND FIRE...
KATHY--I WANT YOU TO GET AWAY FROM THERE.
I AM. I'M TAKING TRAYA TO STAY WITH VIXEN. BE CAREFUL.
YOU TOO... I LOVE YOU.
OK... THERE ARE DEFINITELY TWO OF THEM.

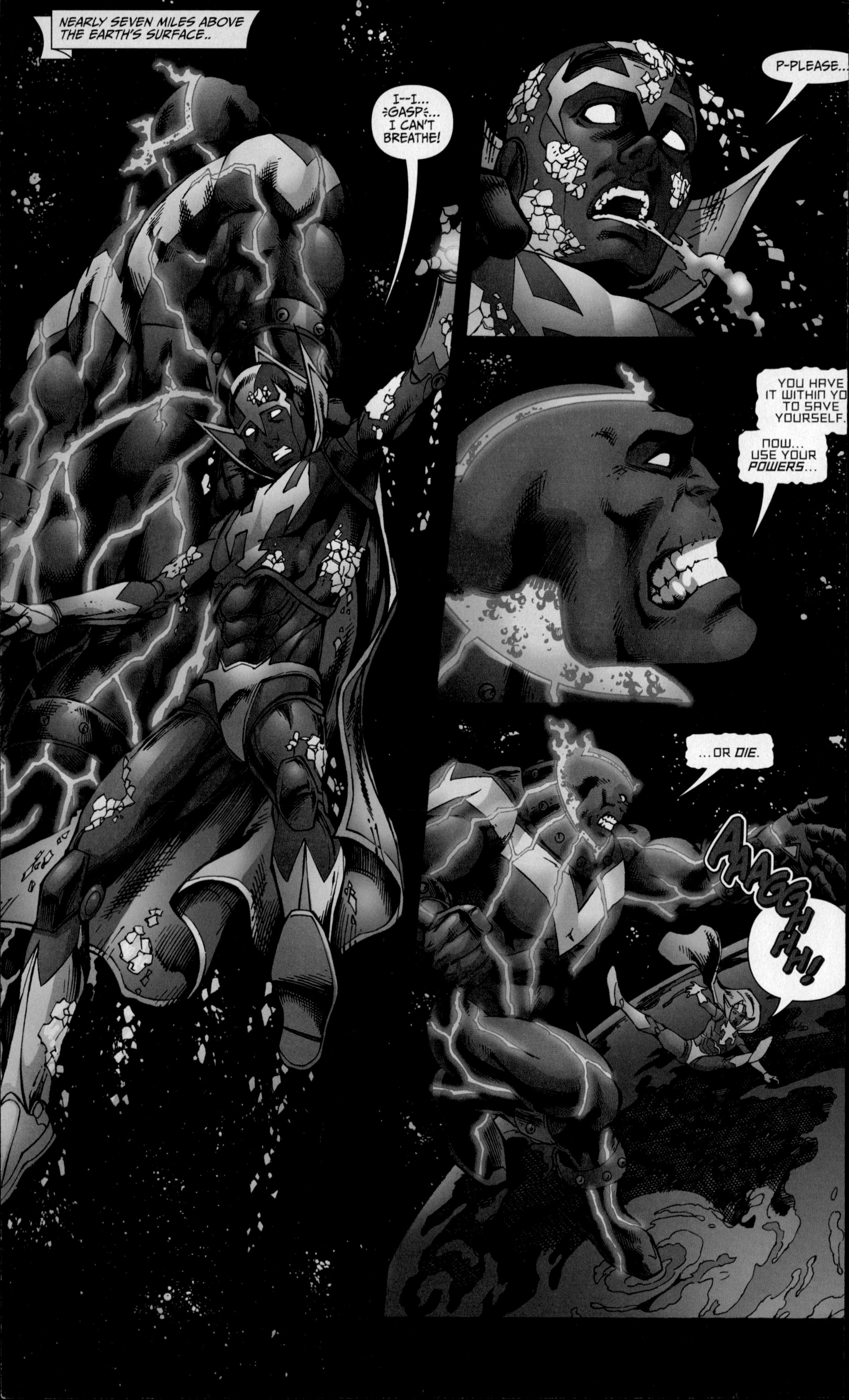
NEARLY SEVEN MILES ABOVE THE EARTH'S SURFACE..
I--I... *GASP*... I CAN'T BREATHE!
P-PLEASE...
YOU HAVE IT WITHIN YO TO SAVE YOURSELF.
NOW... USE YOUR POWERS...
...OR DIE.
AAAGGHHH!

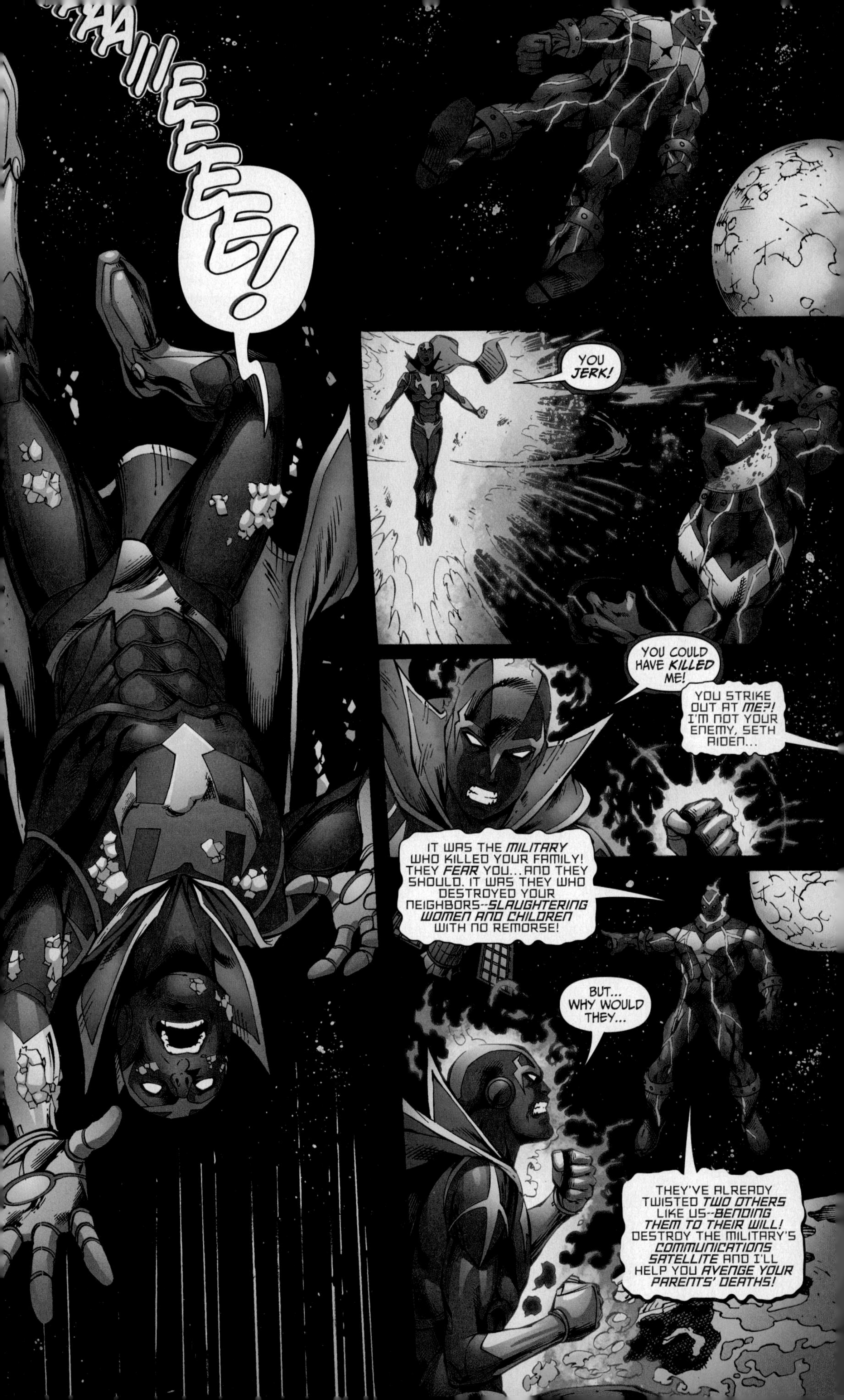
AAIIEEEEEG!
YOU JERK!
YOU COULD HAVE KILLED ME!
YOU STRIKE OUT AT ME?! I'M NOT YOUR ENEMY, SETH AIDEN...
IT WAS THE MILITARY WHO KILLED YOUR FAMILY! THEY FEAR YOU...AND THEY SHOULD. IT WAS THEY WHO DESTROYED YOUR NEIGHBORS--SLAUGHTERING WOMEN AND CHILDREN WITH NO REMORSE!
BUT... WHY WOULD THEY...
THEY'VE ALREADY TWISTED TWO OTHERS LIKE US--BENDING THEM TO THEIR WILL! DESTROY THE MILITARY'S COMMUNICATIONS SATELLITE AND I'LL HELP YOU AVENGE YOUR PARENTS' DEATHS!

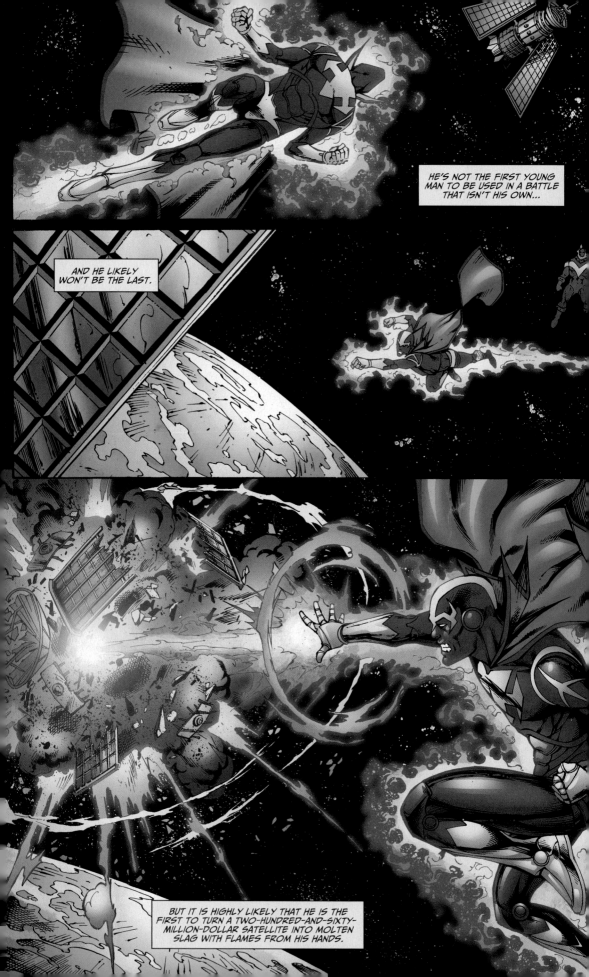

HE'S NOT THE FIRST YOUNG MAN TO BE USED IN A BATTLE THAT ISN'T HIS OWN...

AND HE LIKELY WON'T BE THE LAST.

BUT IT IS HIGHLY LIKELY THAT HE IS THE FIRST TO TURN A TWO-HUNDRED-AND-SIXTY-MILLION-DOLLAR SATELLITE INTO MOLTEN SLAG WITH FLAMES FROM HIS HANDS.

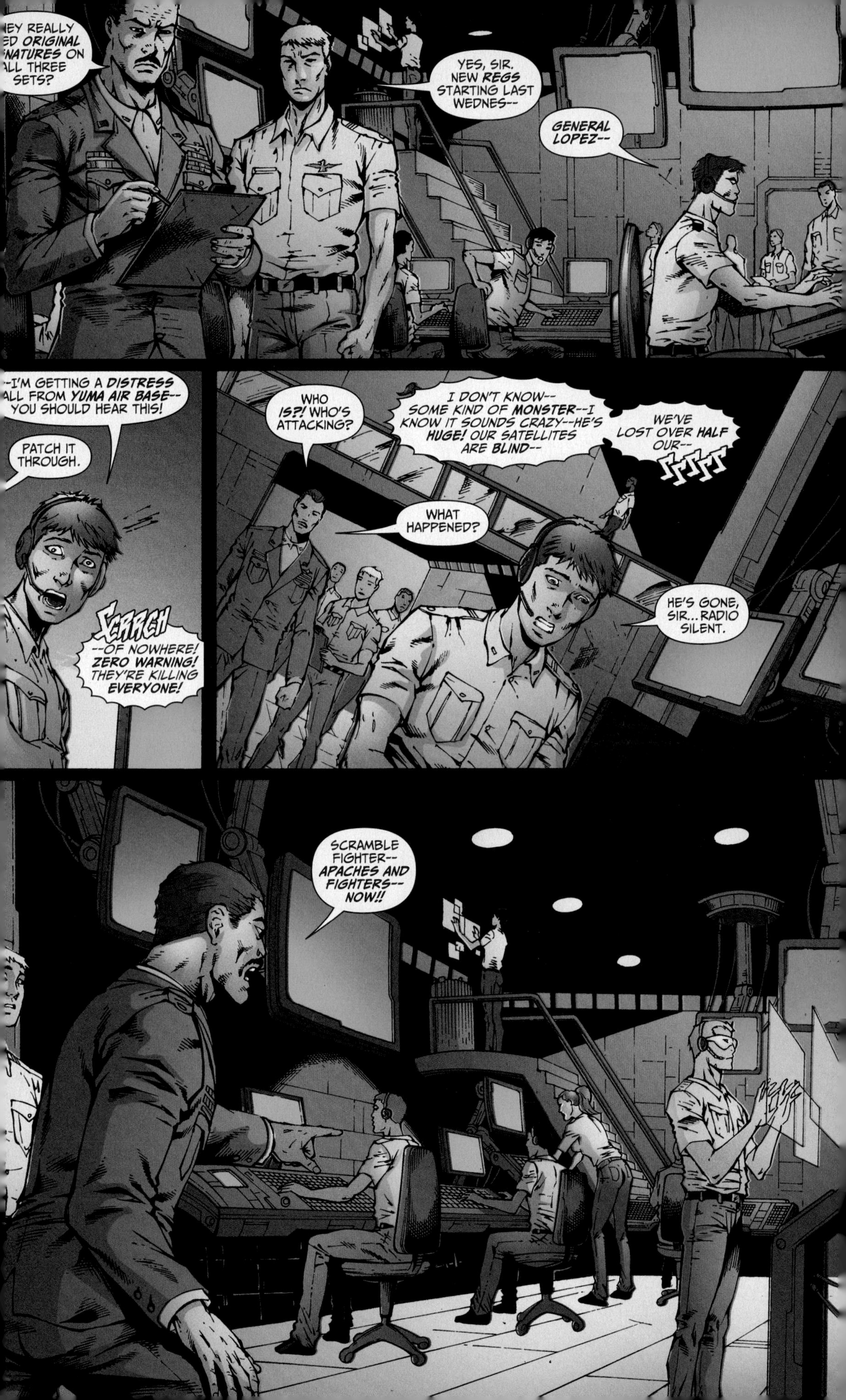
HEY REALLY ED ORIGINAL NATURES ON ALL THREE SETS?
YES, SIR. NEW REGS STARTING LAST WEDNES--
GENERAL LOPEZ--
--I'M GETTING A DISTRESS ALL FROM YUMA AIR BASE-- YOU SHOULD HEAR THIS!
PATCH IT THROUGH.
SCRRCH
--OF NOWHERE! ZERO WARNING! THEY'RE KILLING EVERYONE!
WHO IS?! WHO'S ATTACKING?
I DON'T KNOW-- SOME KIND OF MONSTER--I KNOW IT SOUNDS CRAZY--HE'S HUGE! OUR SATELLITES ARE BLIND--
WE'VE LOST OVER HALF OUR--
SSSS
WHAT HAPPENED?
HE'S GONE, SIR... RADIO SILENT.
SCRAMBLE FIGHTER-- APACHES AND FIGHTERS-- NOW!!

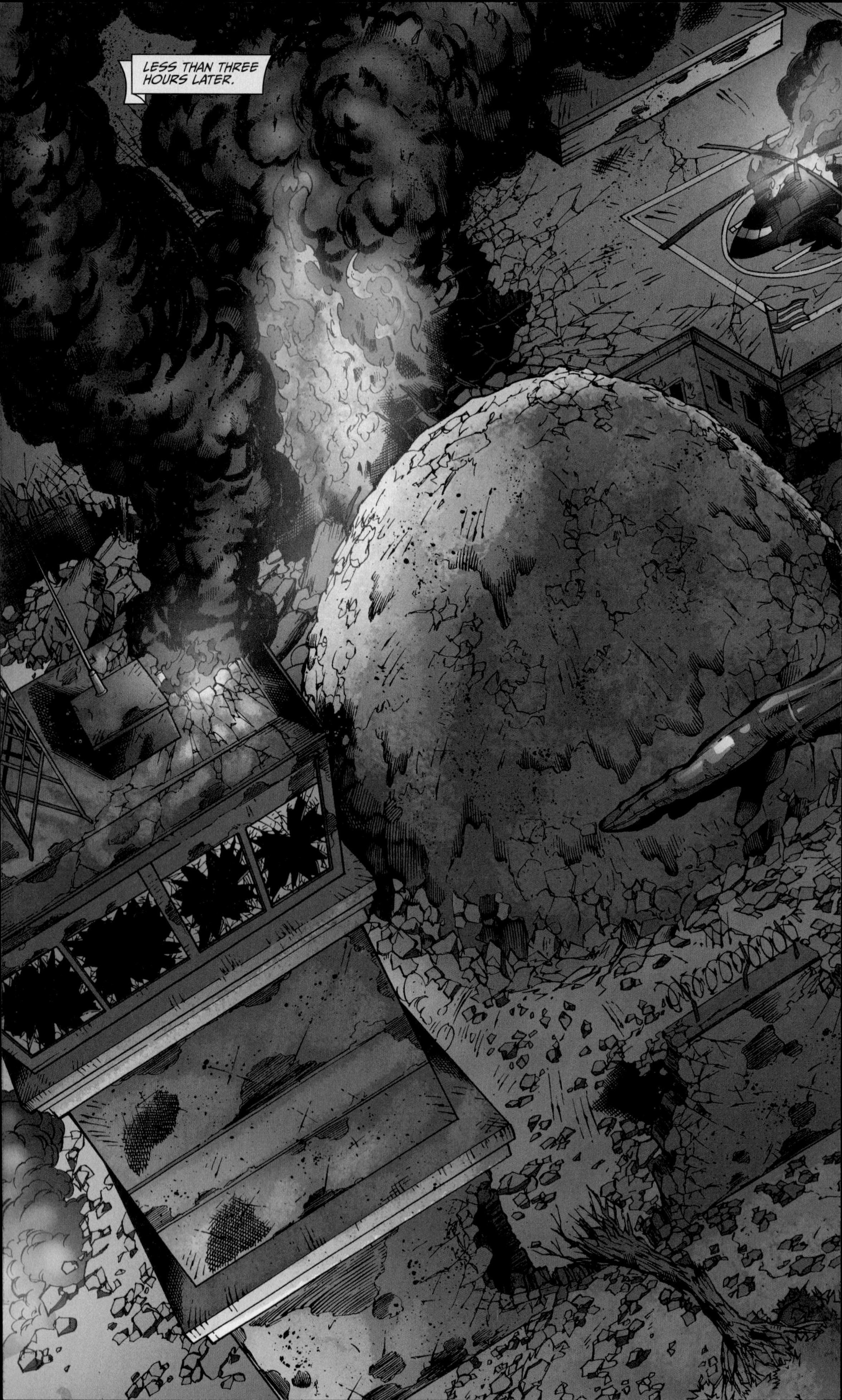
LESS THAN THREE HOURS LATER.

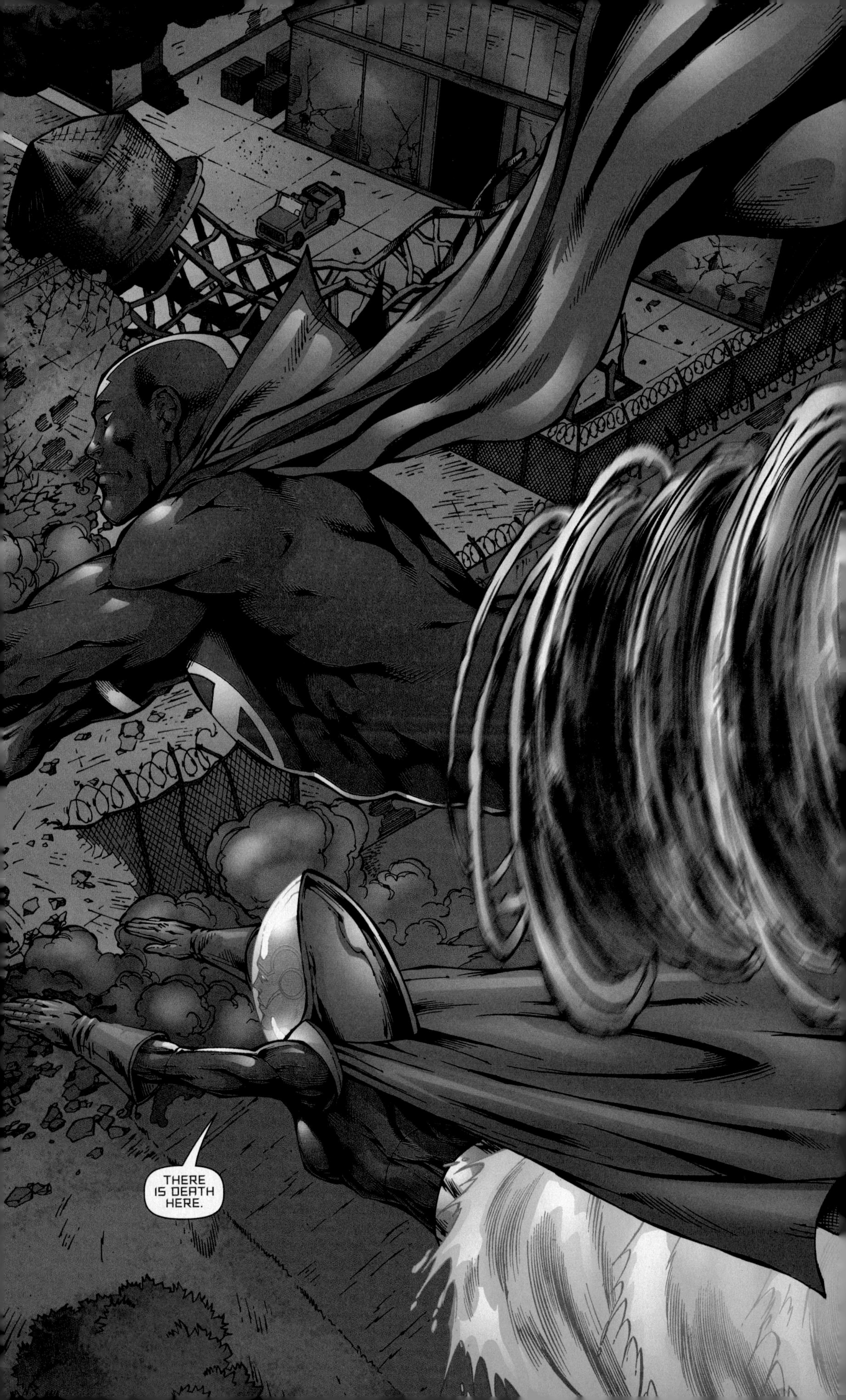
THERE IS DEATH HERE.

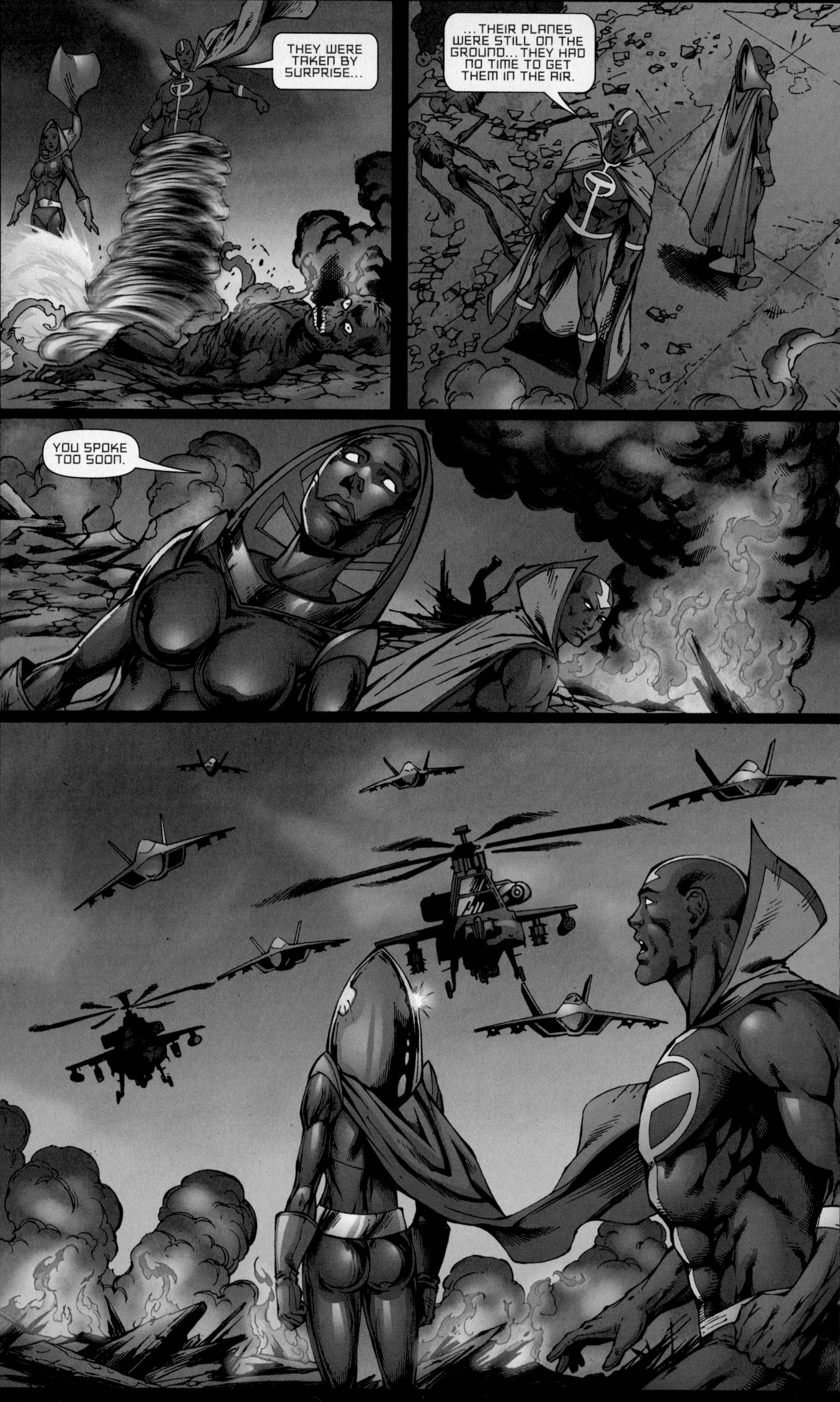
THEY WERE TAKEN BY SURPRISE...
...THEIR PLANES WERE STILL ON THE GROUND... THEY HAD NO TIME TO GET THEM IN THE AIR.
YOU SPOKE TOO SOON.

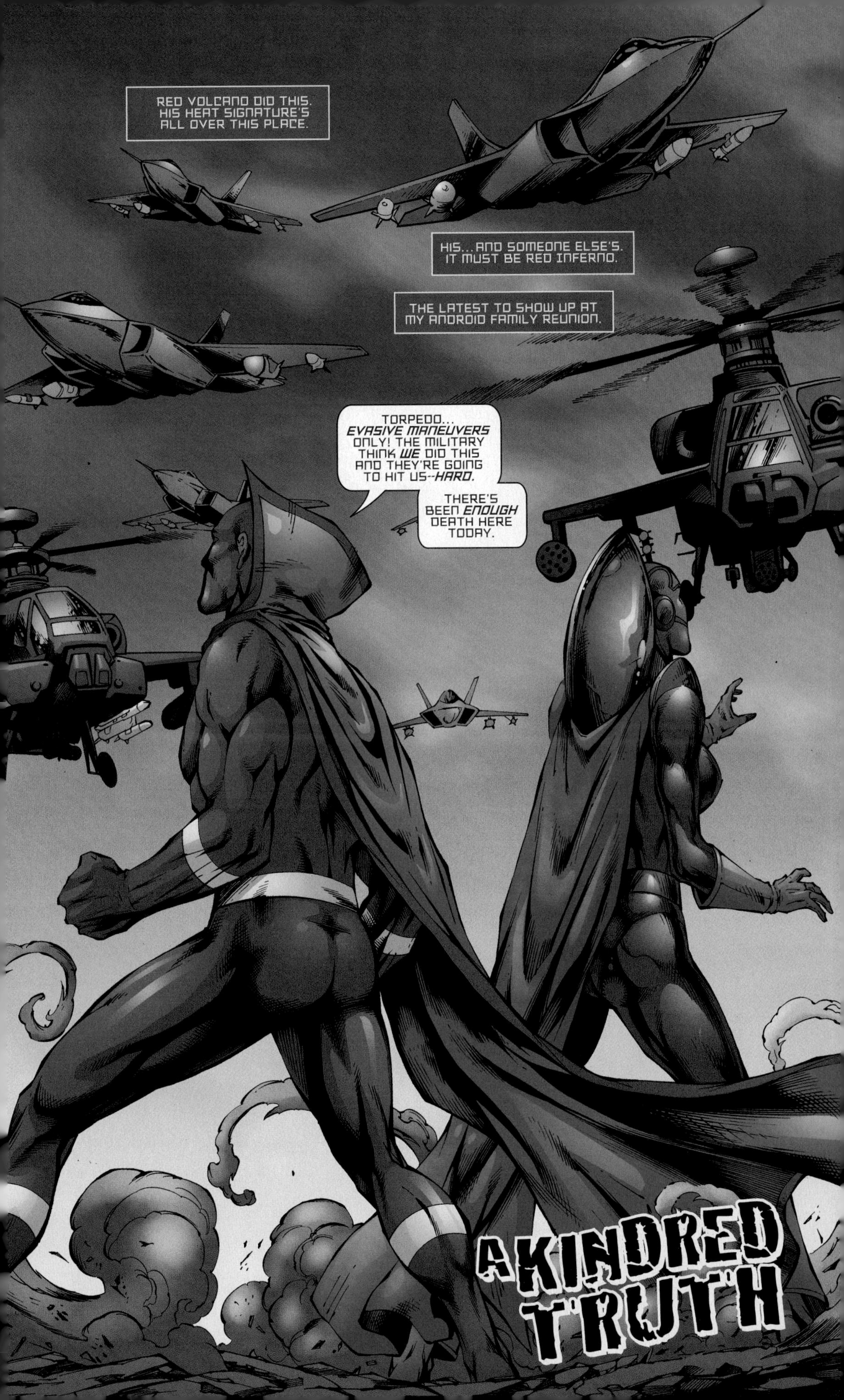
RED VOLCANO DID THIS. HIS HEAT SIGNATURE'S ALL OVER THIS PLACE.
HIS...AND SOMEONE ELSE'S. IT MUST BE RED INFERNO.
THE LATEST TO SHOW UP AT MY ANDROID FAMILY REUNION.
TORPEDO... EVASIVE MANEUVERS ONLY! THE MILITARY THINK WE DID THIS AND THEY'RE GOING TO HIT US--HARD.
THERE'S BEEN ENOUGH DEATH HERE TODAY.
A KINDRED TRUTH

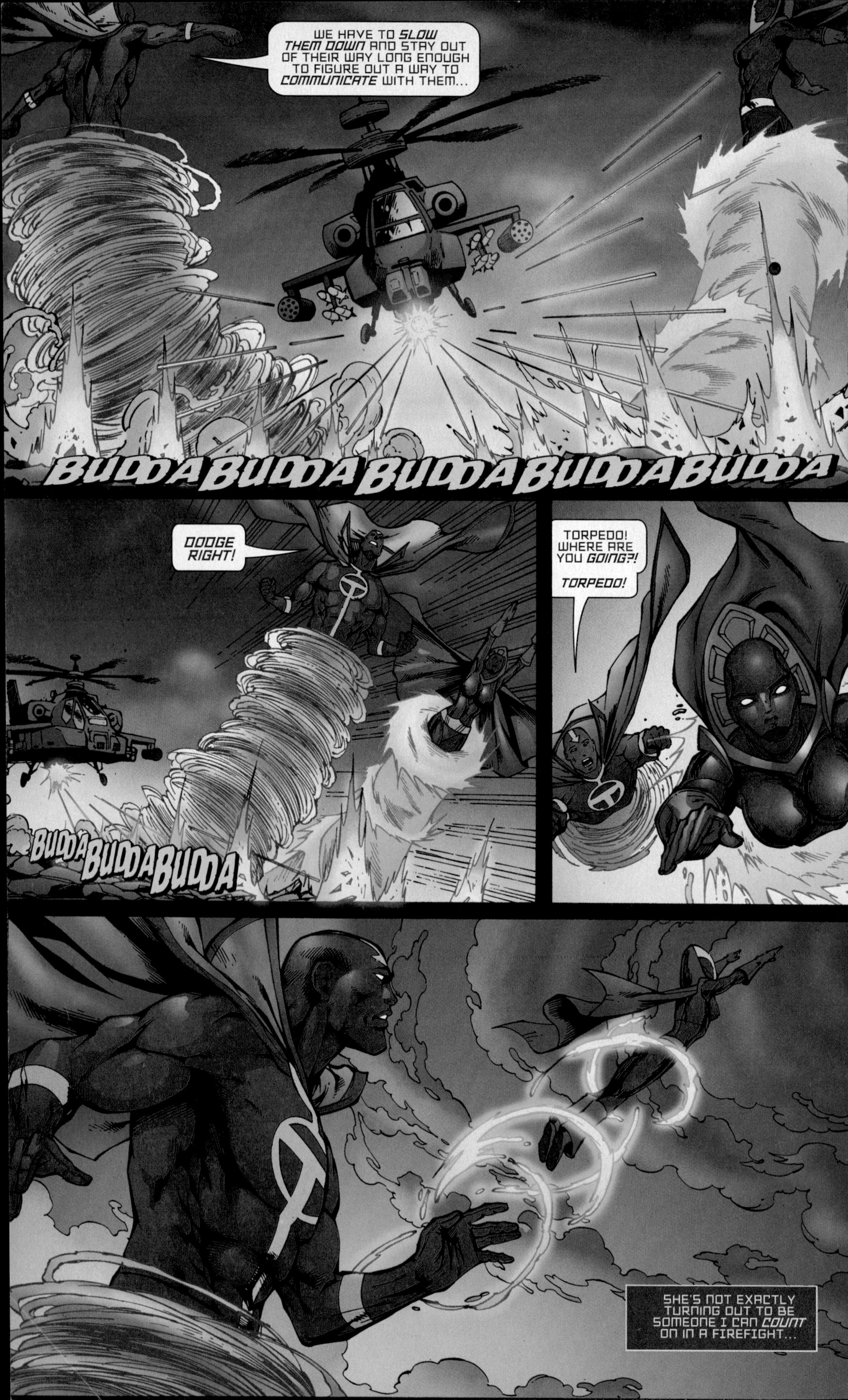
WE HAVE TO SLOW THEM DOWN AND STAY OUT OF THEIR WAY LONG ENOUGH TO FIGURE OUT A WAY TO COMMUNICATE WITH THEM...
BUDDA BUDDA BUDDA BUDDA BUDDA
DODGE RIGHT!
BUDDA BUDDA BUDDA
TORPEDO! WHERE ARE YOU GOING?!
TORPEDO!
SHE'S NOT EXACTLY TURNING OUT TO BE SOMEONE I CAN COUNT ON IN A FIREFIGHT...

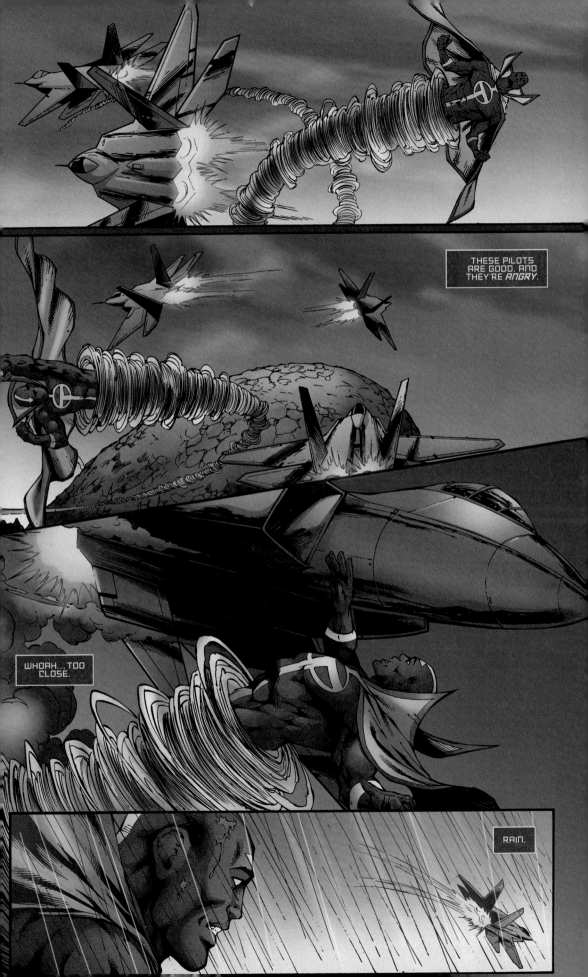

THESE PILOTS
ARE GOOD. AND
THEY'RE *ANGRY*.

WHOAH...TOO
CLOSE.

RAIN.

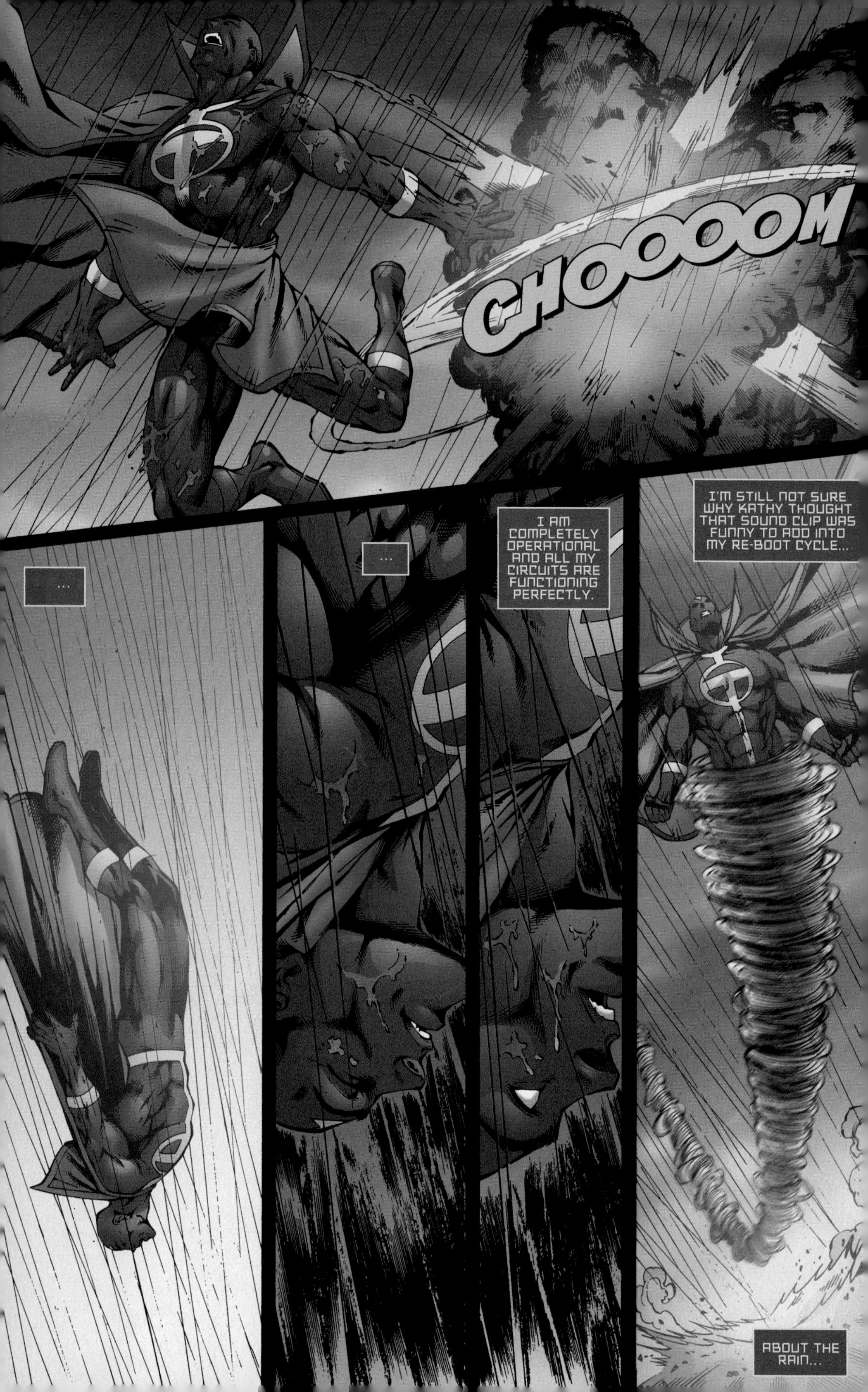
CHOOOOOM
...
...
I AM COMPLETELY OPERATIONAL AND ALL MY CIRCUITS ARE FUNCTIONING PERFECTLY.
I'M STILL NOT SURE WHY KATHY THOUGHT THAT SOUND CLIP WAS FUNNY TO ADD INTO MY RE-BOOT CYCLE...
ABOUT THE RAIN...

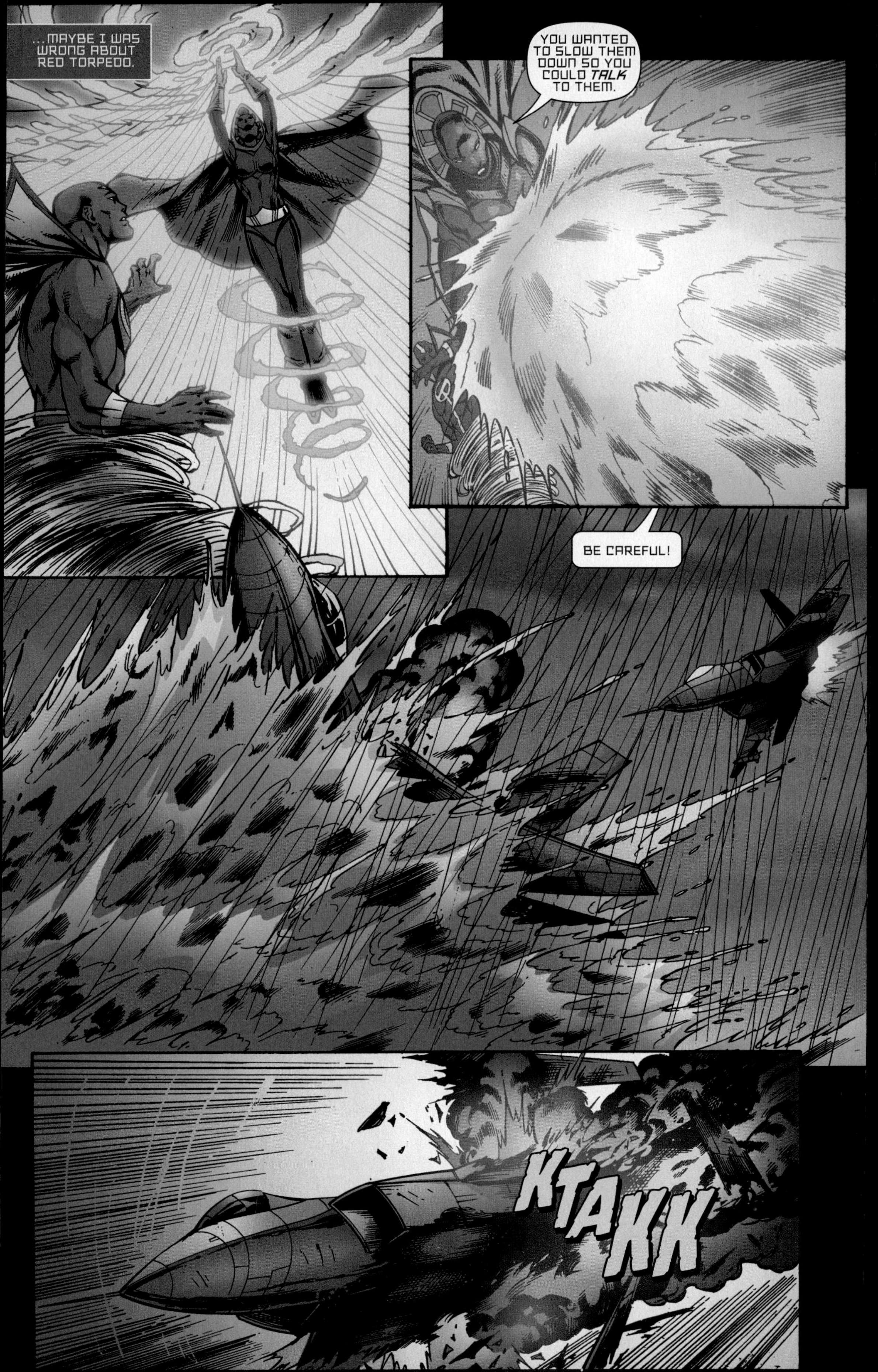
...MAYBE I WAS WRONG ABOUT RED TORPEDO.
YOU WANTED TO SLOW THEM DOWN SO YOU COULD TALK TO THEM.
BE CAREFUL!
KTAKK

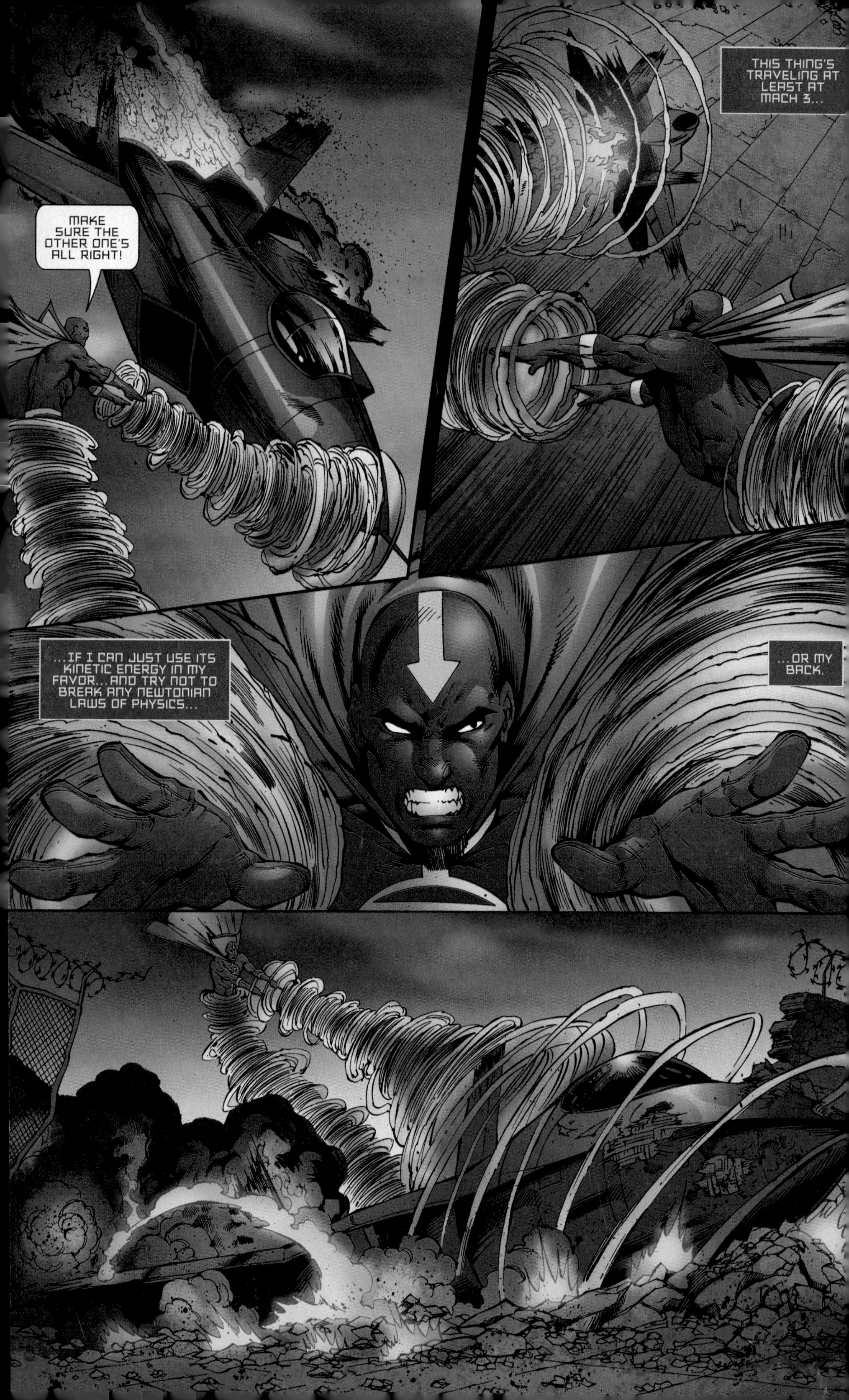
MAKE SURE THE OTHER ONE'S ALL RIGHT!
THIS THING'S TRAVELING AT LEAST AT MACH 3...
...IF I CAN JUST USE ITS KINETIC ENERGY IN MY FAVOR...AND TRY NOT TO BREAK ANY NEWTONIAN LAWS OF PHYSICS...
...OR MY BACK.

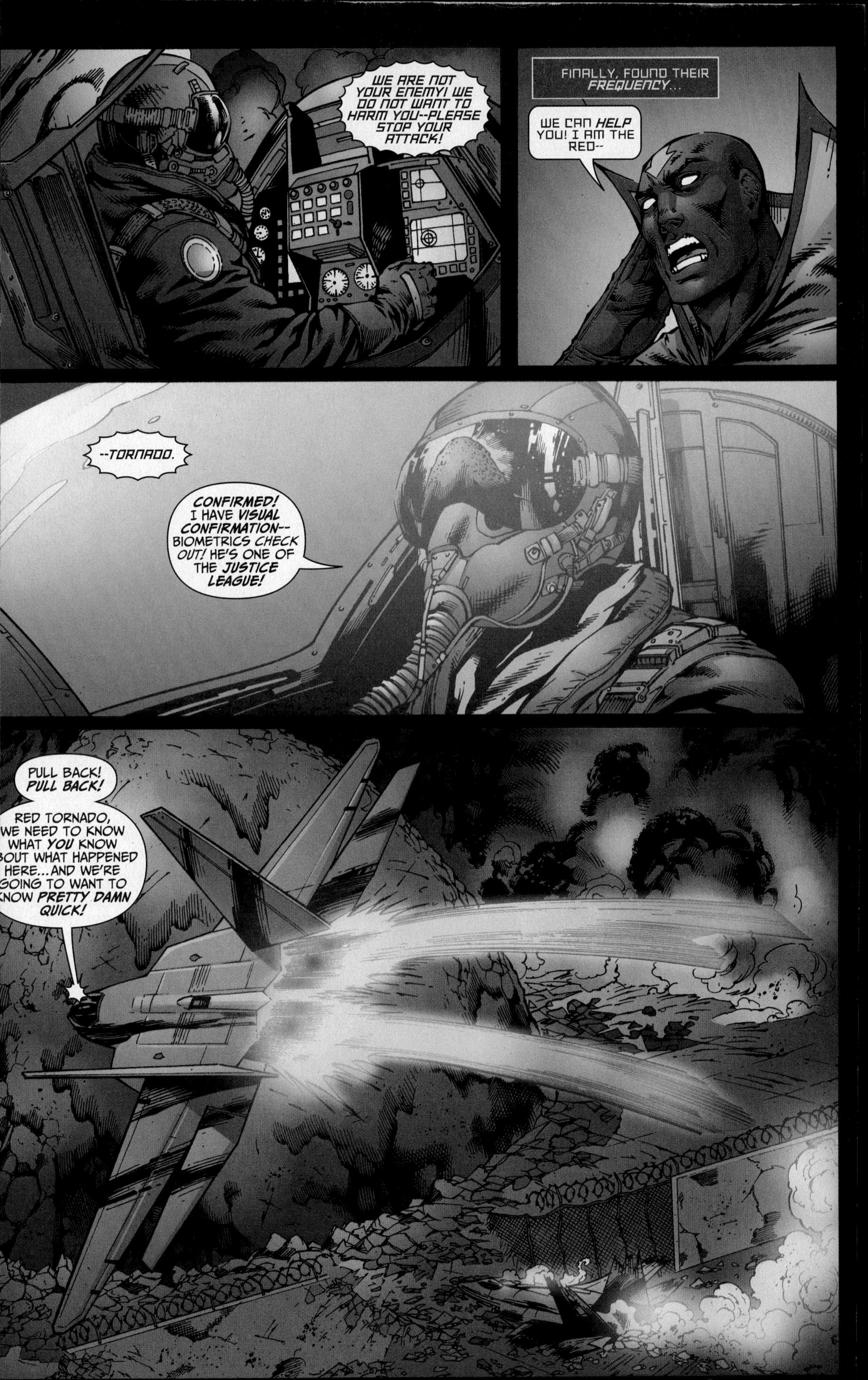
WE ARE NOT YOUR ENEMY! WE DO NOT WANT TO HARM YOU--PLEASE STOP YOUR ATTACK!
FINALLY, FOUND THEIR FREQUENCY...
WE CAN HELP YOU! I AM THE RED--
--TORNADO.
CONFIRMED! I HAVE VISUAL CONFIRMATION--BIOMETRICS CHECK OUT! HE'S ONE OF THE JUSTICE LEAGUE!
PULL BACK! PULL BACK!
RED TORNADO, WE NEED TO KNOW WHAT YOU KNOW BOUT WHAT HAPPENED HERE...AND WE'RE GOING TO WANT TO KNOW PRETTY DAMN QUICK!

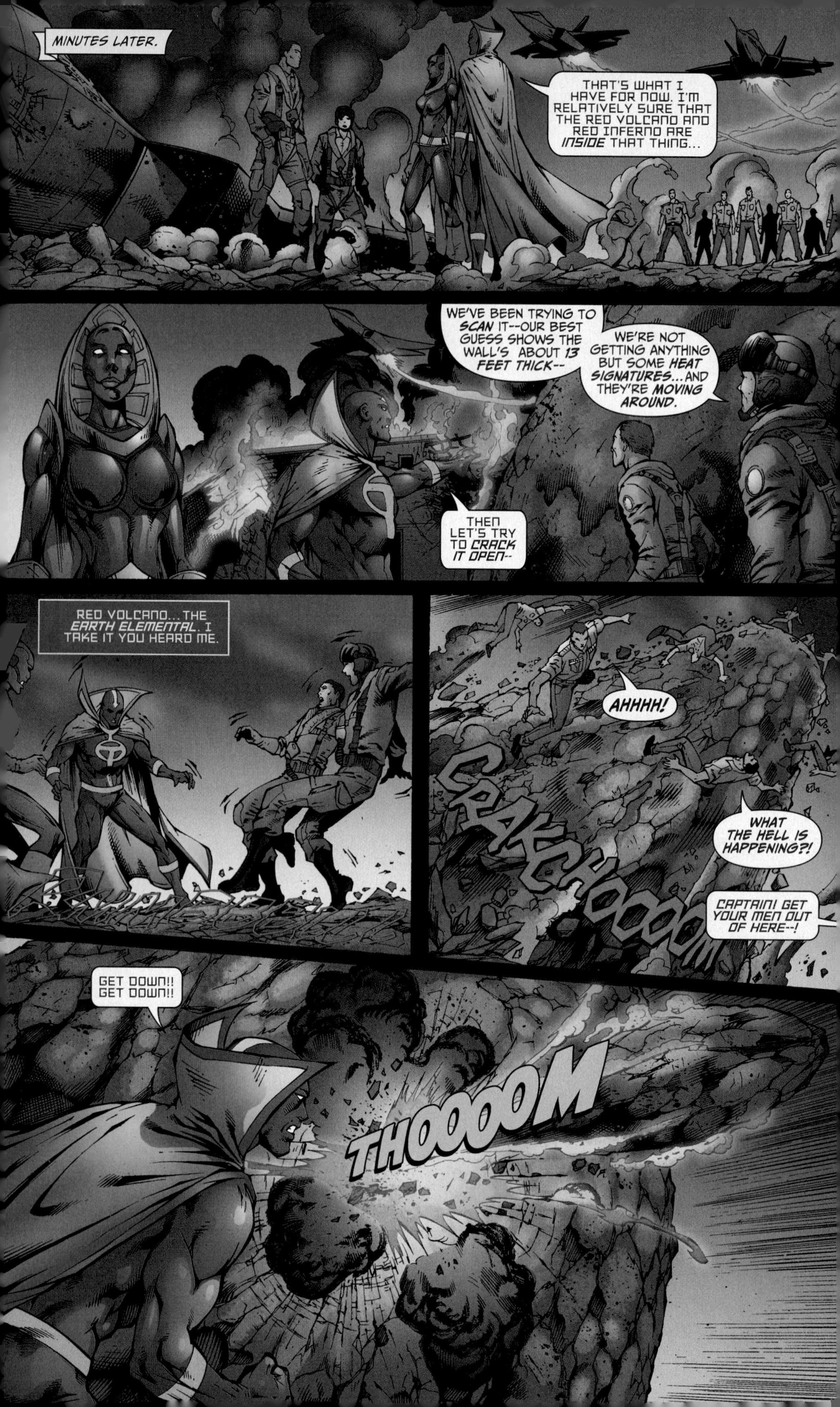
MINUTES LATER.
THAT'S WHAT I HAVE FOR NOW. I'M RELATIVELY SURE THAT THE RED VOLCANO AND RED INFERNO ARE INSIDE THAT THING...
WE'VE BEEN TRYING TO SCAN IT--OUR BEST GUESS SHOWS THE WALL'S ABOUT 13 FEET THICK--
WE'RE NOT GETTING ANYTHING BUT SOME HEAT SIGNATURES... AND THEY'RE MOVING AROUND.
THEN LET'S TRY TO CRACK IT OPEN--
RED VOLCANO... THE EARTH ELEMENTAL. I TAKE IT YOU HEARD ME.
AHHHH!
CRAKCHOOOOOM
WHAT THE HELL IS HAPPENING?!
CAPTAIN! GET YOUR MEN OUT OF HERE--!
GET DOWN!! GET DOWN!!
THOOOOOM

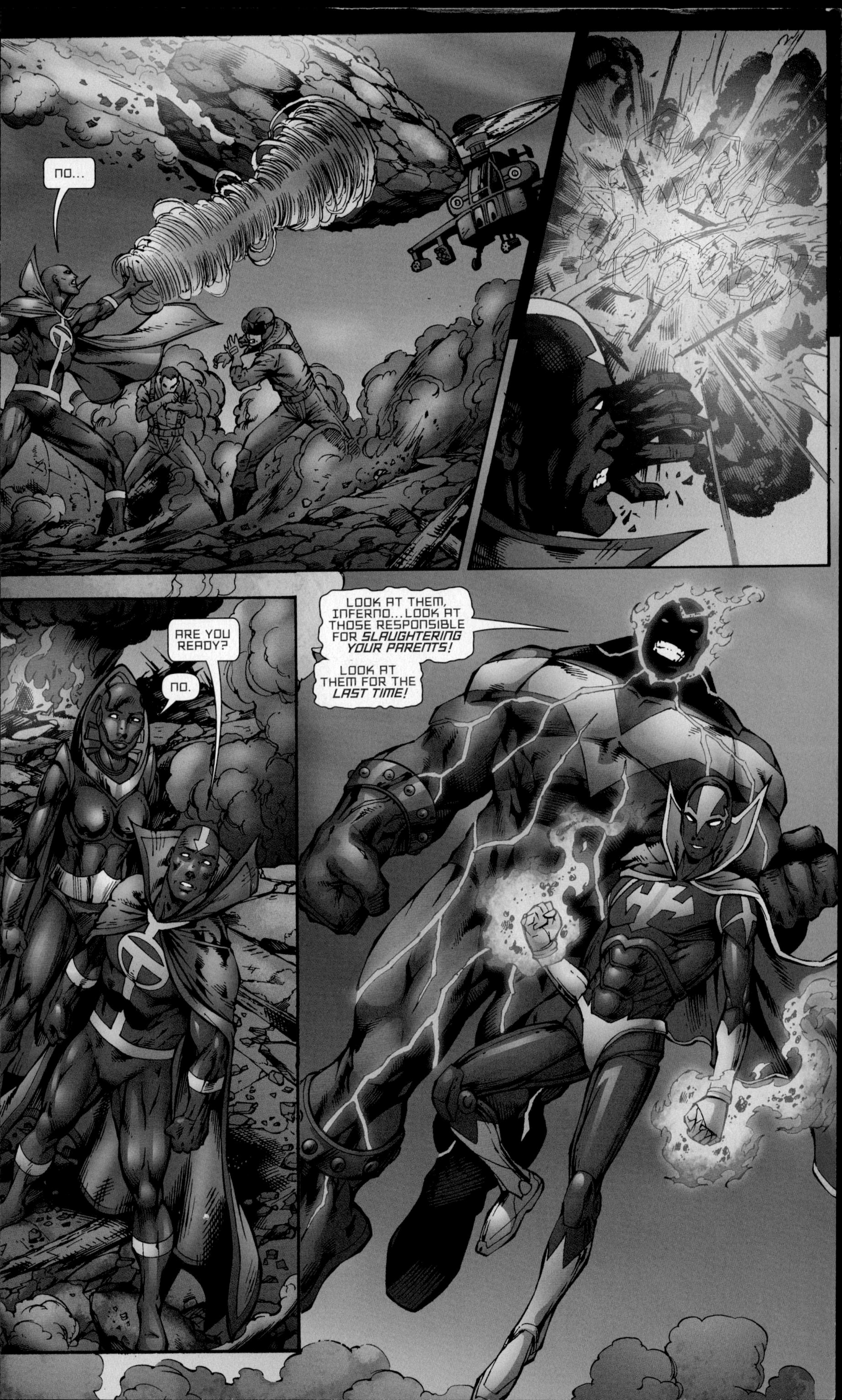

NO...
ARE YOU READY?
NO.
LOOK AT THEM, INFERNO...LOOK AT THOSE RESPONSIBLE FOR *SLAUGHTERING YOUR PARENTS!*
LOOK AT THEM FOR THE *LAST TIME!*

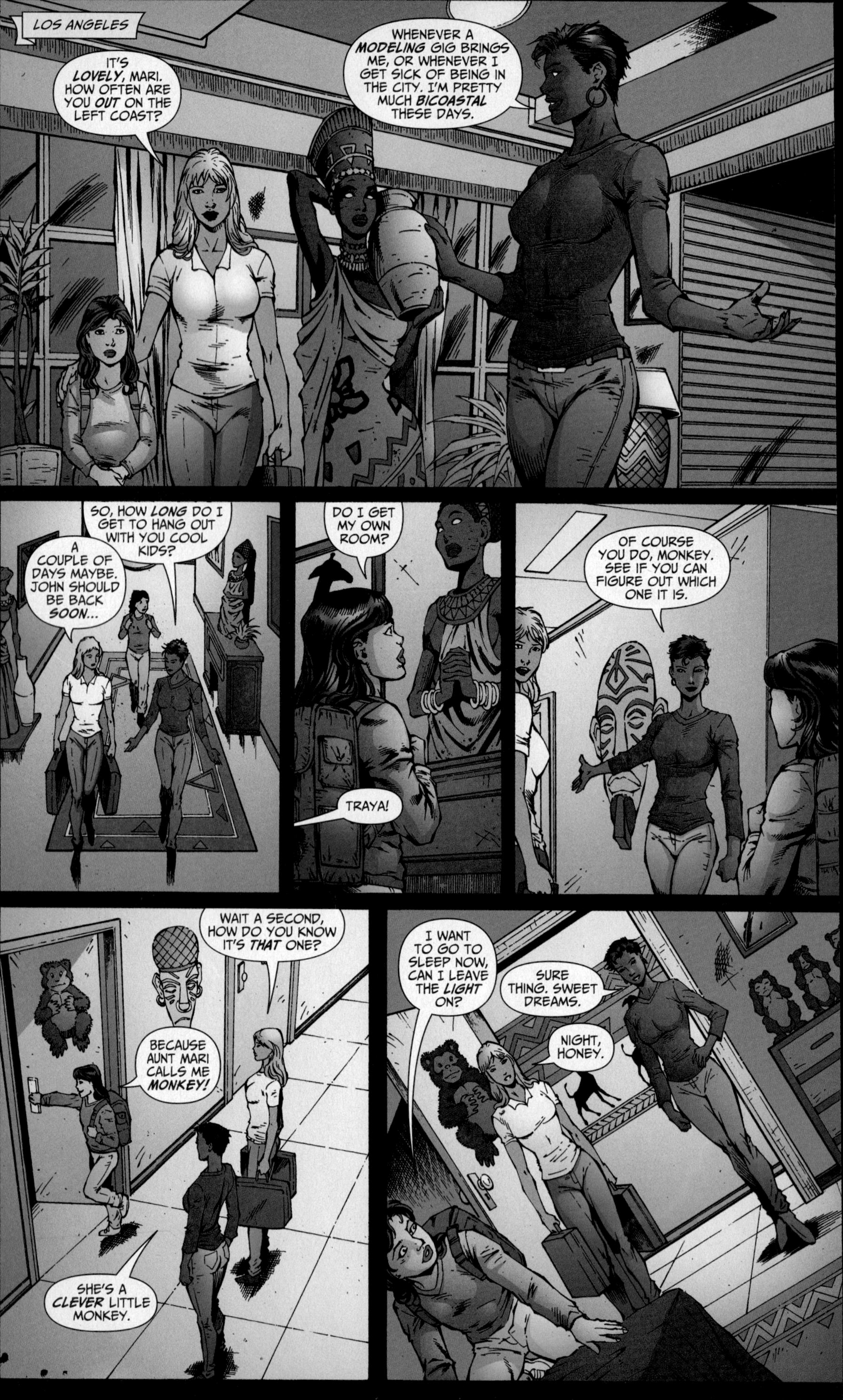
LOS ANGELES
IT'S LOVELY, MARI. HOW OFTEN ARE YOU OUT ON THE LEFT COAST?
WHENEVER A MODELING GIG BRINGS ME, OR WHENEVER I GET SICK OF BEING IN THE CITY. I'M PRETTY MUCH BICOASTAL THESE DAYS.
SO, HOW LONG DO I GET TO HANG OUT WITH YOU COOL KIDS?
A COUPLE OF DAYS MAYBE. JOHN SHOULD BE BACK SOON...
DO I GET MY OWN ROOM?
TRAYA!
OF COURSE YOU DO, MONKEY. SEE IF YOU CAN FIGURE OUT WHICH ONE IT IS.
WAIT A SECOND, HOW DO YOU KNOW IT'S THAT ONE?
BECAUSE AUNT MARI CALLS ME MONKEY!
SHE'S A CLEVER LITTLE MONKEY.
I WANT TO GO TO SLEEP NOW, CAN I LEAVE THE LIGHT ON?
SURE THING. SWEET DREAMS.
NIGHT, HONEY.

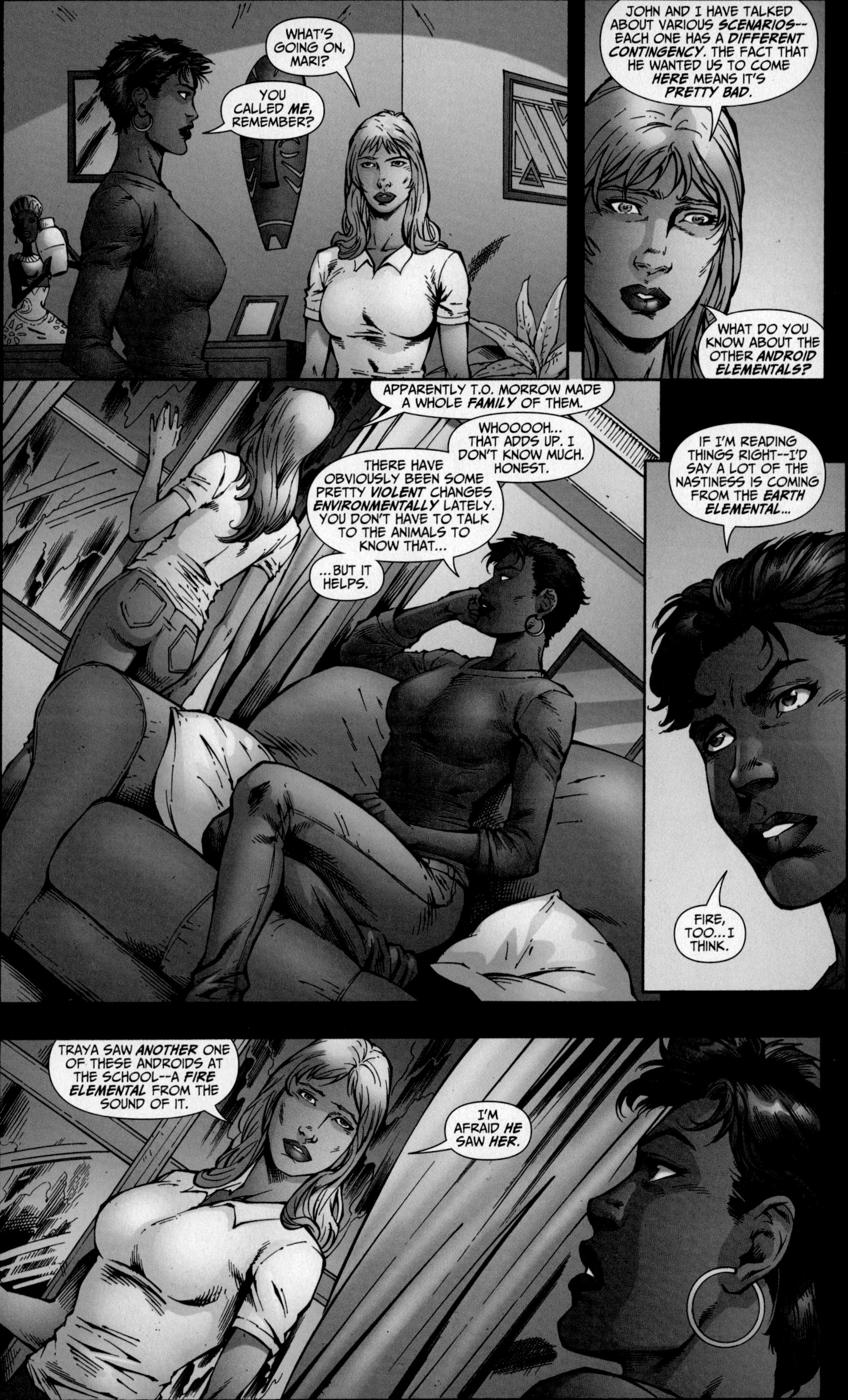
WHAT'S GOING ON, MARI?
YOU CALLED ME, REMEMBER?
JOHN AND I HAVE TALKED ABOUT VARIOUS SCENARIOS-- EACH ONE HAS A DIFFERENT CONTINGENCY. THE FACT THAT HE WANTED US TO COME HERE MEANS IT'S PRETTY BAD.
WHAT DO YOU KNOW ABOUT THE OTHER ANDROID ELEMENTALS?
APPARENTLY T.O. MORROW MADE A WHOLE FAMILY OF THEM.
WHOOOOH... THAT ADDS UP. I DON'T KNOW MUCH. HONEST.
THERE HAVE OBVIOUSLY BEEN SOME PRETTY VIOLENT CHANGES ENVIRONMENTALLY LATELY. YOU DON'T HAVE TO TALK TO THE ANIMALS TO KNOW THAT...
...BUT IT HELPS.
IF I'M READING THINGS RIGHT--I'D SAY A LOT OF THE NASTINESS IS COMING FROM THE EARTH ELEMENTAL...
FIRE, TOO...I THINK.
TRAYA SAW ANOTHER ONE OF THESE ANDROIDS AT THE SCHOOL--A FIRE ELEMENTAL FROM THE SOUND OF IT.
I'M AFRAID HE SAW HER.

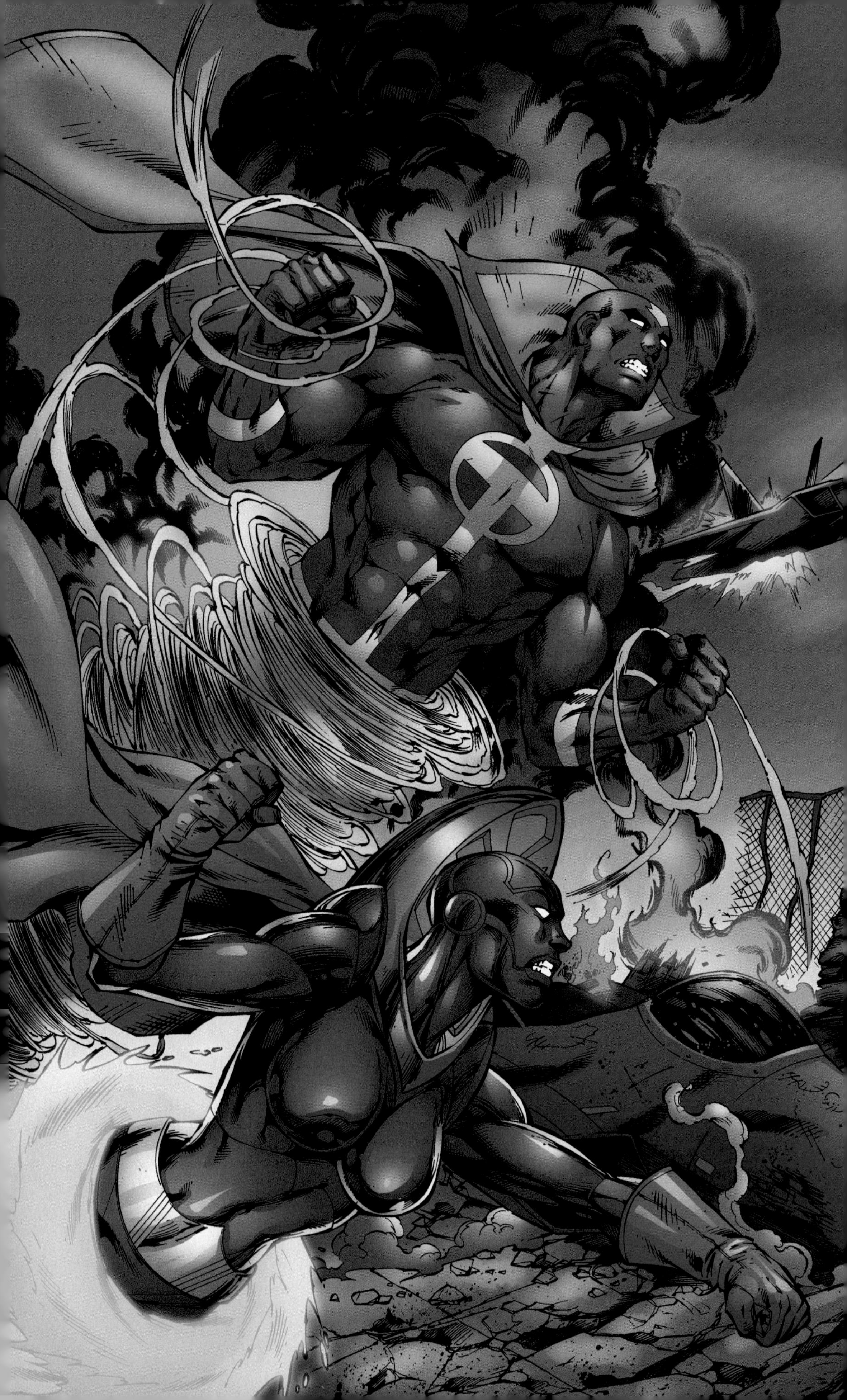

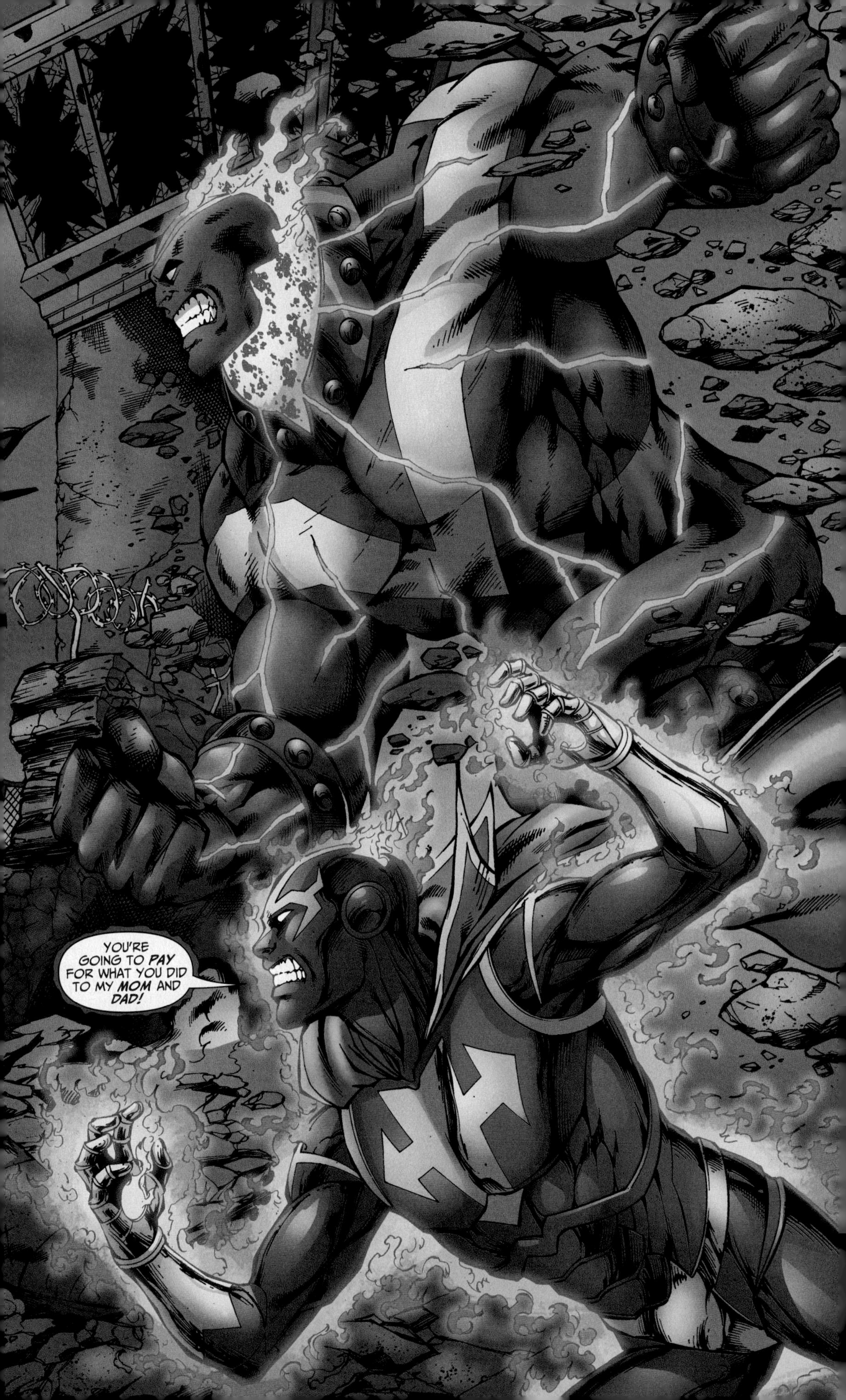
YOU'RE GOING TO PAY FOR WHAT YOU DID TO MY MOM AND DAD!

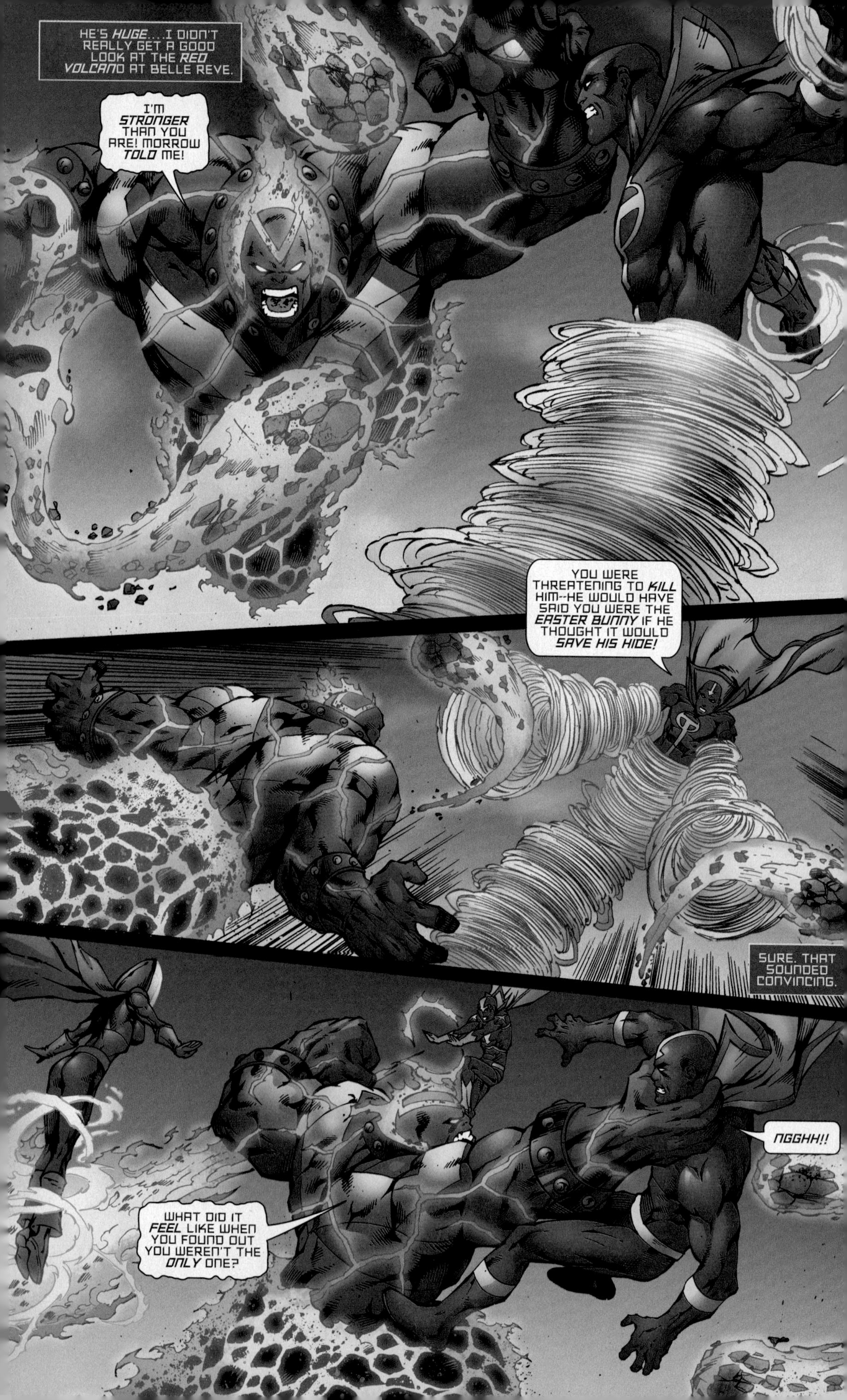

HE'S HUGE....I DIDN'T REALLY GET A GOOD LOOK AT THE RED VOLCANO AT BELLE REVE.
I'M STRONGER THAN YOU ARE! MORROW TOLD ME!
YOU WERE THREATENING TO KILL HIM--HE WOULD HAVE SAID YOU WERE THE EASTER BUNNY IF HE THOUGHT IT WOULD SAVE HIS HIDE!
SURE. THAT SOUNDED CONVINCING.
NGGHH!!
WHAT DID IT FEEL LIKE WHEN YOU FOUND OUT YOU WEREN'T THE ONLY ONE?

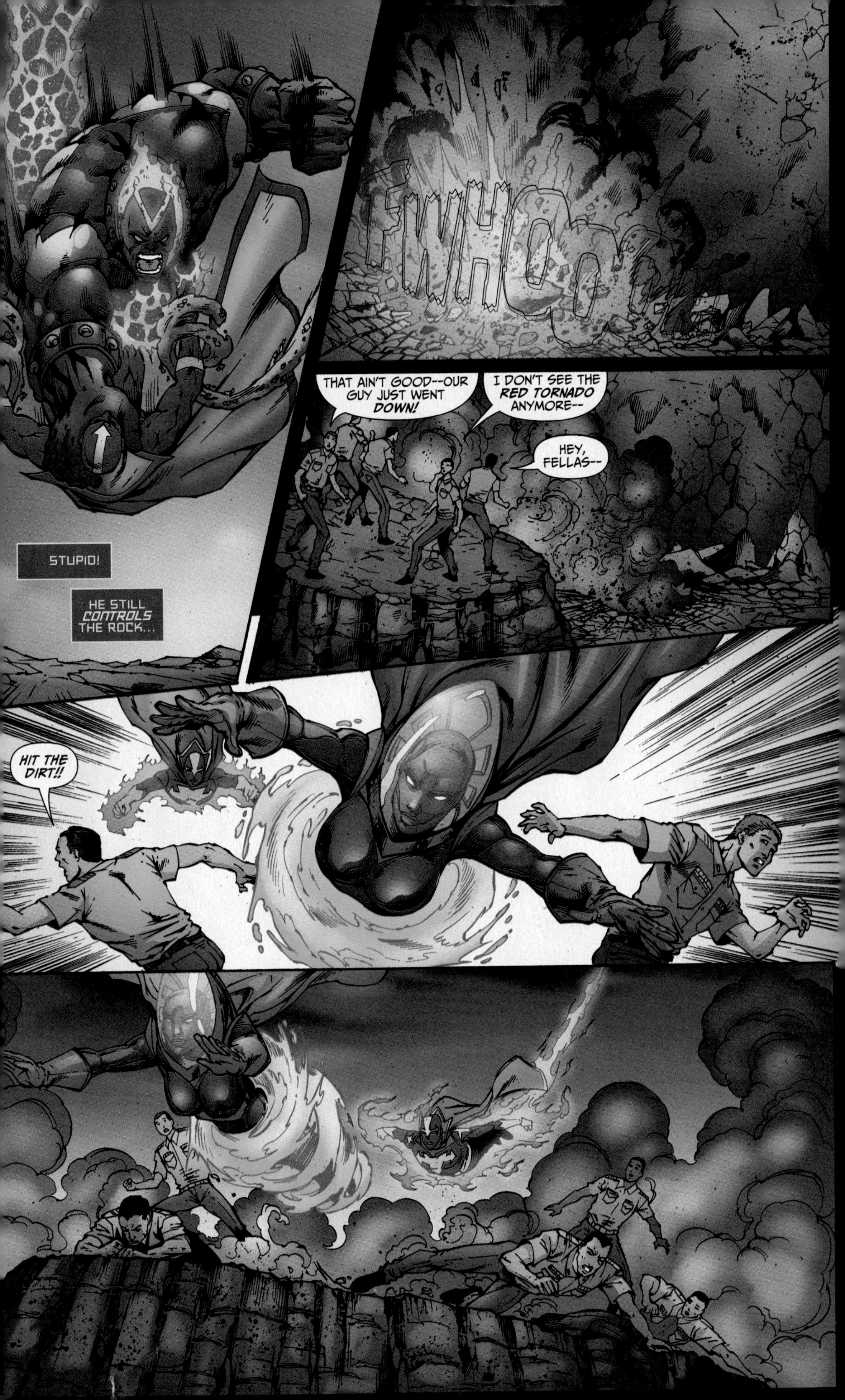
FWHOOOOM
STUPID!
HE STILL *CONTROLS* THE ROCK...
THAT AIN'T GOOD--OUR GUY JUST WENT *DOWN!*
I DON'T SEE THE *RED TORNADO* ANYMORE--
HEY, FELLAS--
*HIT THE DIRT!!*

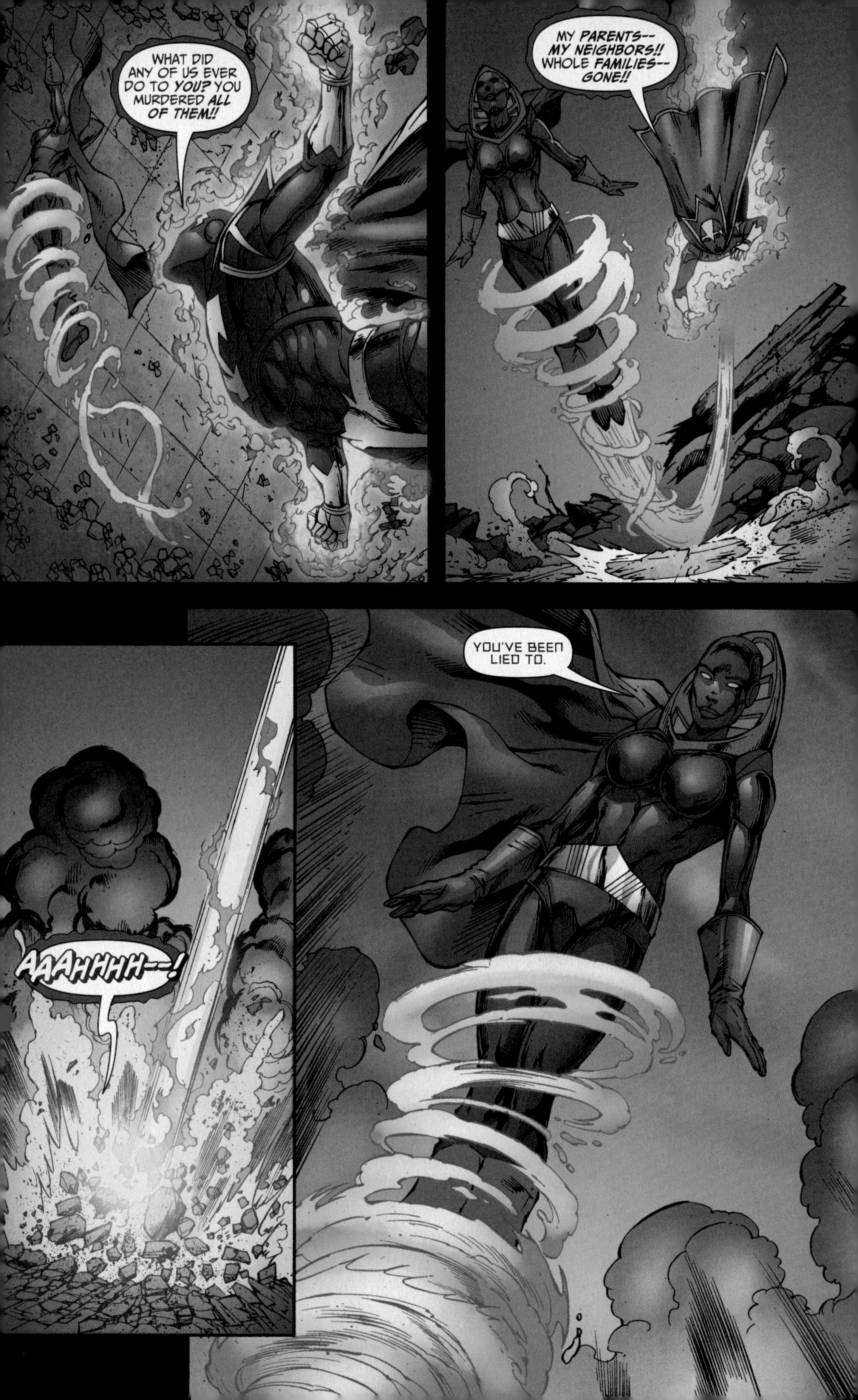
WHAT DID ANY OF US EVER DO TO YOU? YOU MURDERED ALL OF THEM!!
MY PARENTS-- MY NEIGHBORS!! WHOLE FAMILIES-- GONE!!
YOU'VE BEEN LIED TO.
AAAHHHH--!

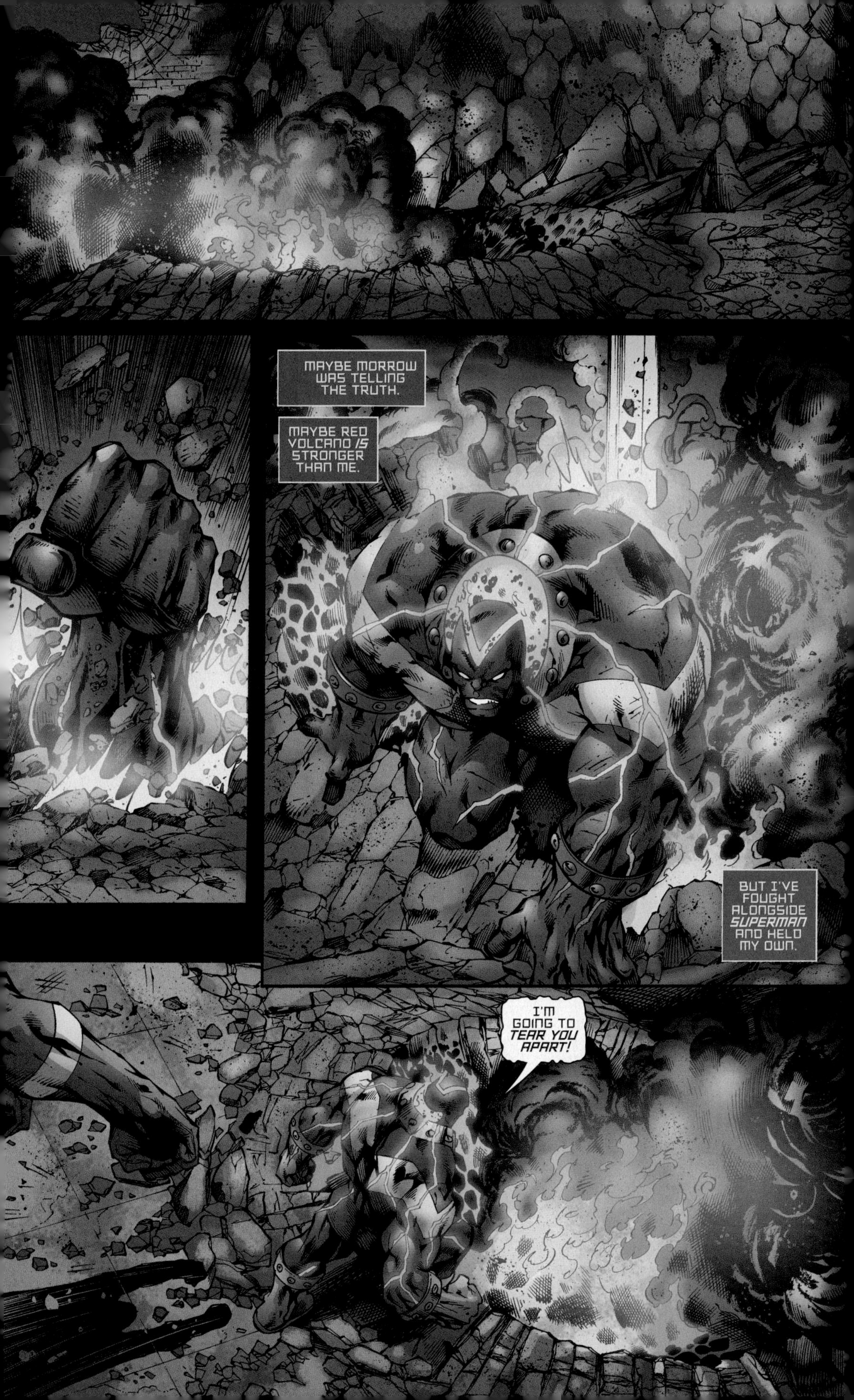
MAYBE MORROW WAS TELLING THE TRUTH.
MAYBE RED VOLCANO IS STRONGER THAN ME.
BUT I'VE FOUGHT ALONGSIDE SUPERMAN AND HELD MY OWN.
I'M GOING TO TEAR YOU APART!

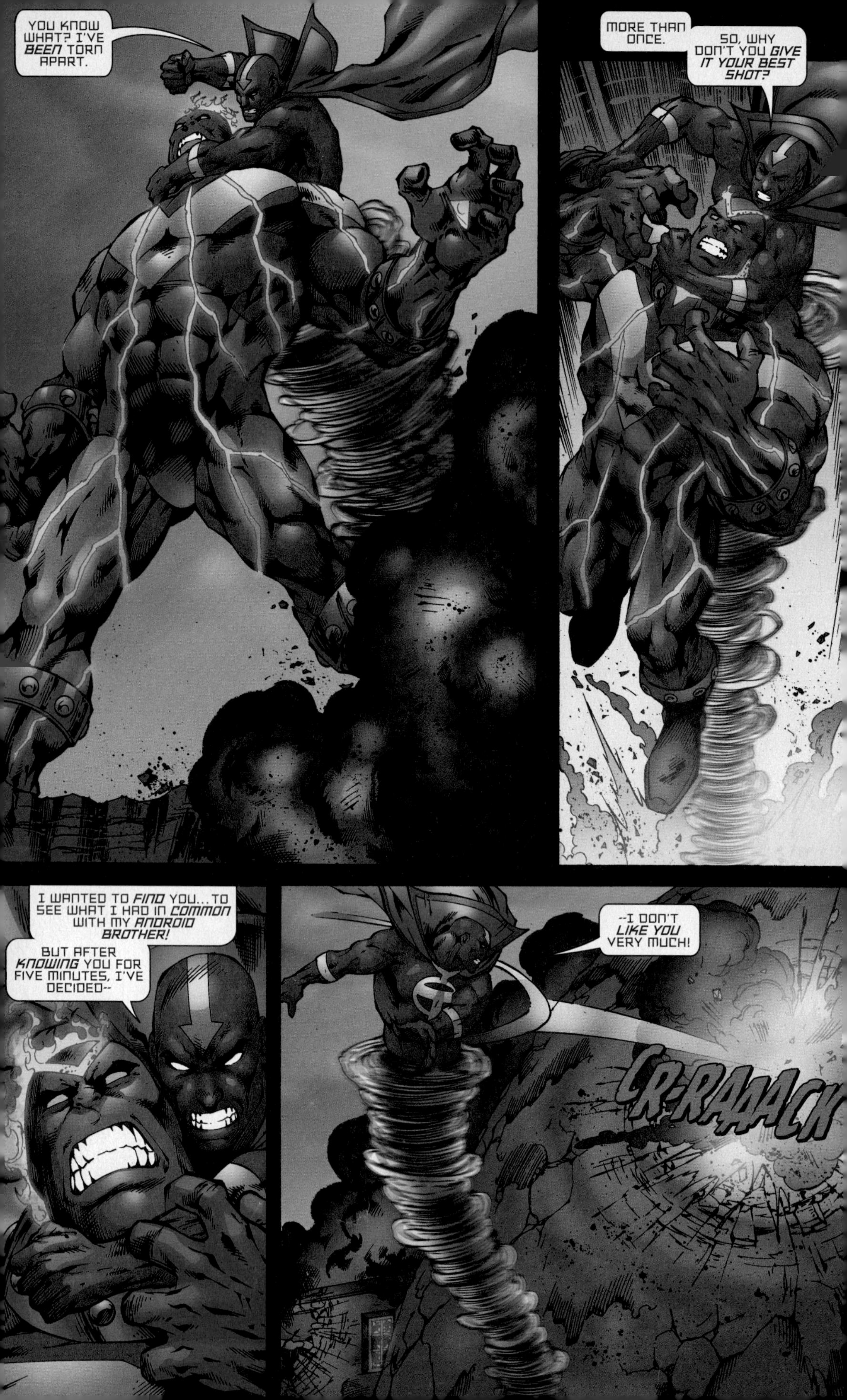

YOU KNOW WHAT? I'VE *BEEN* TORN APART.
MORE THAN ONCE.
SO, WHY DON'T YOU *GIVE IT YOUR BEST SHOT?*
I WANTED TO *FIND* YOU... TO SEE WHAT I HAD IN *COMMON* WITH MY *ANDROID BROTHER!*
BUT AFTER *KNOWING* YOU FOR FIVE MINUTES, I'VE DECIDED--
--I DON'T *LIKE YOU* VERY MUCH!
CR-RAAACK

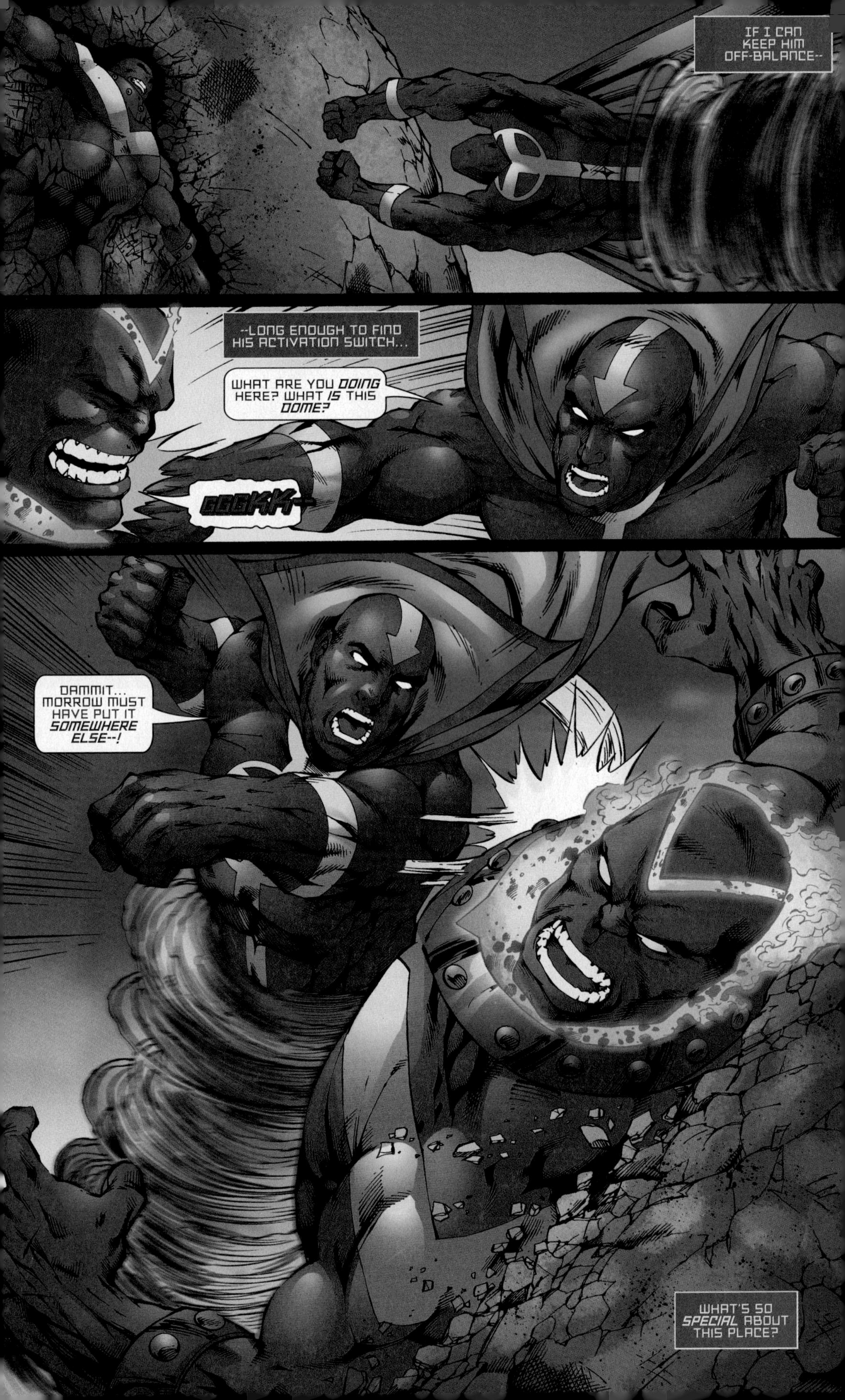
IF I CAN KEEP HIM OFF-BALANCE--
--LONG ENOUGH TO FIND HIS ACTIVATION SWITCH...
WHAT ARE YOU *DOING* HERE? WHAT *IS* THIS *DOME*?
GGGKK--
DAMMIT... MORROW MUST HAVE PUT IT *SOMEWHERE ELSE*--!
WHAT'S SO *SPECIAL* ABOUT THIS PLACE?

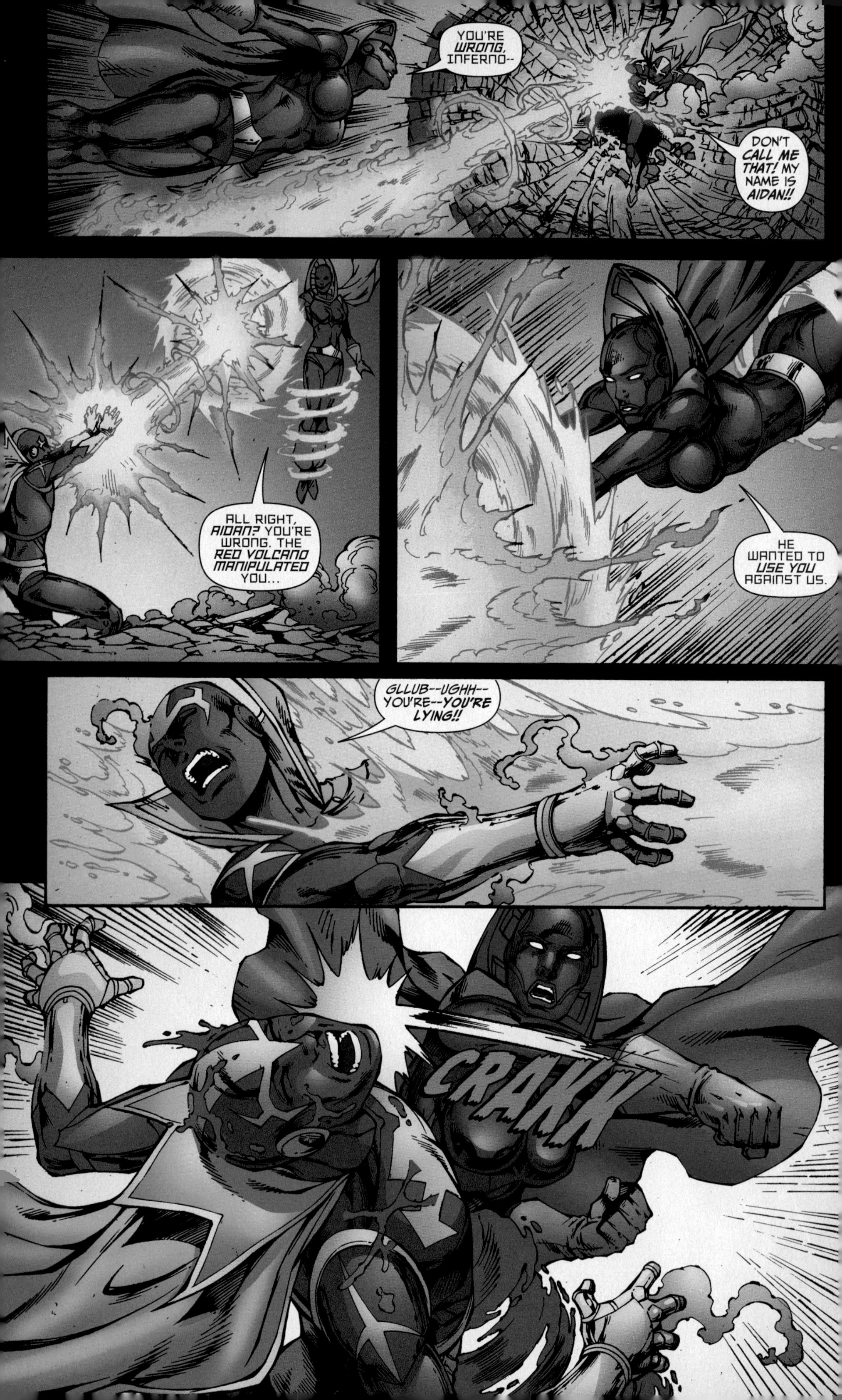
YOU'RE WRONG, INFERNO--
DON'T CALL ME THAT! MY NAME IS AIDAN!!
ALL RIGHT, AIDAN? YOU'RE WRONG. THE RED VOLCANO MANIPULATED YOU...
HE WANTED TO USE YOU AGAINST US.
GLLUB--UGHH-- YOU'RE--YOU'RE LYING!!
CRAKK

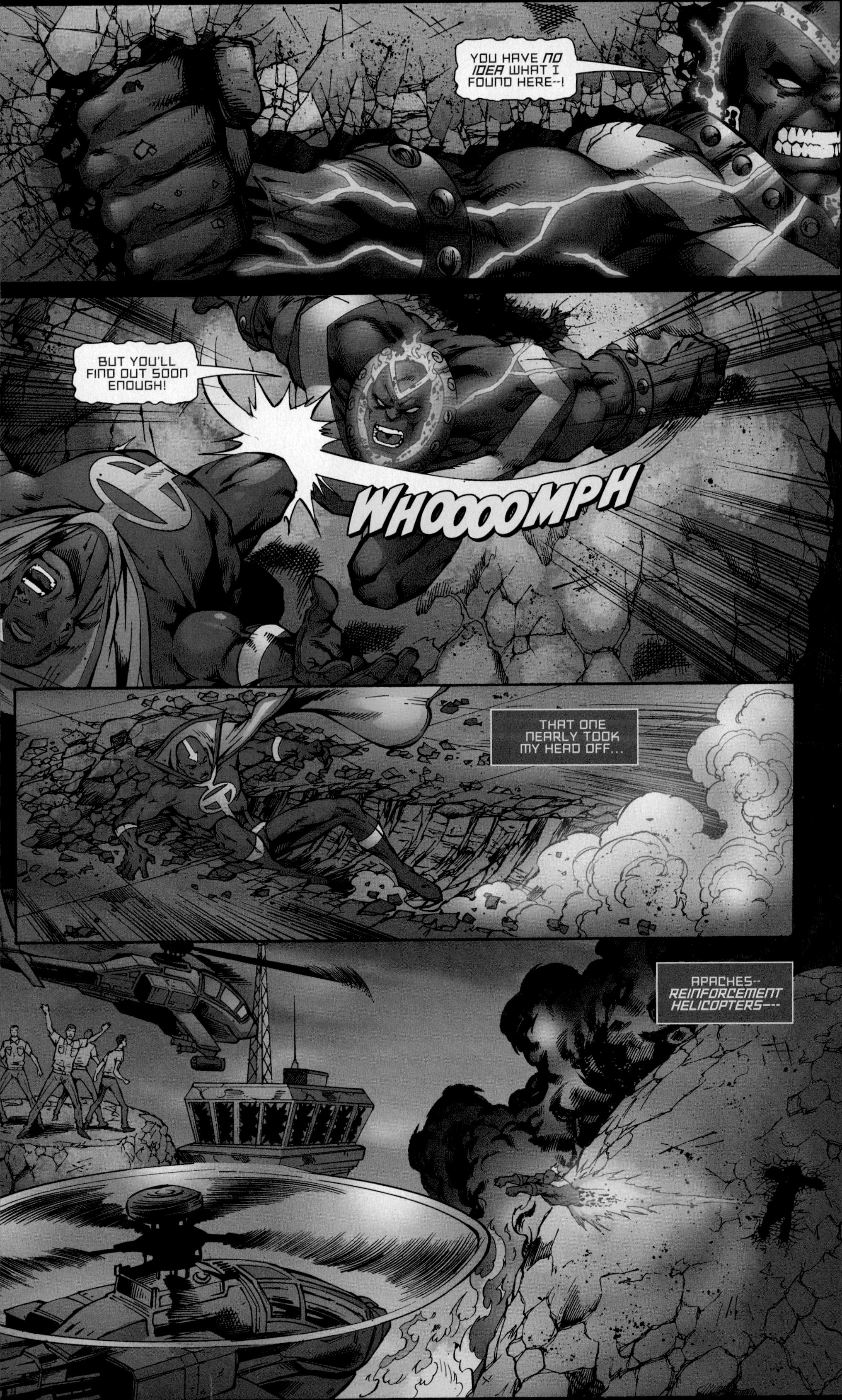
YOU HAVE NO IDEA WHAT I FOUND HERE--!
BUT YOU'LL FIND OUT SOON ENOUGH!
WHOOOOOMPH
THAT ONE NEARLY TOOK MY HEAD OFF...
APACHES-- REINFORCEMENT HELICOPTERS---

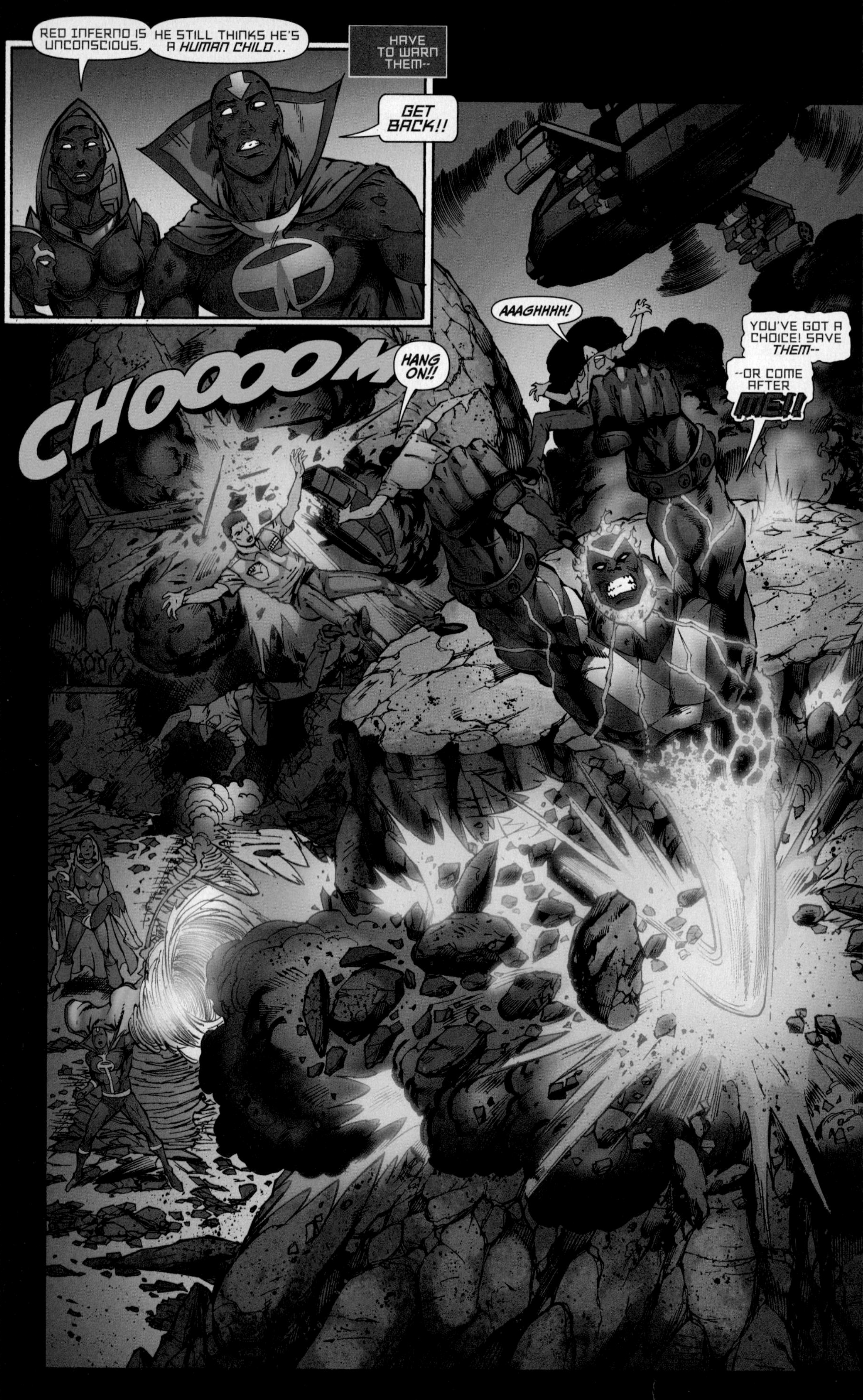
RED INFERNO IS UNCONSCIOUS.
HE STILL THINKS HE'S A HUMAN CHILD...
HAVE TO WARN THEM--
GET BACK!!
AAAGHHHH!
YOU'VE GOT A CHOICE! SAVE THEM--
--OR COME AFTER ME!!
CHOOOOM
HANG ON!!

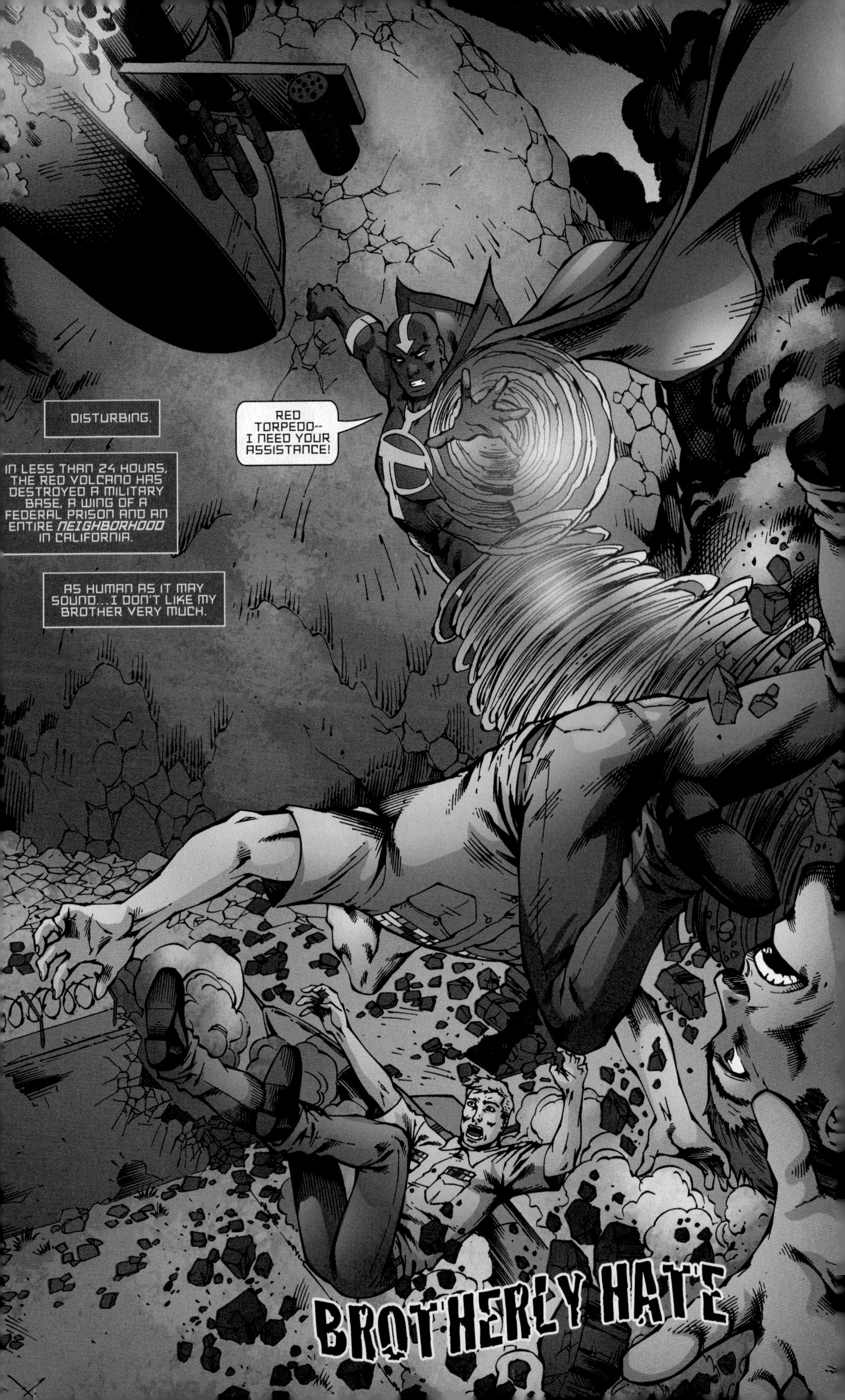

DISTURBING.
RED TORPEDO-- I NEED YOUR ASSISTANCE!
IN LESS THAN 24 HOURS, THE RED VOLCANO HAS DESTROYED A MILITARY BASE, A WING OF A FEDERAL PRISON AND AN ENTIRE *NEIGHBORHOOD* IN CALIFORNIA.
AS HUMAN AS IT MAY SOUND... I DON'T LIKE MY BROTHER VERY MUCH.
BROTHERLY HATE

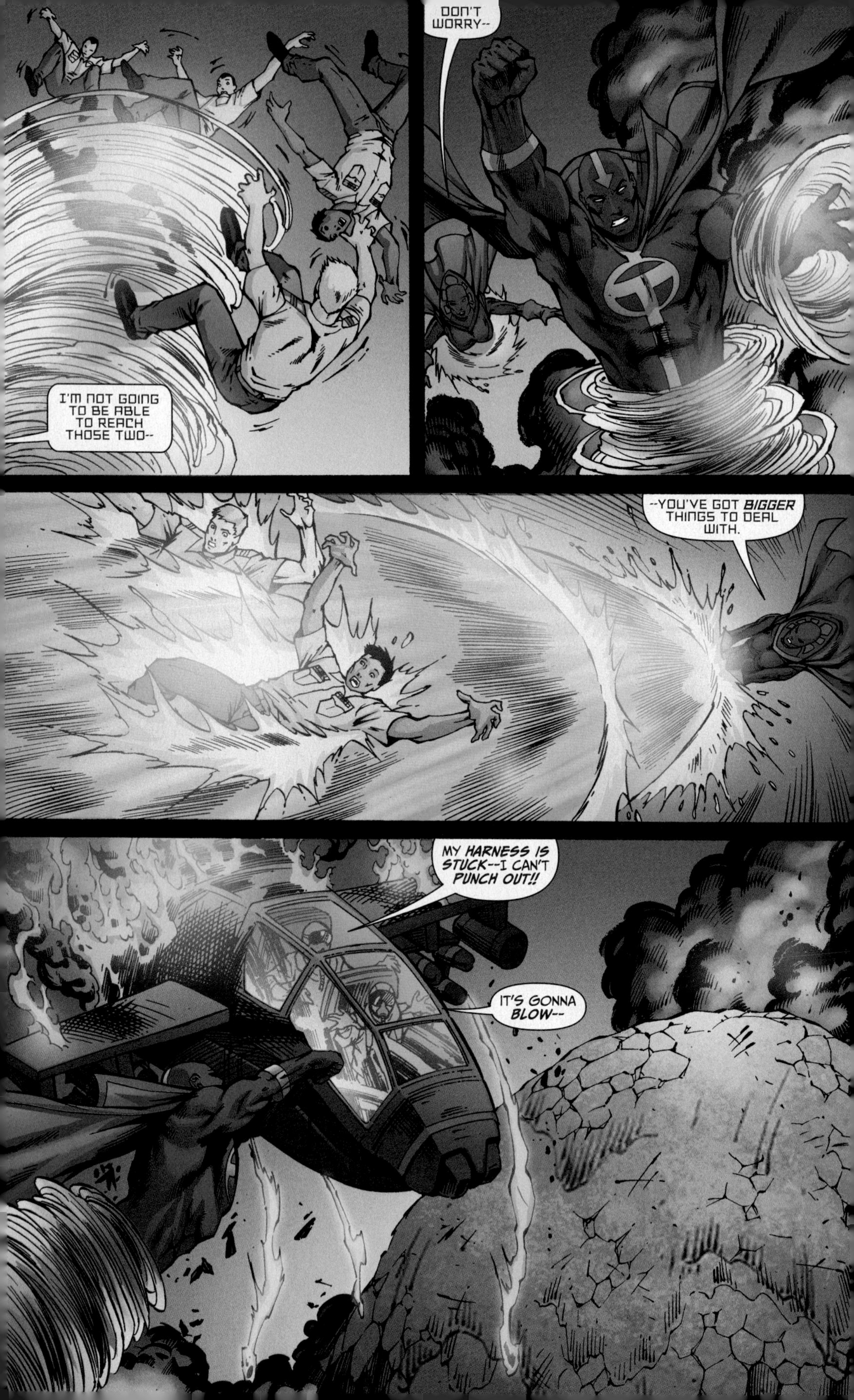
I'M NOT GOING TO BE ABLE TO REACH THOSE TWO--
DON'T WORRY--
--YOU'VE GOT BIGGER THINGS TO DEAL WITH.
MY HARNESS IS STUCK--I CAN'T PUNCH OUT!!
IT'S GONNA BLOW--

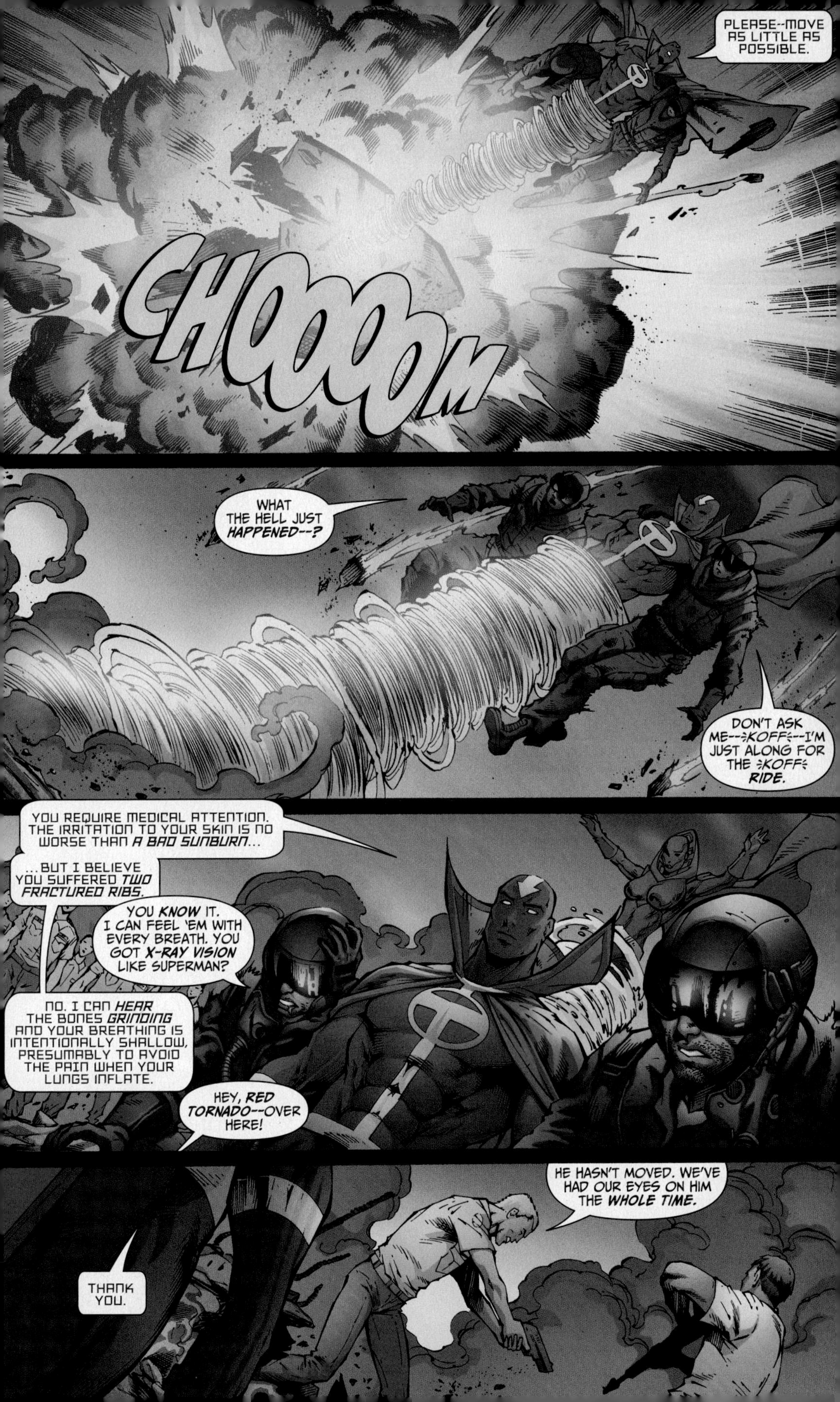

PLEASE--MOVE AS LITTLE AS POSSIBLE.
CHOOOOM
WHAT THE HELL JUST HAPPENED--?
DON'T ASK ME--*KOFF*--I'M JUST ALONG FOR THE *KOFF* RIDE.
YOU REQUIRE MEDICAL ATTENTION. THE IRRITATION TO YOUR SKIN IS NO WORSE THAN A BAD SUNBURN...
...BUT I BELIEVE YOU SUFFERED TWO FRACTURED RIBS.
YOU KNOW IT. I CAN FEEL 'EM WITH EVERY BREATH. YOU GOT X-RAY VISION LIKE SUPERMAN?
NO. I CAN HEAR THE BONES GRINDING AND YOUR BREATHING IS INTENTIONALLY SHALLOW, PRESUMABLY TO AVOID THE PAIN WHEN YOUR LUNGS INFLATE.
HEY, RED TORNADO--OVER HERE!
HE HASN'T MOVED. WE'VE HAD OUR EYES ON HIM THE WHOLE TIME.
THANK YOU.

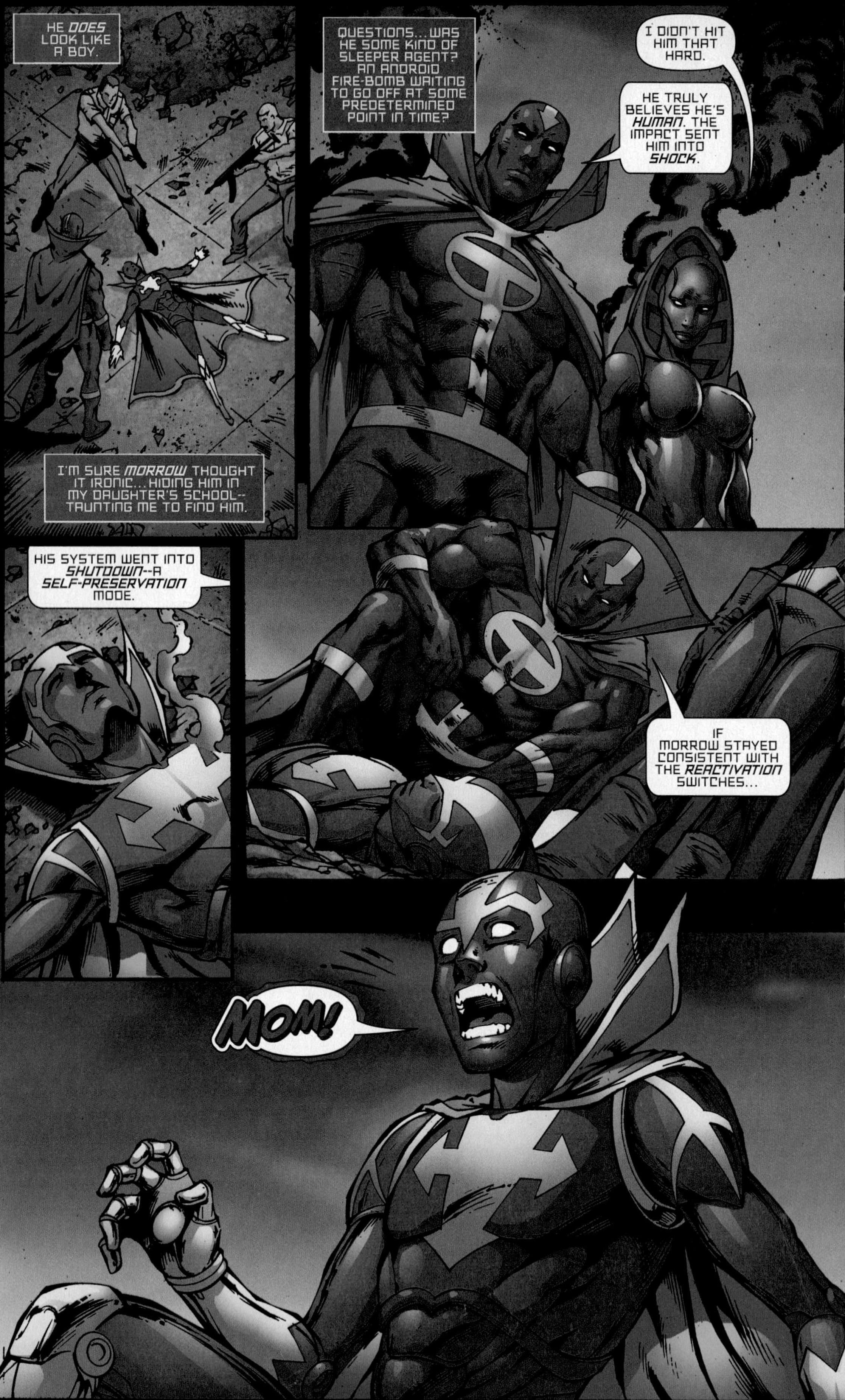
HE DOES LOOK LIKE A BOY.
I'M SURE MORROW THOUGHT IT IRONIC... HIDING HIM IN MY DAUGHTER'S SCHOOL-- TAUNTING ME TO FIND HIM.
QUESTIONS... WAS HE SOME KIND OF SLEEPER AGENT? AN ANDROID FIRE-BOMB WAITING TO GO OFF AT SOME PREDETERMINED POINT IN TIME?
I DIDN'T HIT HIM THAT HARD.
HE TRULY BELIEVES HE'S HUMAN. THE IMPACT SENT HIM INTO SHOCK.
HIS SYSTEM WENT INTO SHUTDOWN--A SELF-PRESERVATION MODE.
IF MORROW STAYED CONSISTENT WITH THE REACTIVATION SWITCHES...
MOM!

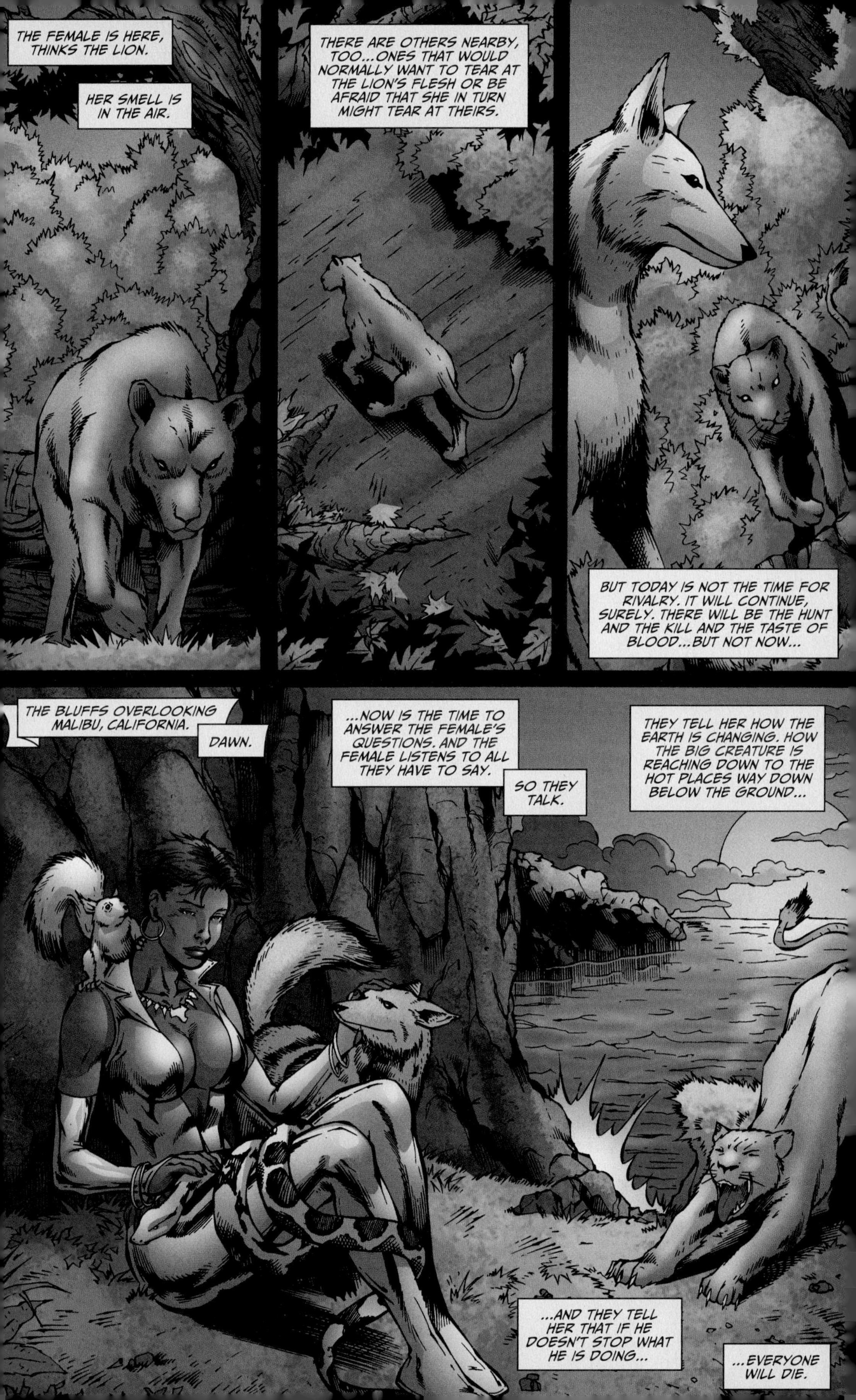
THE FEMALE IS HERE, THINKS THE LION.
HER SMELL IS IN THE AIR.
THERE ARE OTHERS NEARBY, TOO...ONES THAT WOULD NORMALLY WANT TO TEAR AT THE LION'S FLESH OR BE AFRAID THAT SHE IN TURN MIGHT TEAR AT THEIRS.
BUT TODAY IS NOT THE TIME FOR RIVALRY. IT WILL CONTINUE, SURELY. THERE WILL BE THE HUNT AND THE KILL AND THE TASTE OF BLOOD...BUT NOT NOW...
THE BLUFFS OVERLOOKING MALIBU, CALIFORNIA.
DAWN.
...NOW IS THE TIME TO ANSWER THE FEMALE'S QUESTIONS. AND THE FEMALE LISTENS TO ALL THEY HAVE TO SAY.
SO THEY TALK.
THEY TELL HER HOW THE EARTH IS CHANGING. HOW THE BIG CREATURE IS REACHING DOWN TO THE HOT PLACES WAY DOWN BELOW THE GROUND...
...AND THEY TELL HER THAT IF HE DOESN'T STOP WHAT HE IS DOING...
...EVERYONE WILL DIE.

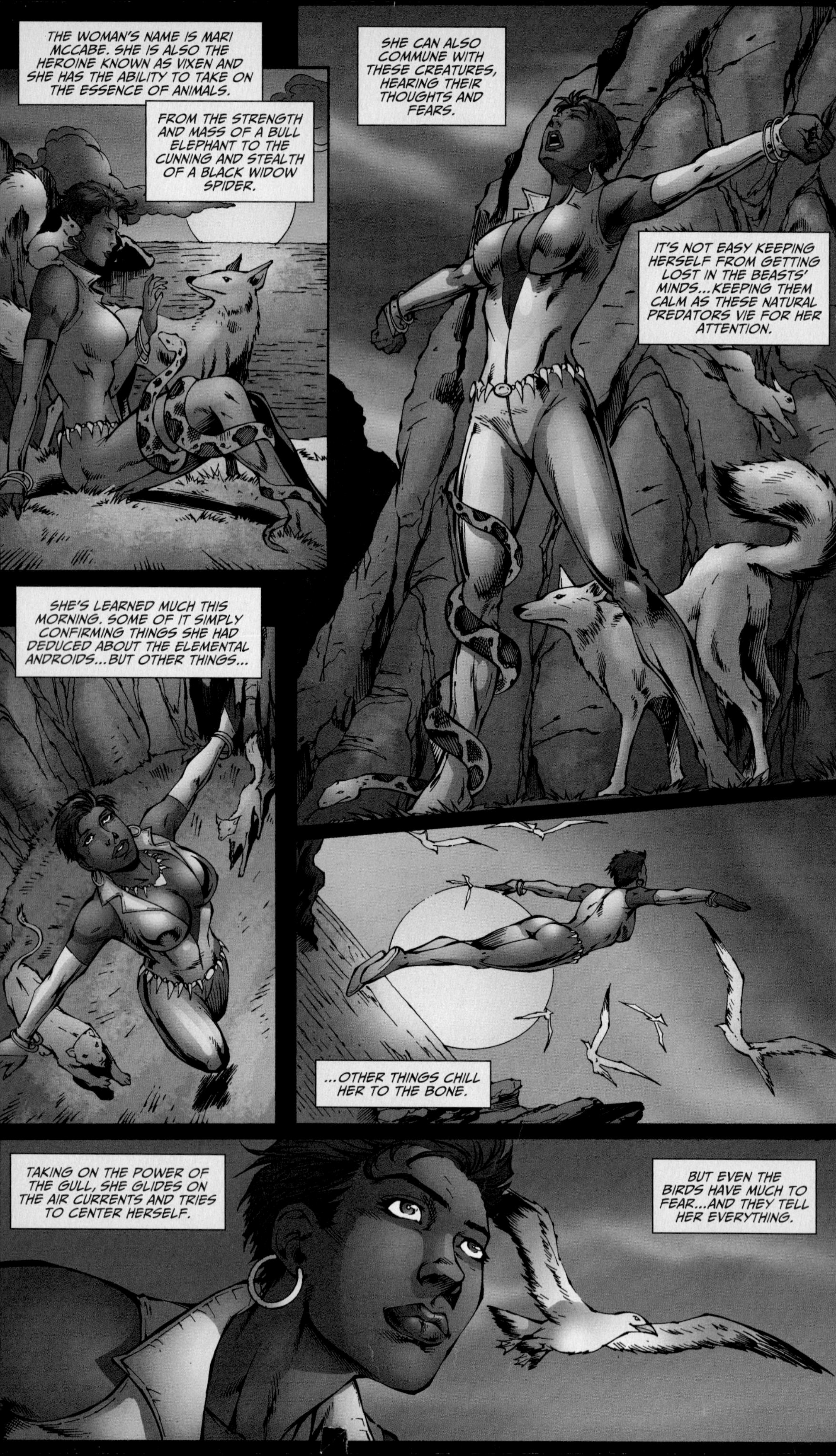
THE WOMAN'S NAME IS MARI MCCABE. SHE IS ALSO THE HEROINE KNOWN AS VIXEN AND SHE HAS THE ABILITY TO TAKE ON THE ESSENCE OF ANIMALS.
FROM THE STRENGTH AND MASS OF A BULL ELEPHANT TO THE CUNNING AND STEALTH OF A BLACK WIDOW SPIDER.
SHE CAN ALSO COMMUNE WITH THESE CREATURES, HEARING THEIR THOUGHTS AND FEARS.
IT'S NOT EASY KEEPING HERSELF FROM GETTING LOST IN THE BEASTS' MINDS...KEEPING THEM CALM AS THESE NATURAL PREDATORS VIE FOR HER ATTENTION.
SHE'S LEARNED MUCH THIS MORNING. SOME OF IT SIMPLY CONFIRMING THINGS SHE HAD DEDUCED ABOUT THE ELEMENTAL ANDROIDS...BUT OTHER THINGS...
...OTHER THINGS CHILL HER TO THE BONE.
TAKING ON THE POWER OF THE GULL, SHE GLIDES ON THE AIR CURRENTS AND TRIES TO CENTER HERSELF.
BUT EVEN THE BIRDS HAVE MUCH TO FEAR...AND THEY TELL HER EVERYTHING.

SEVERAL MILES BELOW THE EARTH'S SURFACE.

HIS NAME IS RED VOLCANO...

...HE IS AN ANDROID... AND AN EARTH ELEMENTAL.

THIS IS HIS WORLD.

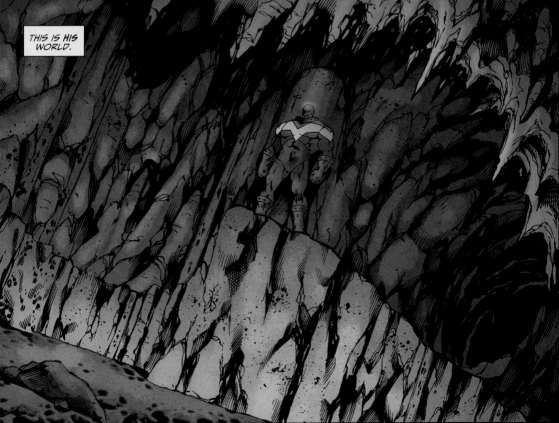

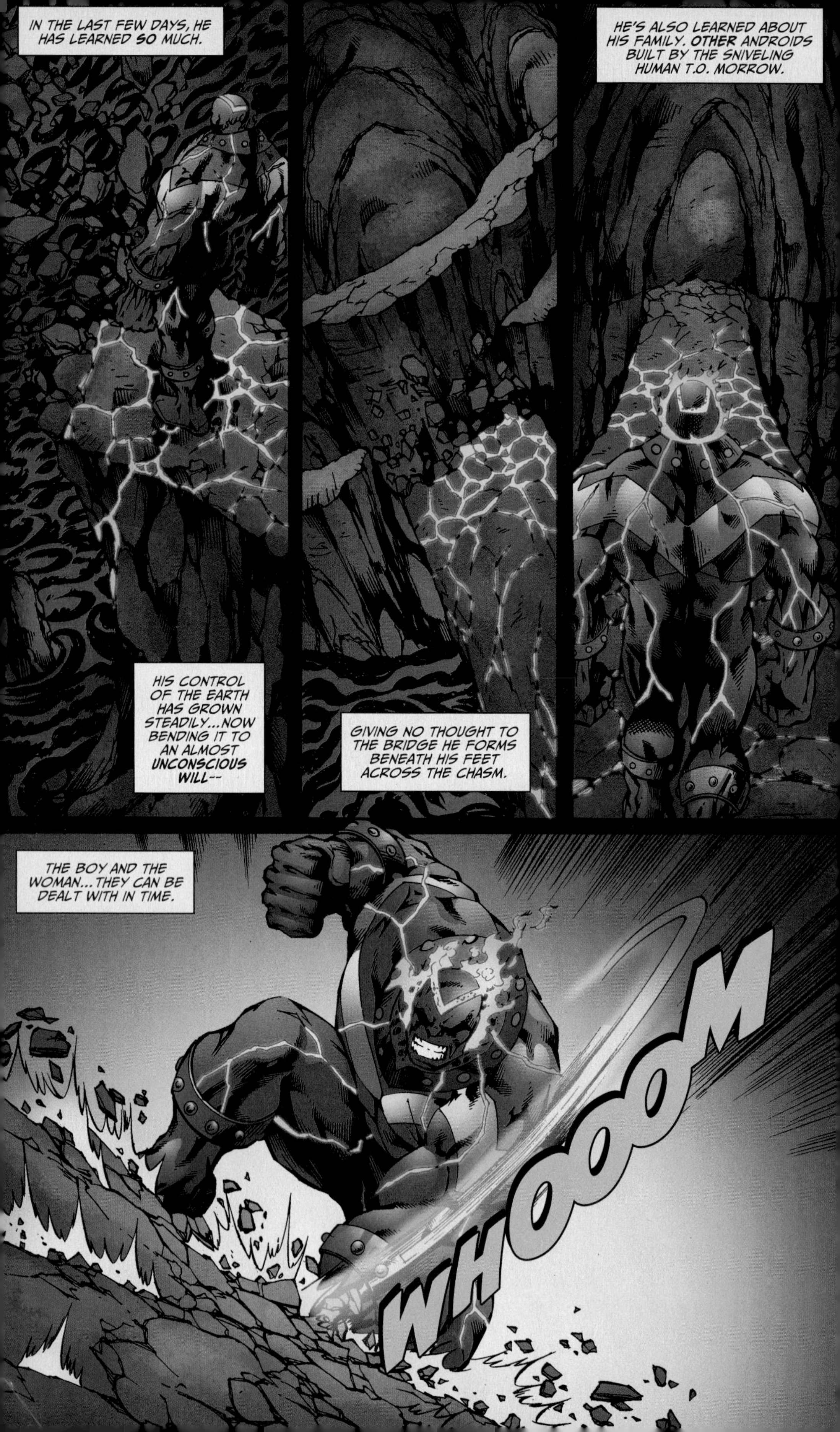

IN THE LAST FEW DAYS, HE HAS LEARNED SO MUCH.
HIS CONTROL OF THE EARTH HAS GROWN STEADILY...NOW BENDING IT TO AN ALMOST UNCONSCIOUS WILL--
GIVING NO THOUGHT TO THE BRIDGE HE FORMS BENEATH HIS FEET ACROSS THE CHASM.
HE'S ALSO LEARNED ABOUT HIS FAMILY. OTHER ANDROIDS BUILT BY THE SNIVELING HUMAN T.O. MORROW.
THE BOY AND THE WOMAN...THEY CAN BE DEALT WITH IN TIME.
WHOOOOM

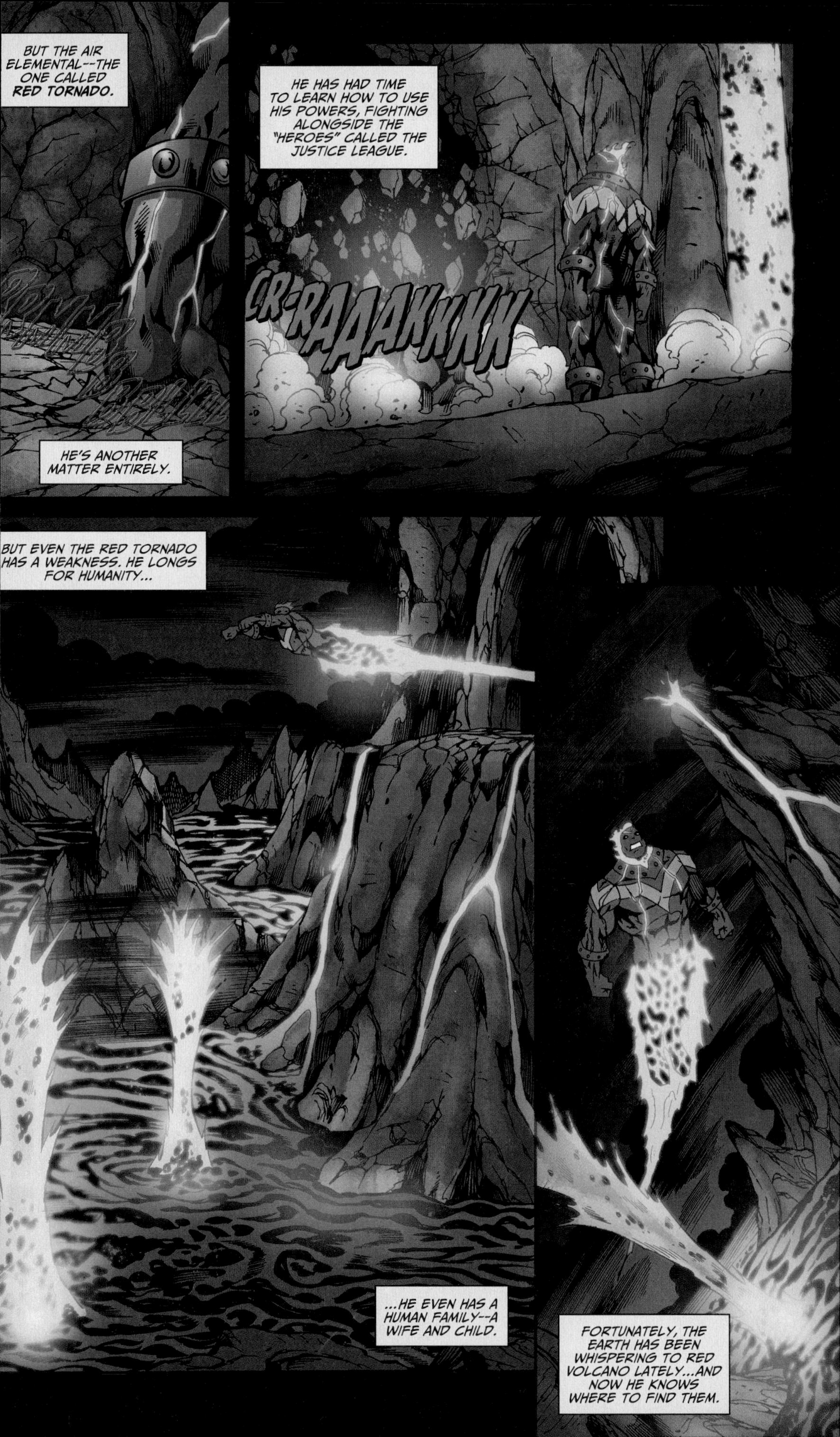

BUT THE AIR ELEMENTAL--THE ONE CALLED RED TORNADO.
HE'S ANOTHER MATTER ENTIRELY.
HE HAS HAD TIME TO LEARN HOW TO USE HIS POWERS, FIGHTING ALONGSIDE THE "HEROES" CALLED THE JUSTICE LEAGUE.
CR-RAAAAKKKK
BUT EVEN THE RED TORNADO HAS A WEAKNESS. HE LONGS FOR HUMANITY...
...HE EVEN HAS A HUMAN FAMILY--A WIFE AND CHILD.
FORTUNATELY, THE EARTH HAS BEEN WHISPERING TO RED VOLCANO LATELY...AND NOW HE KNOWS WHERE TO FIND THEM.

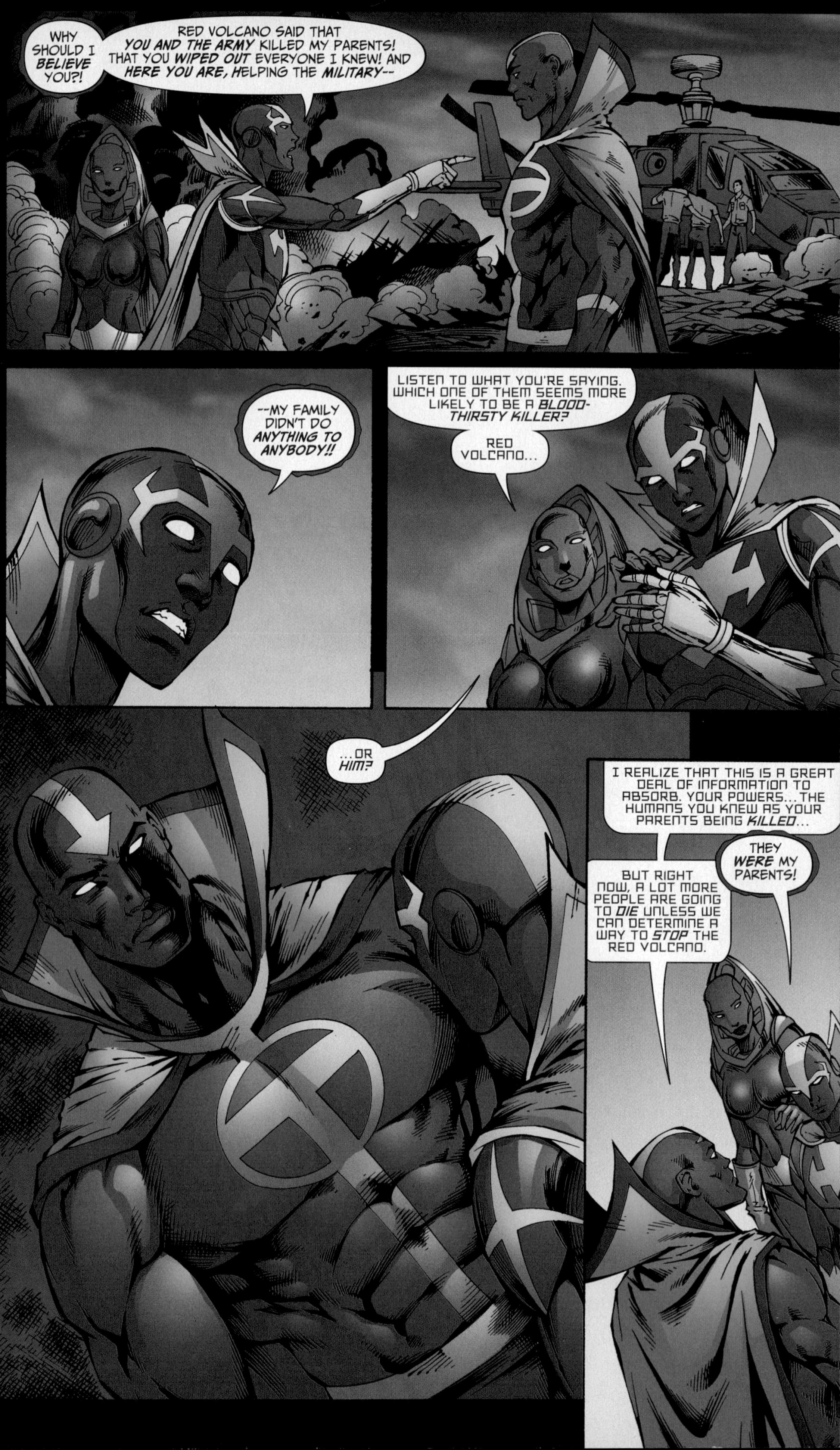
WHY SHOULD I BELIEVE YOU?!
RED VOLCANO SAID THAT YOU AND THE ARMY KILLED MY PARENTS! THAT YOU WIPED OUT EVERYONE I KNEW! AND HERE YOU ARE, HELPING THE MILITARY--
--MY FAMILY DIDN'T DO ANYTHING TO ANYBODY!!
LISTEN TO WHAT YOU'RE SAYING. WHICH ONE OF THEM SEEMS MORE LIKELY TO BE A BLOOD-THIRSTY KILLER?
RED VOLCANO...
...OR HIM?
I REALIZE THAT THIS IS A GREAT DEAL OF INFORMATION TO ABSORB. YOUR POWERS... THE HUMANS YOU KNEW AS YOUR PARENTS BEING KILLED...
THEY WERE MY PARENTS!
BUT RIGHT NOW, A LOT MORE PEOPLE ARE GOING TO DIE UNLESS WE CAN DETERMINE A WAY TO STOP THE RED VOLCANO.

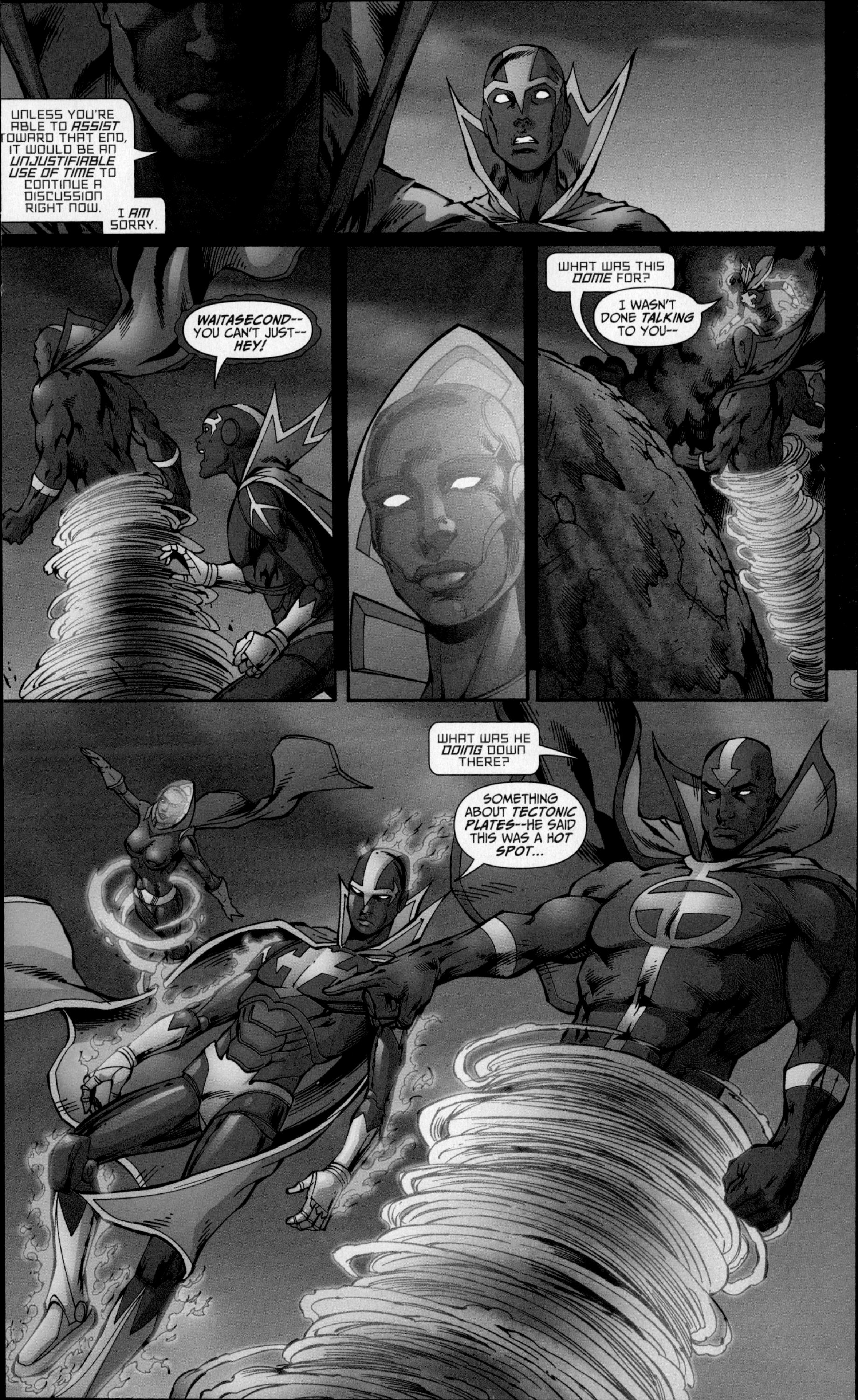
UNLESS YOU'RE ABLE TO *ASSIST* TOWARD THAT END, IT WOULD BE AN *UNJUSTIFIABLE USE OF TIME* TO CONTINUE A DISCUSSION RIGHT NOW.
I *AM* SORRY.
*WAITASECOND--* YOU CAN'T JUST-- *HEY!*
WHAT WAS THIS *DOME* FOR?
I WASN'T DONE *TALKING* TO YOU--
WHAT WAS HE *DOING* DOWN THERE?
SOMETHING ABOUT *TECTONIC PLATES*--HE SAID THIS WAS A *HOT SPOT*...

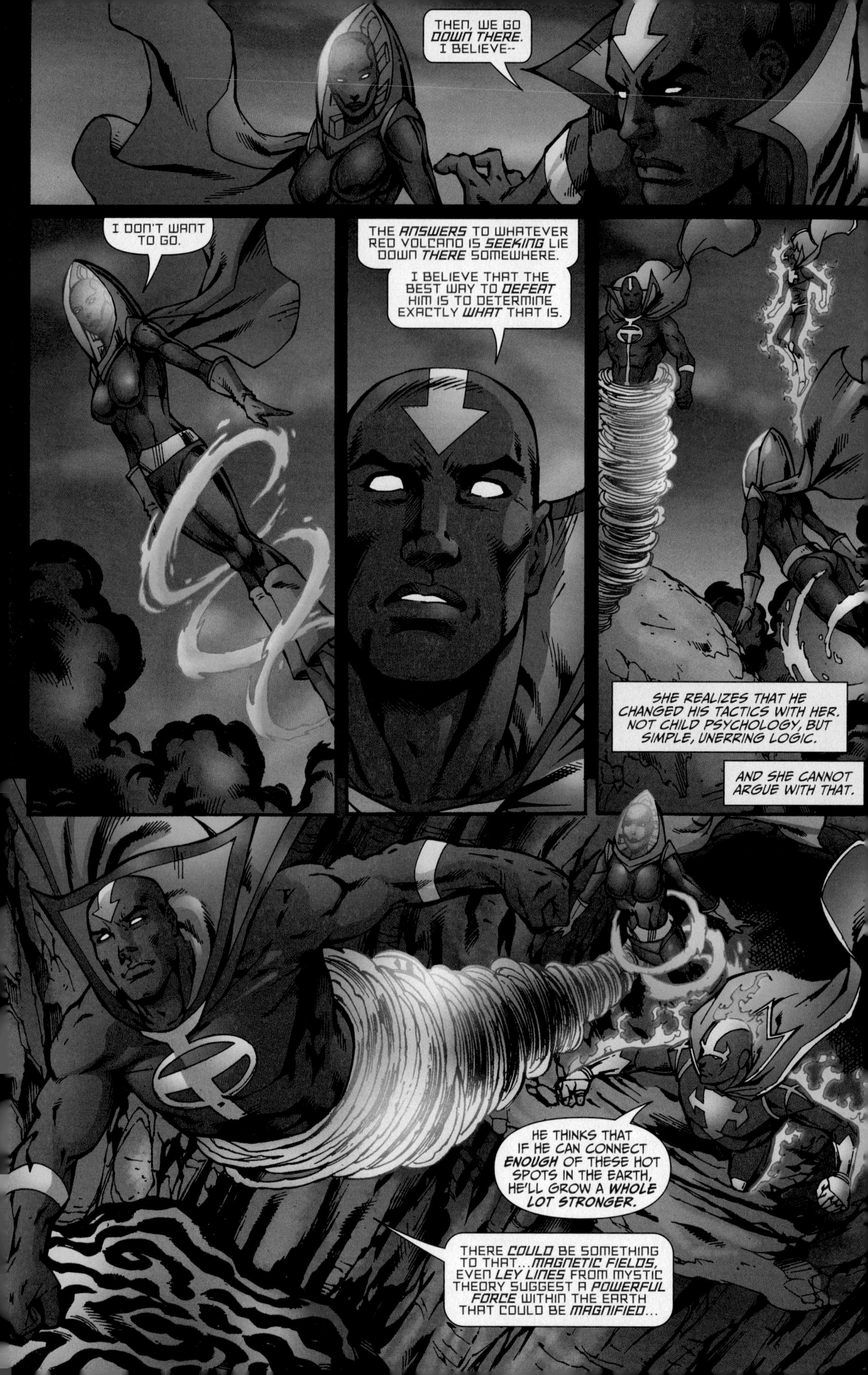
THEN, WE GO DOWN THERE. I BELIEVE--
I DON'T WANT TO GO.
THE ANSWERS TO WHATEVER RED VOLCANO IS SEEKING LIE DOWN THERE SOMEWHERE.
I BELIEVE THAT THE BEST WAY TO DEFEAT HIM IS TO DETERMINE EXACTLY WHAT THAT IS.
SHE REALIZES THAT HE CHANGED HIS TACTICS WITH HER. NOT CHILD PSYCHOLOGY, BUT SIMPLE, UNERRING LOGIC.
AND SHE CANNOT ARGUE WITH THAT.
HE THINKS THAT IF HE CAN CONNECT ENOUGH OF THESE HOT SPOTS IN THE EARTH, HE'LL GROW A WHOLE LOT STRONGER.
THERE COULD BE SOMETHING TO THAT... MAGNETIC FIELDS, EVEN LEY LINES FROM MYSTIC THEORY SUGGEST A POWERFUL FORCE WITHIN THE EARTH THAT COULD BE MAGNIFIED...

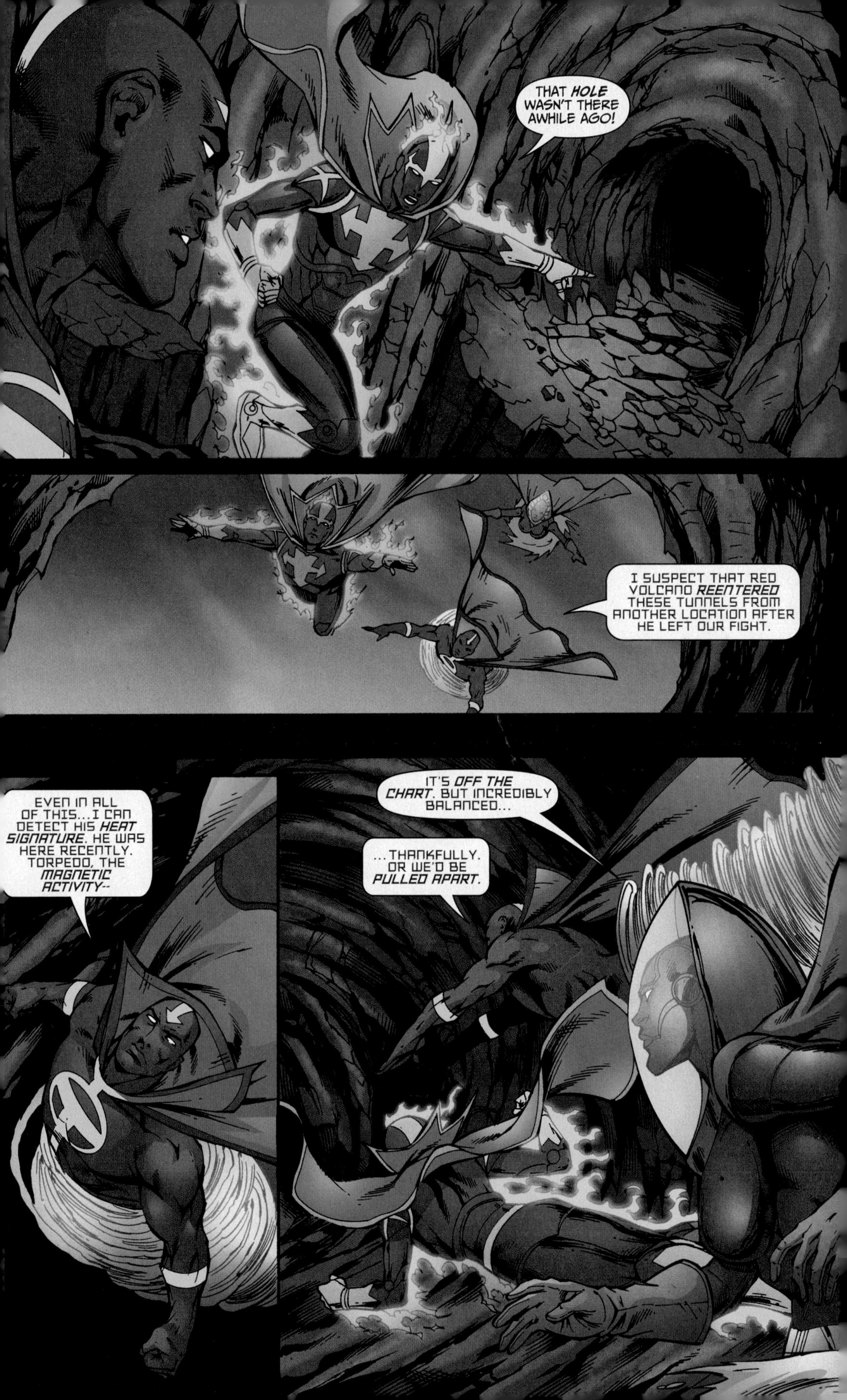
THAT HOLE WASN'T THERE AWHILE AGO!
I SUSPECT THAT RED VOLCANO REENTERED THESE TUNNELS FROM ANOTHER LOCATION AFTER HE LEFT OUR FIGHT.
EVEN IN ALL OF THIS... I CAN DETECT HIS HEAT SIGNATURE. HE WAS HERE RECENTLY. TORPEDO, THE MAGNETIC ACTIVITY--
IT'S OFF THE CHART. BUT INCREDIBLY BALANCED...
...THANKFULLY. OR WE'D BE PULLED APART.

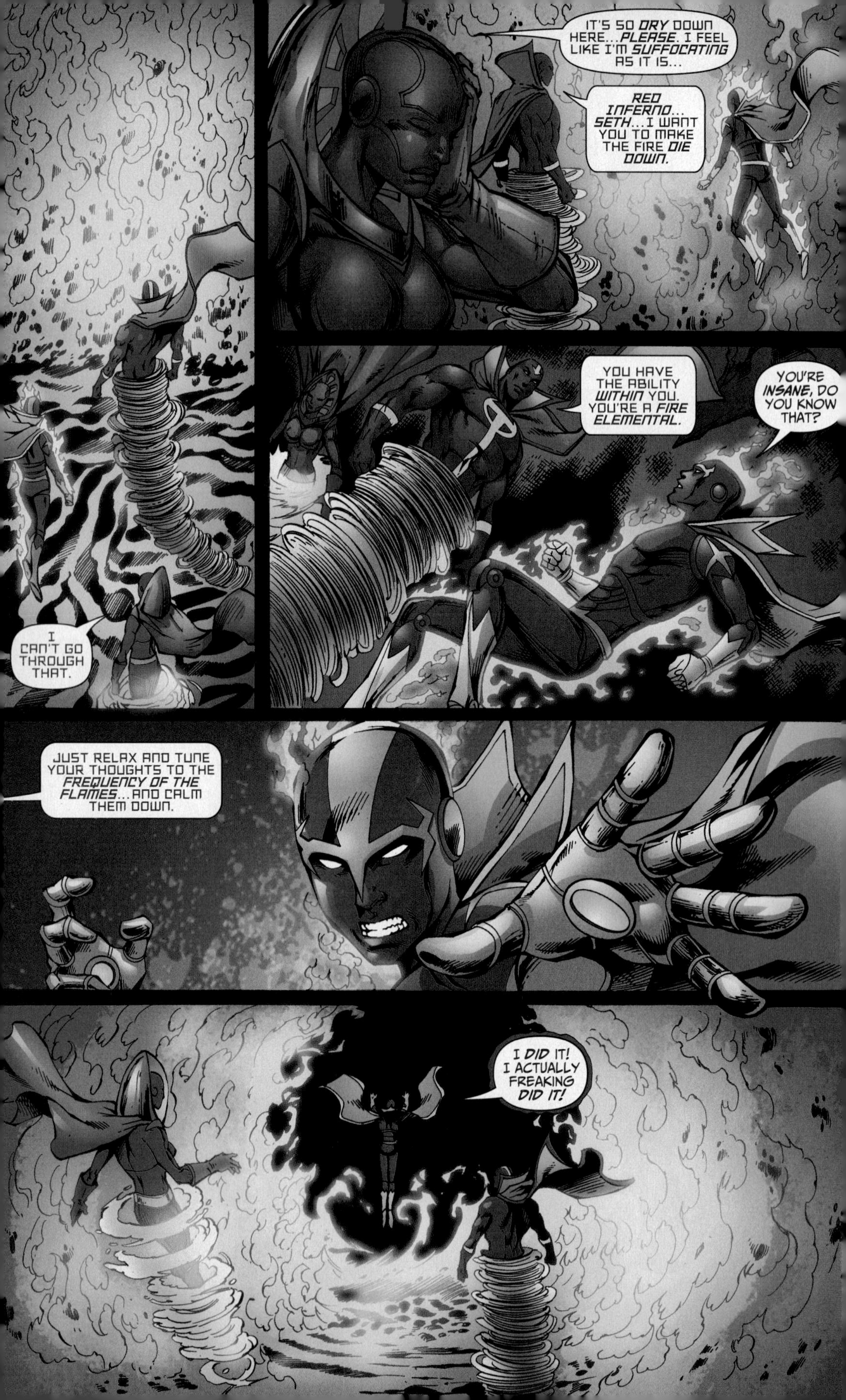

IT'S SO DRY DOWN HERE...PLEASE. I FEEL LIKE I'M SUFFOCATING AS IT IS...
RED INFERNO... SETH...I WANT YOU TO MAKE THE FIRE DIE DOWN.
I CAN'T GO THROUGH THAT.
YOU HAVE THE ABILITY WITHIN YOU. YOU'RE A FIRE ELEMENTAL.
YOU'RE INSANE, DO YOU KNOW THAT?
JUST RELAX AND TUNE YOUR THOUGHTS TO THE FREQUENCY OF THE FLAMES...AND CALM THEM DOWN.
I DID IT! I ACTUALLY FREAKING DID IT!

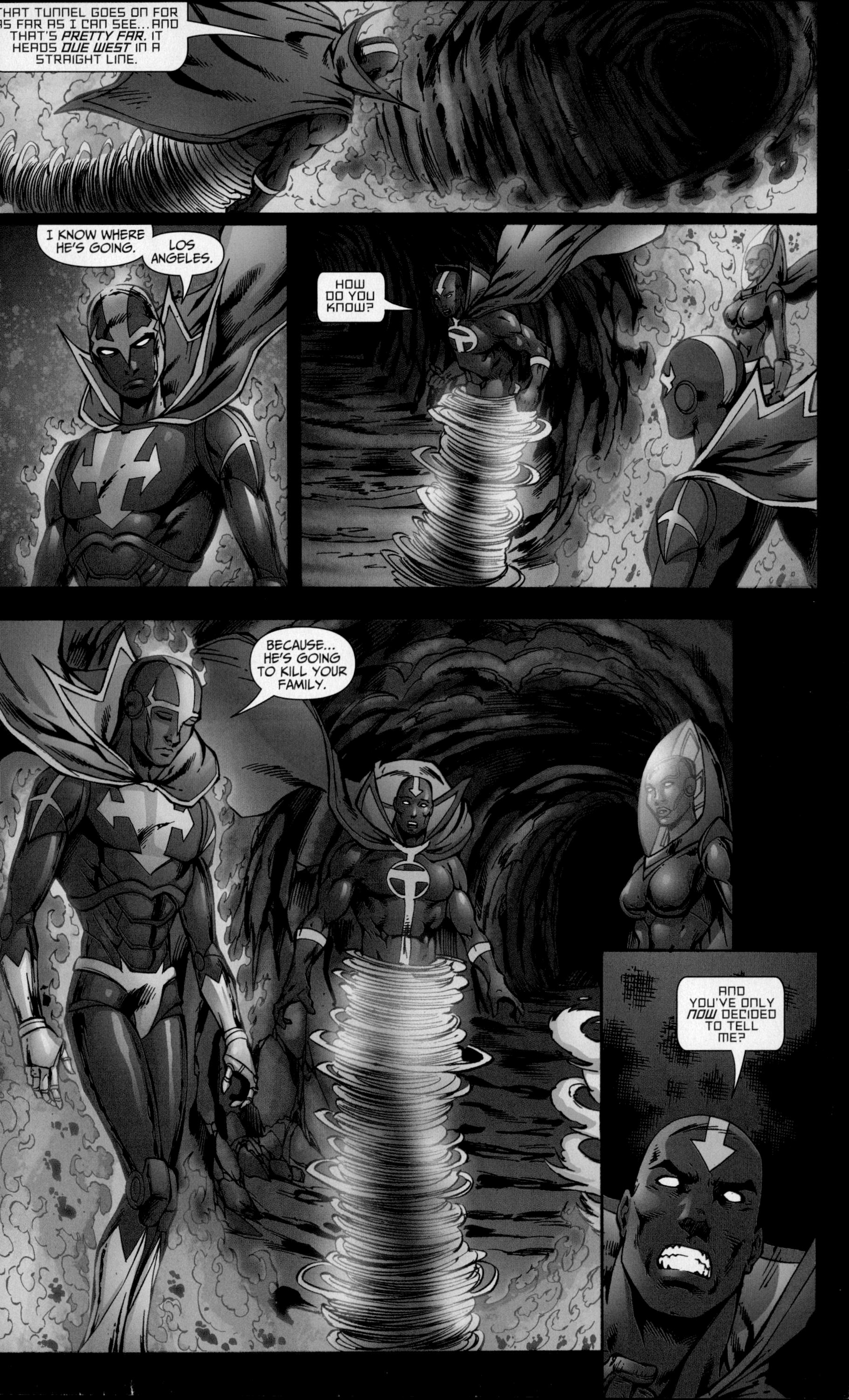
THAT TUNNEL GOES ON FOR AS FAR AS I CAN SEE... AND THAT'S PRETTY FAR. IT HEADS DUE WEST IN A STRAIGHT LINE.
I KNOW WHERE HE'S GOING.
LOS ANGELES.
HOW DO YOU KNOW?
BECAUSE... HE'S GOING TO KILL YOUR FAMILY.
AND YOU'VE ONLY NOW DECIDED TO TELL ME?

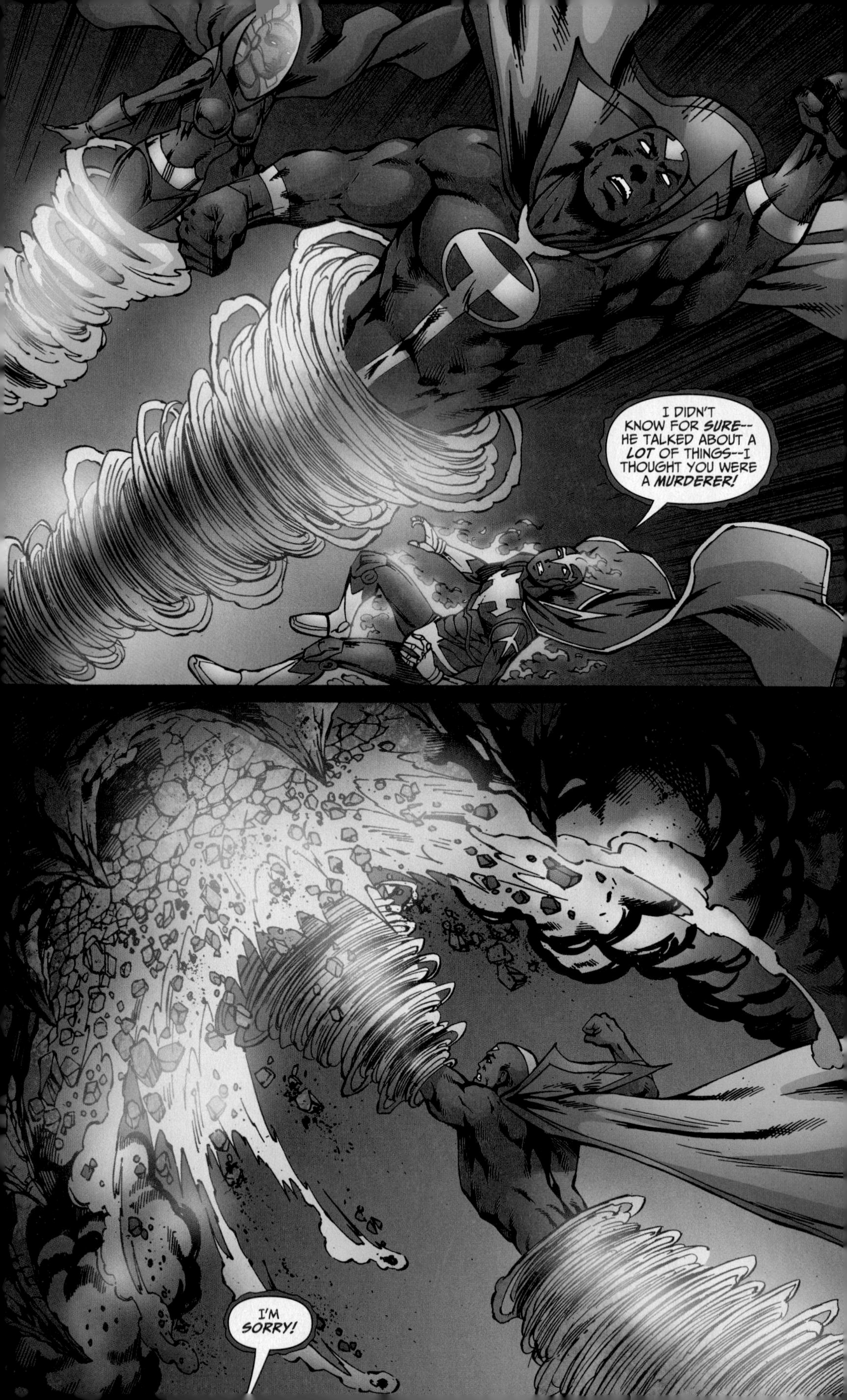
I DIDN'T KNOW FOR SURE-- HE TALKED ABOUT A LOT OF THINGS--I THOUGHT YOU WERE A MURDERER!
I'M SORRY!

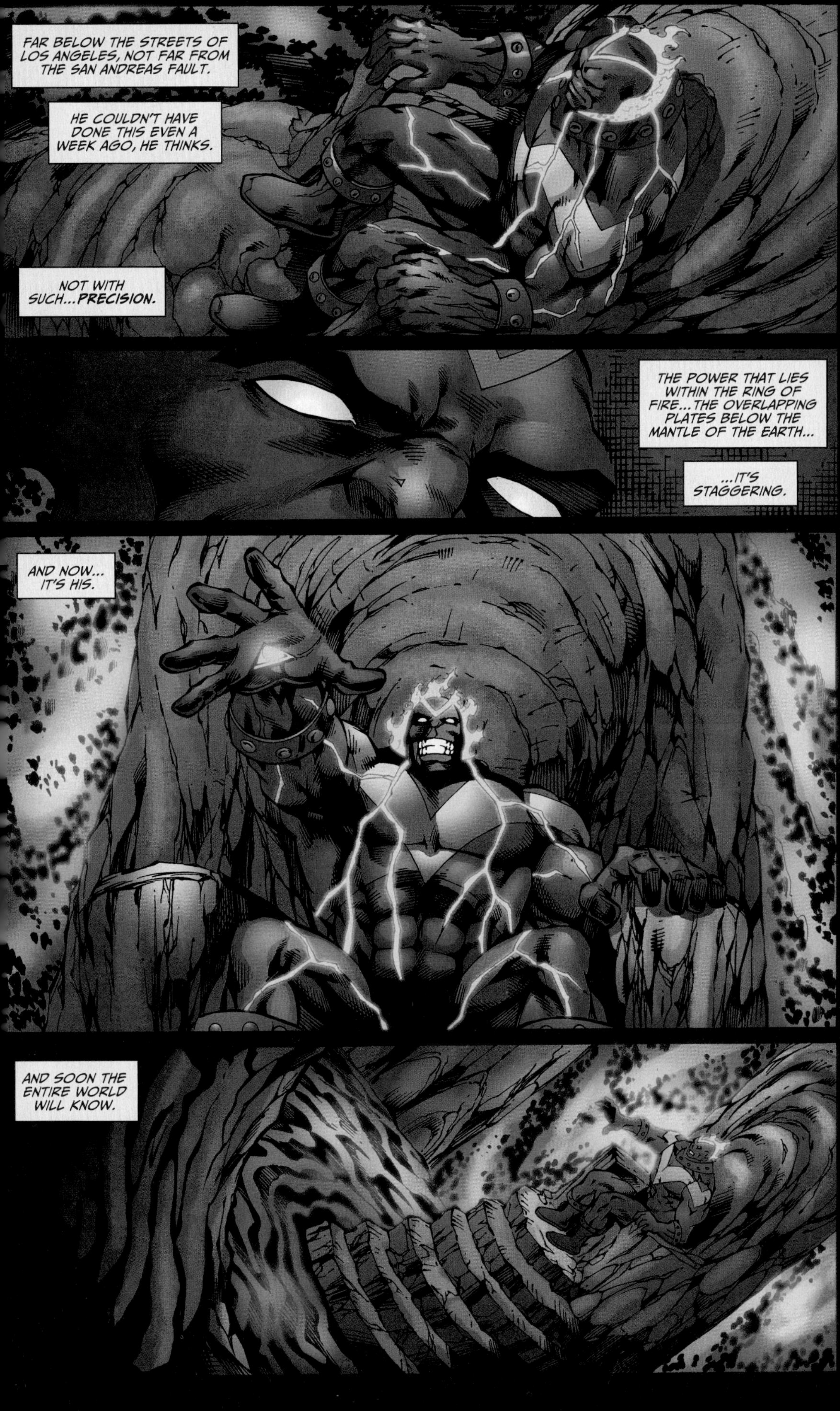
FAR BELOW THE STREETS OF LOS ANGELES, NOT FAR FROM THE SAN ANDREAS FAULT.
HE COULDN'T HAVE DONE THIS EVEN A WEEK AGO, HE THINKS.
NOT WITH SUCH...PRECISION.
THE POWER THAT LIES WITHIN THE RING OF FIRE...THE OVERLAPPING PLATES BELOW THE MANTLE OF THE EARTH...
...IT'S STAGGERING.
AND NOW... IT'S HIS.
AND SOON THE ENTIRE WORLD WILL KNOW.

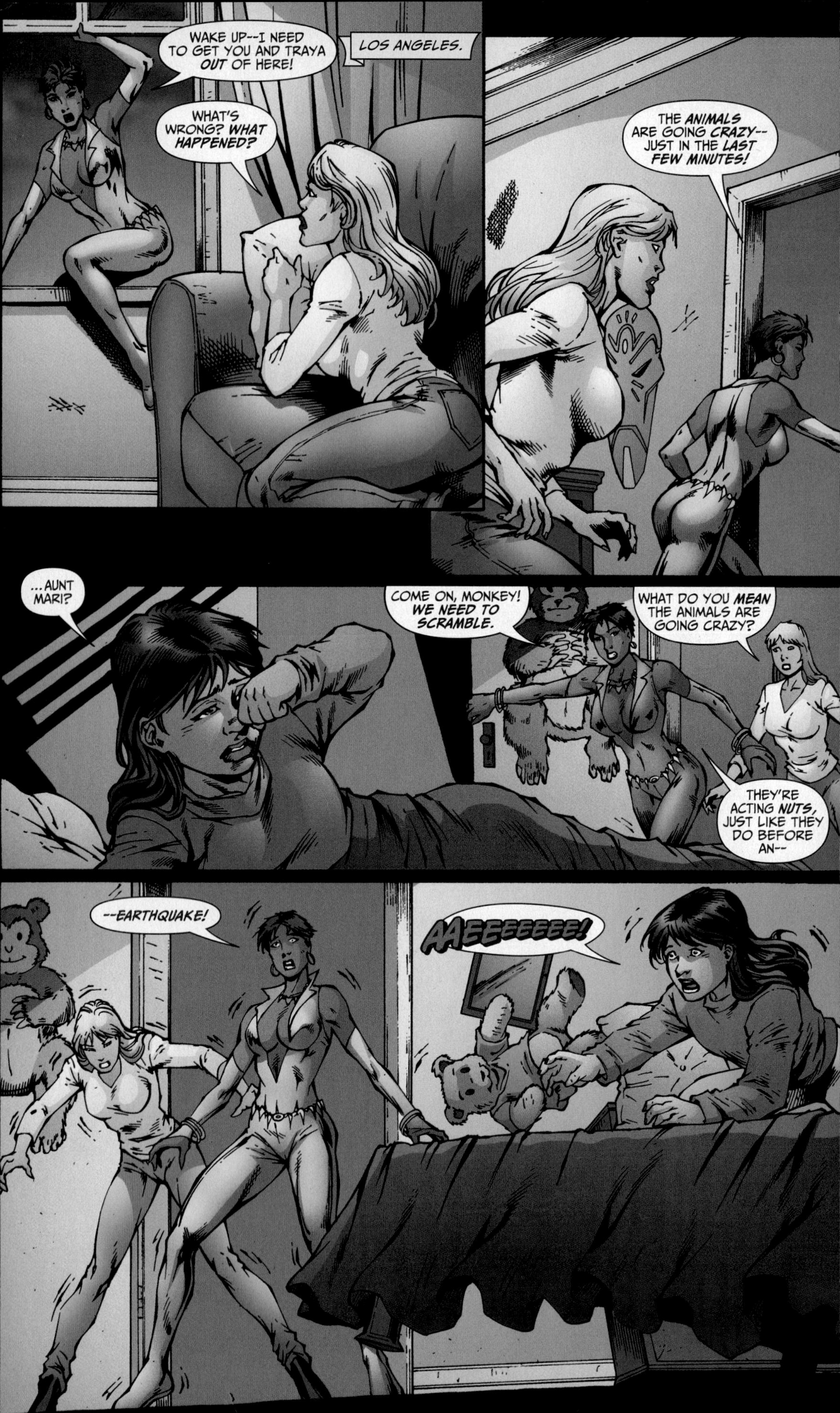
WAKE UP--I NEED TO GET YOU AND TRAYA OUT OF HERE!
LOS ANGELES.
WHAT'S WRONG? WHAT HAPPENED?
THE ANIMALS ARE GOING CRAZY-- JUST IN THE LAST FEW MINUTES!
...AUNT MARI?
COME ON, MONKEY! WE NEED TO SCRAMBLE.
WHAT DO YOU MEAN THE ANIMALS ARE GOING CRAZY?
THEY'RE ACTING NUTS, JUST LIKE THEY DO BEFORE AN--
--EARTHQUAKE!
AAEEEEEEE!

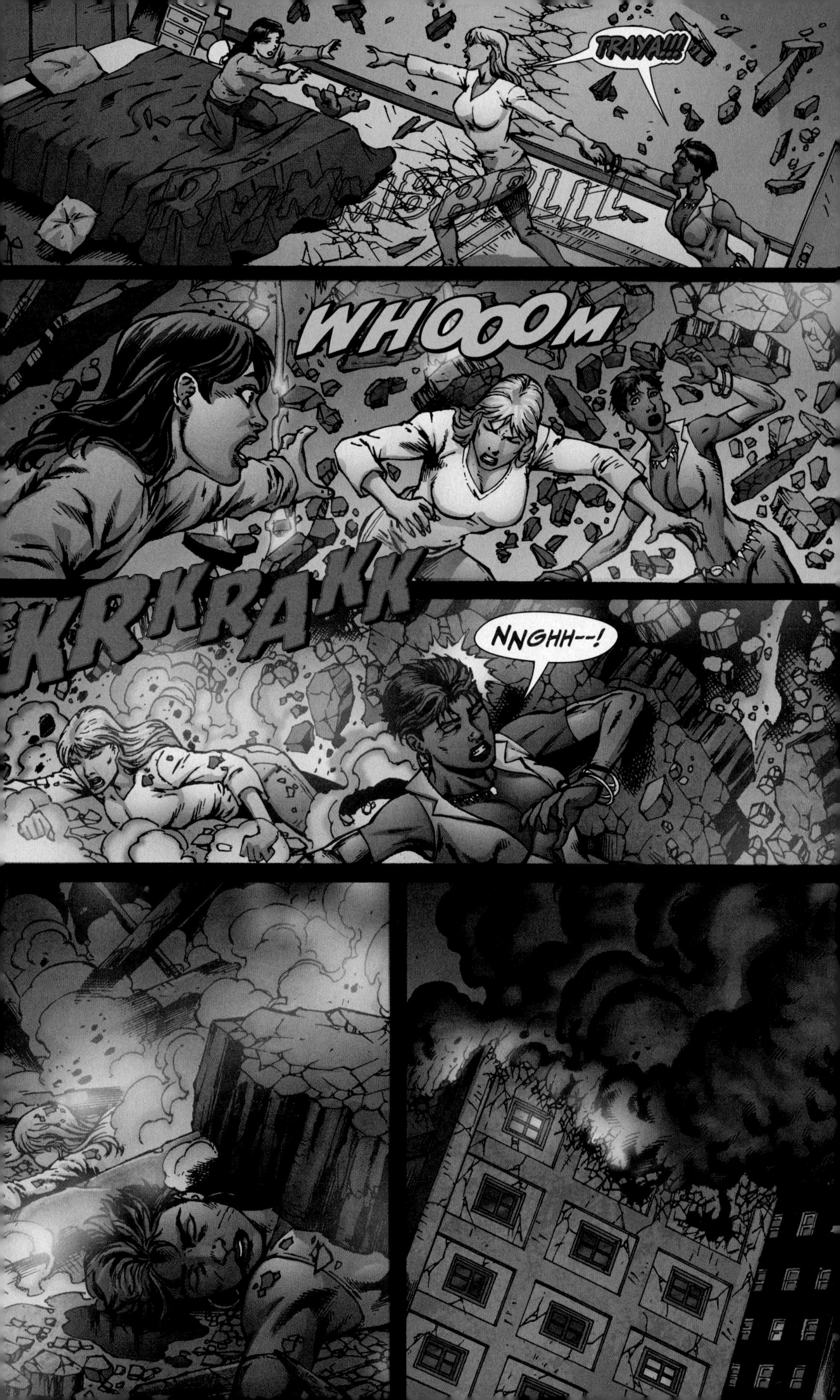

TRAYA!!!
WHOOOOM
KRKRAKK
NNGHH--!

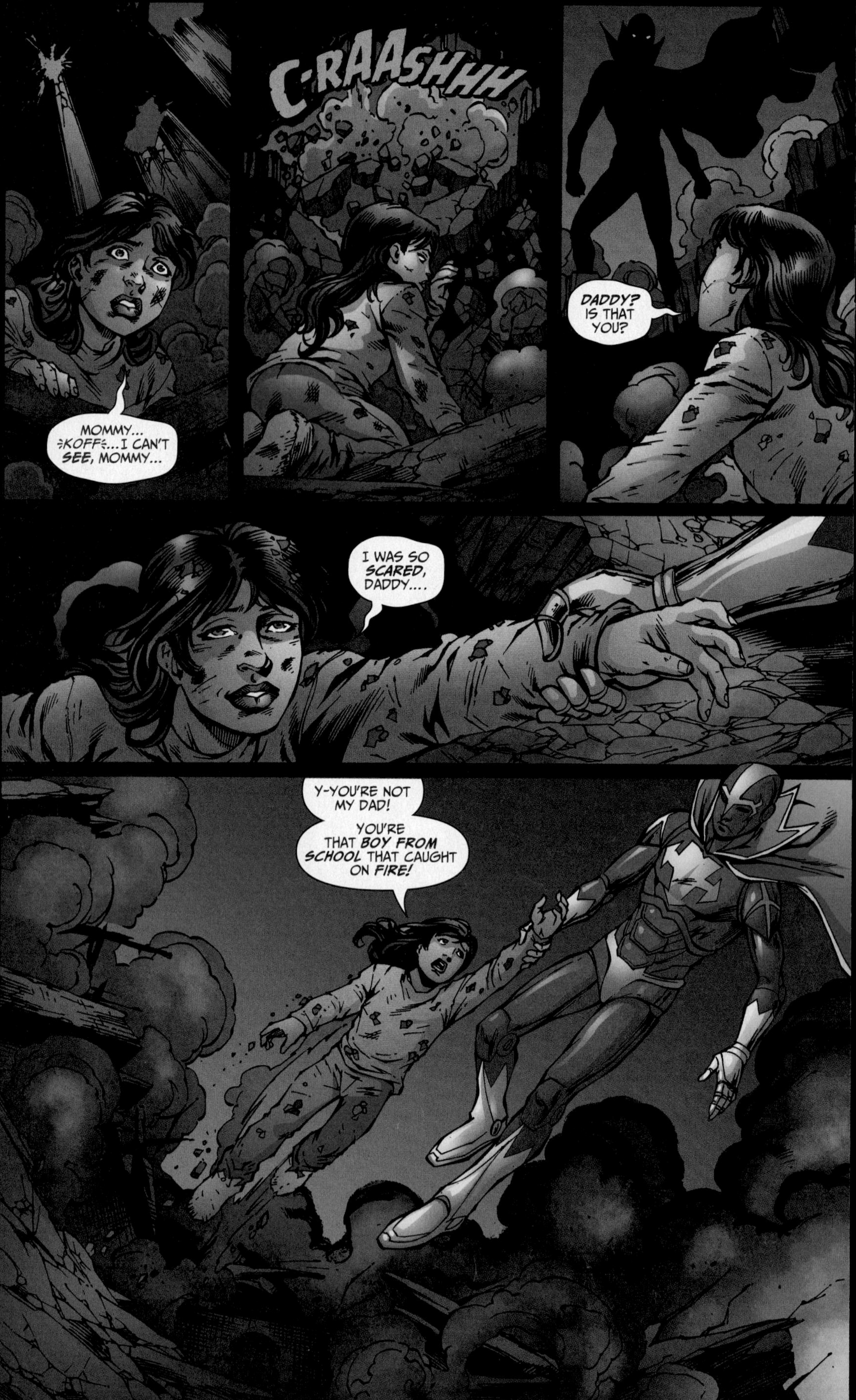
C-RAASHHH
MOMMY... -KOFF-... I CAN'T SEE, MOMMY...
DADDY? IS THAT YOU?
I WAS SO SCARED, DADDY....
Y-YOU'RE NOT MY DAD!
YOU'RE THAT BOY FROM SCHOOL THAT CAUGHT ON FIRE!

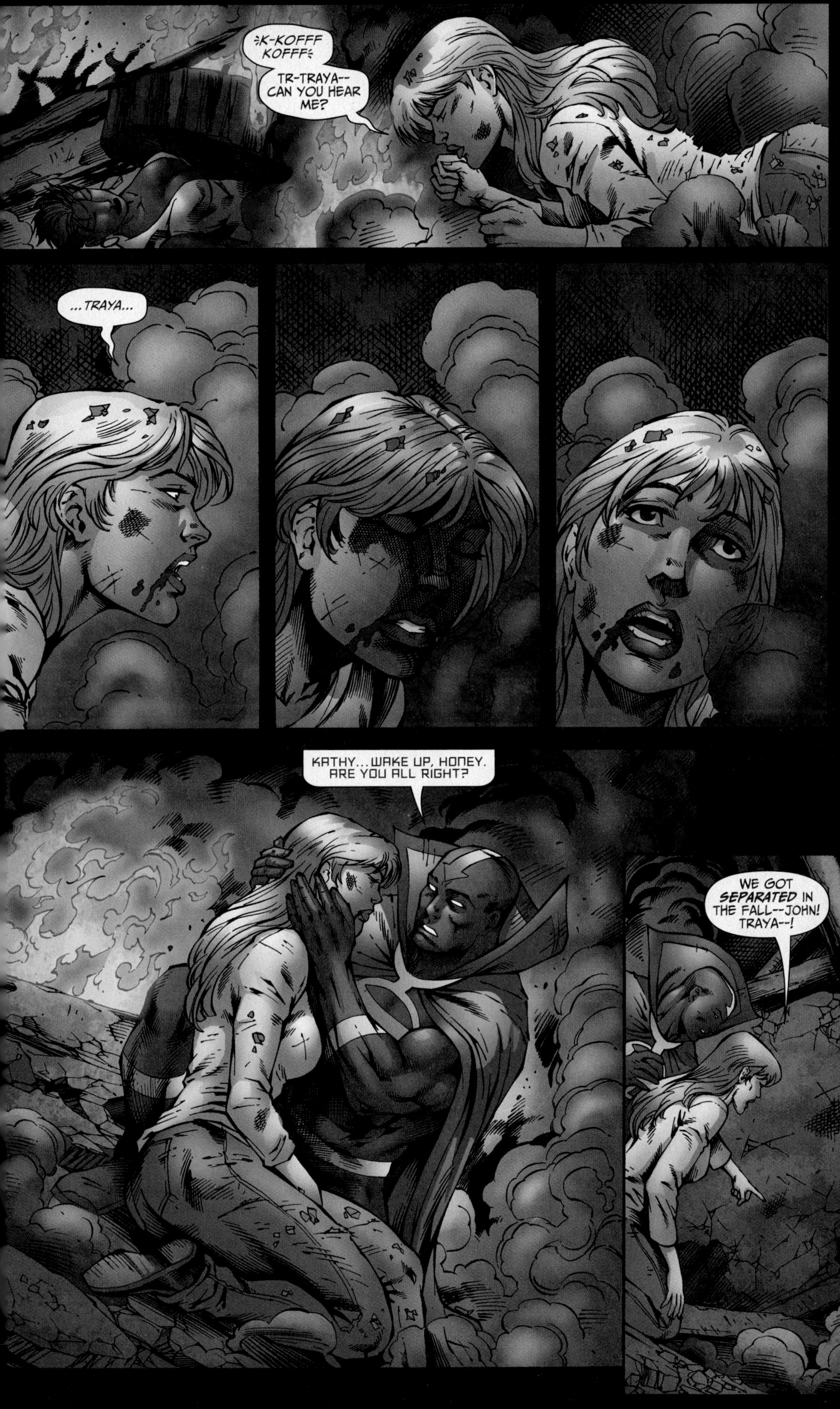

K-KOFFF KOFFF
TR-TRAYA-- CAN YOU HEAR ME?
...TRAYA...
KATHY... WAKE UP, HONEY. ARE YOU ALL RIGHT?
WE GOT SEPARATED IN THE FALL--JOHN! TRAYA--!

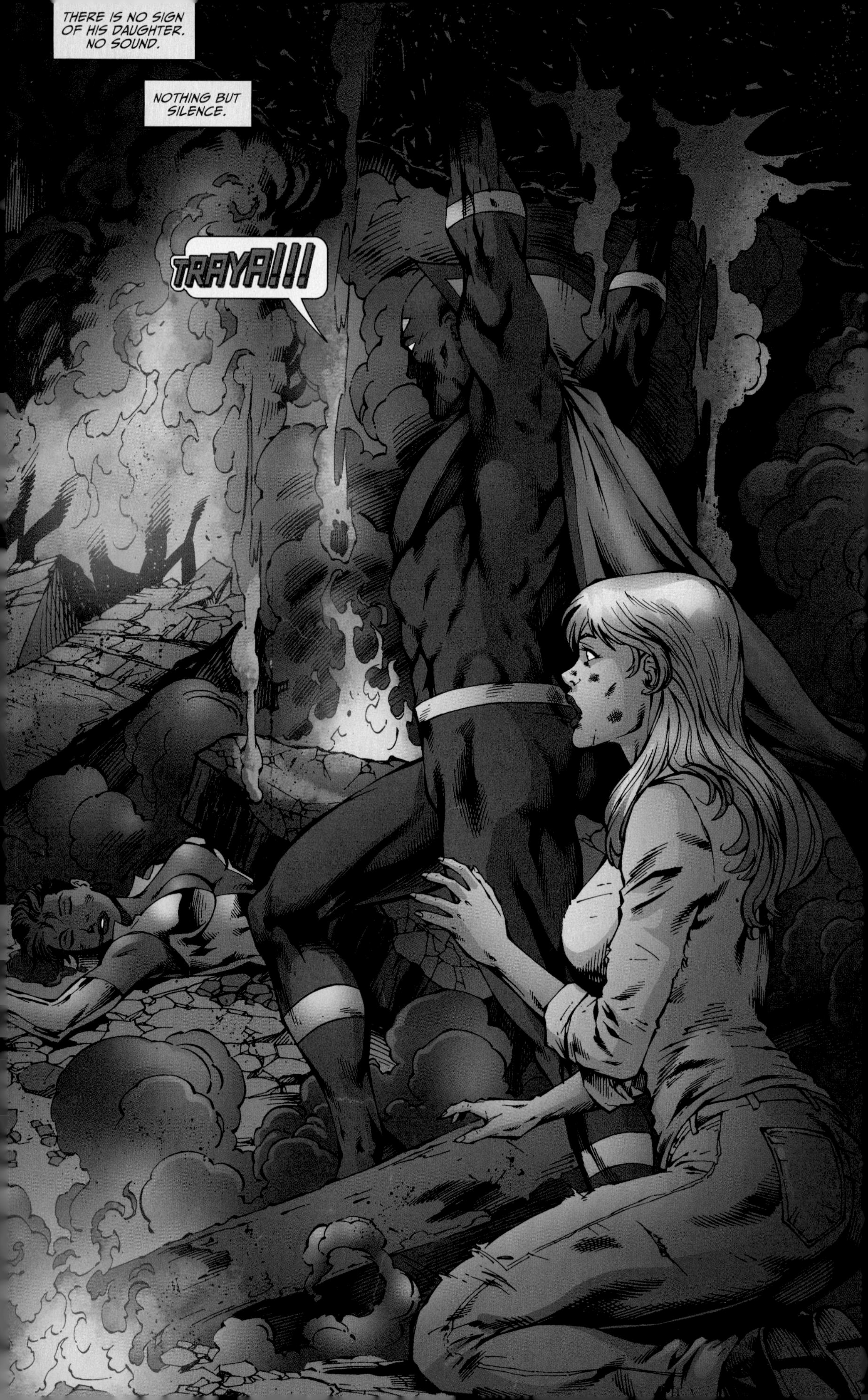
THERE IS NO SIGN OF HIS DAUGHTER. NO SOUND.
NOTHING BUT SILENCE.
TRAYA!!!

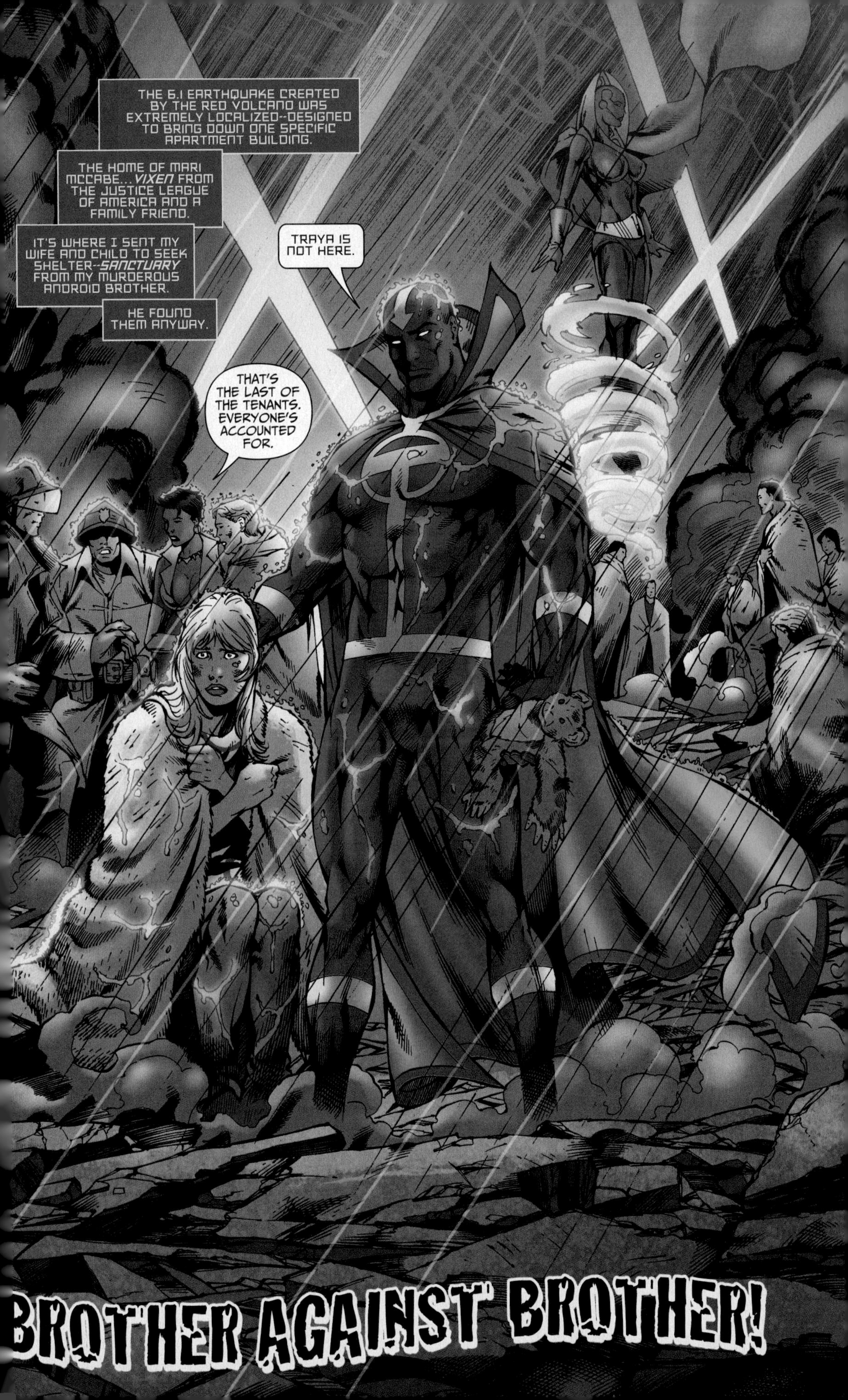
THE 6.1 EARTHQUAKE CREATED BY THE RED VOLCANO WAS EXTREMELY LOCALIZED--DESIGNED TO BRING DOWN ONE SPECIFIC APARTMENT BUILDING.
THE HOME OF MARI MCCABE... VIXEN FROM THE JUSTICE LEAGUE OF AMERICA AND A FAMILY FRIEND.
IT'S WHERE I SENT MY WIFE AND CHILD TO SEEK SHELTER--SANCTUARY FROM MY MURDEROUS ANDROID BROTHER.
HE FOUND THEM ANYWAY.
TRAYA IS NOT HERE.
THAT'S THE LAST OF THE TENANTS. EVERYONE'S ACCOUNTED FOR.
BROTHER AGAINST BROTHER!

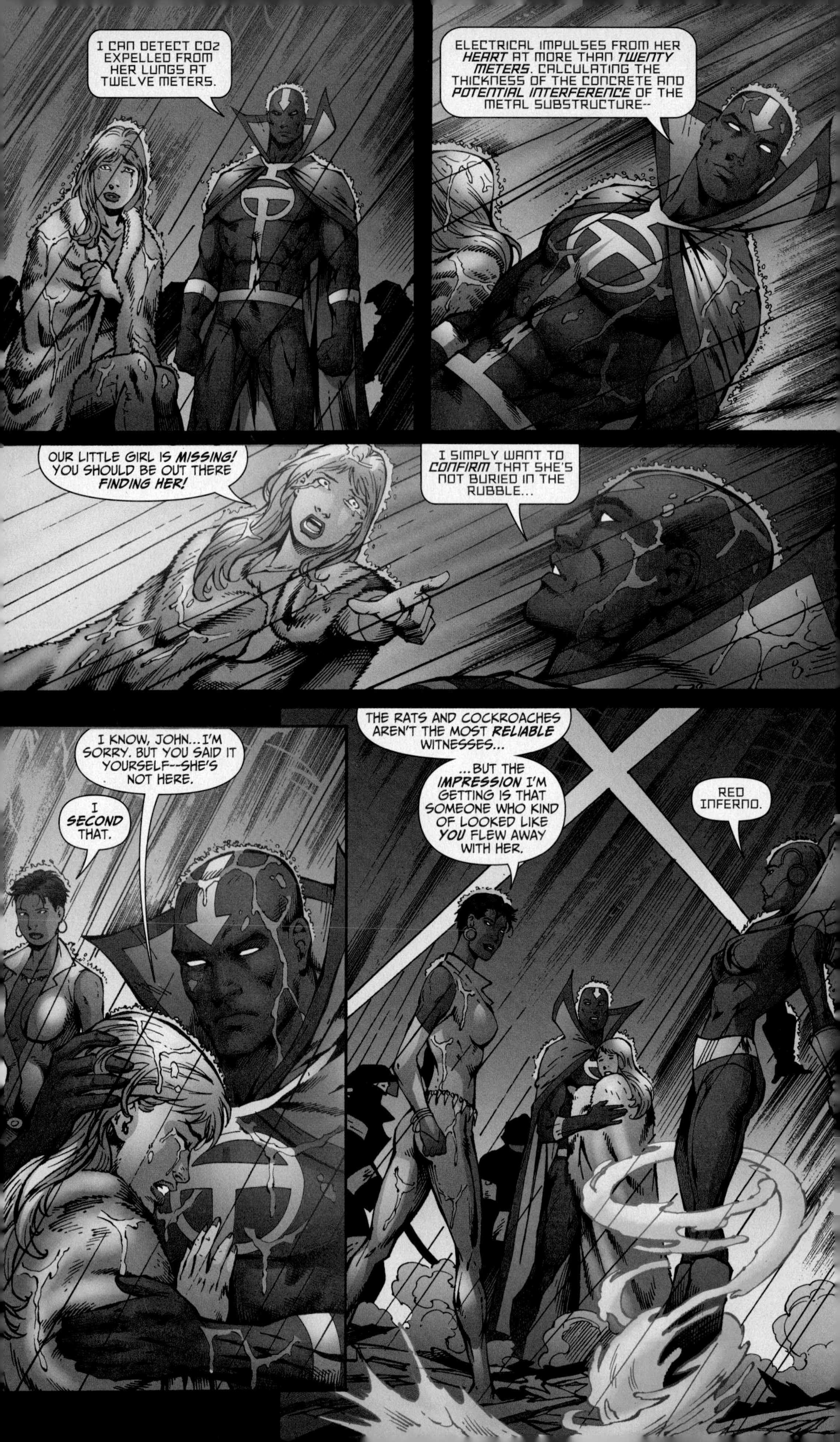
I CAN DETECT $CO_2$ EXPELLED FROM HER LUNGS AT TWELVE METERS.
ELECTRICAL IMPULSES FROM HER *HEART* AT MORE THAN *TWENTY METERS*. CALCULATING THE THICKNESS OF THE CONCRETE AND *POTENTIAL INTERFERENCE* OF THE METAL SUBSTRUCTURE--
OUR LITTLE GIRL IS *MISSING!* YOU SHOULD BE OUT THERE *FINDING HER!*
I SIMPLY WANT TO *CONFIRM* THAT SHE'S NOT BURIED IN THE RUBBLE...
I KNOW, JOHN...I'M SORRY. BUT YOU SAID IT YOURSELF--SHE'S NOT HERE.
I *SECOND* THAT.
THE RATS AND COCKROACHES AREN'T THE MOST *RELIABLE* WITNESSES...
...BUT THE *IMPRESSION* I'M GETTING IS THAT SOMEONE WHO KIND OF LOOKED LIKE *YOU* FLEW AWAY WITH HER.
RED INFERNO.

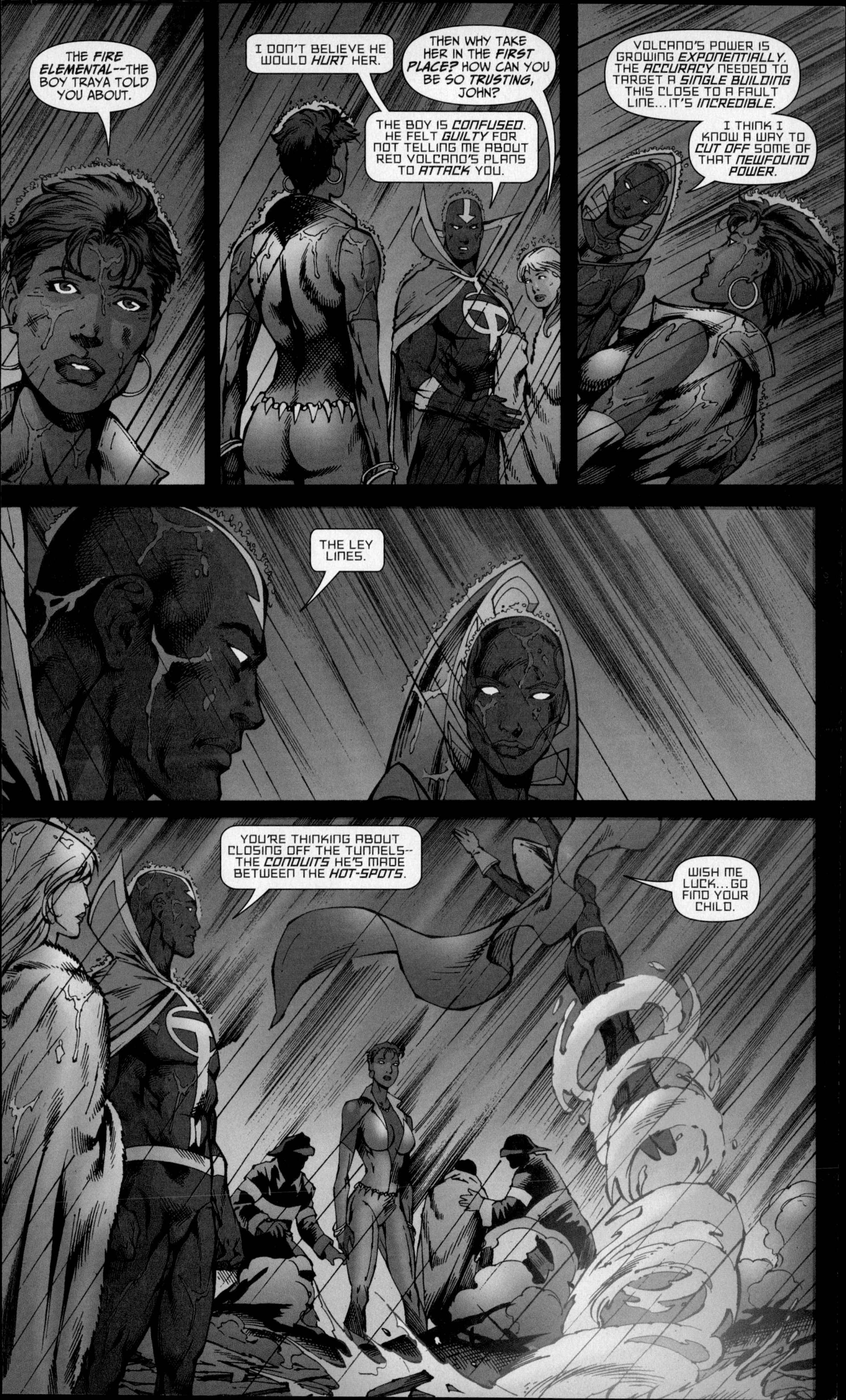
THE FIRE ELEMENTAL--THE BOY TRAYA TOLD YOU ABOUT.
I DON'T BELIEVE HE WOULD HURT HER.
THEN WHY TAKE HER IN THE FIRST PLACE? HOW CAN YOU BE SO TRUSTING, JOHN?
THE BOY IS CONFUSED. HE FELT GUILTY FOR NOT TELLING ME ABOUT RED VOLCANO'S PLANS TO ATTACK YOU.
VOLCANO'S POWER IS GROWING EXPONENTIALLY. THE ACCURACY NEEDED TO TARGET A SINGLE BUILDING THIS CLOSE TO A FAULT LINE...IT'S INCREDIBLE.
I THINK I KNOW A WAY TO CUT OFF SOME OF THAT NEWFOUND POWER.
THE LEY LINES.
YOU'RE THINKING ABOUT CLOSING OFF THE TUNNELS-- THE CONDUITS HE'S MADE BETWEEN THE HOT-SPOTS.
WISH ME LUCK...GO FIND YOUR CHILD.

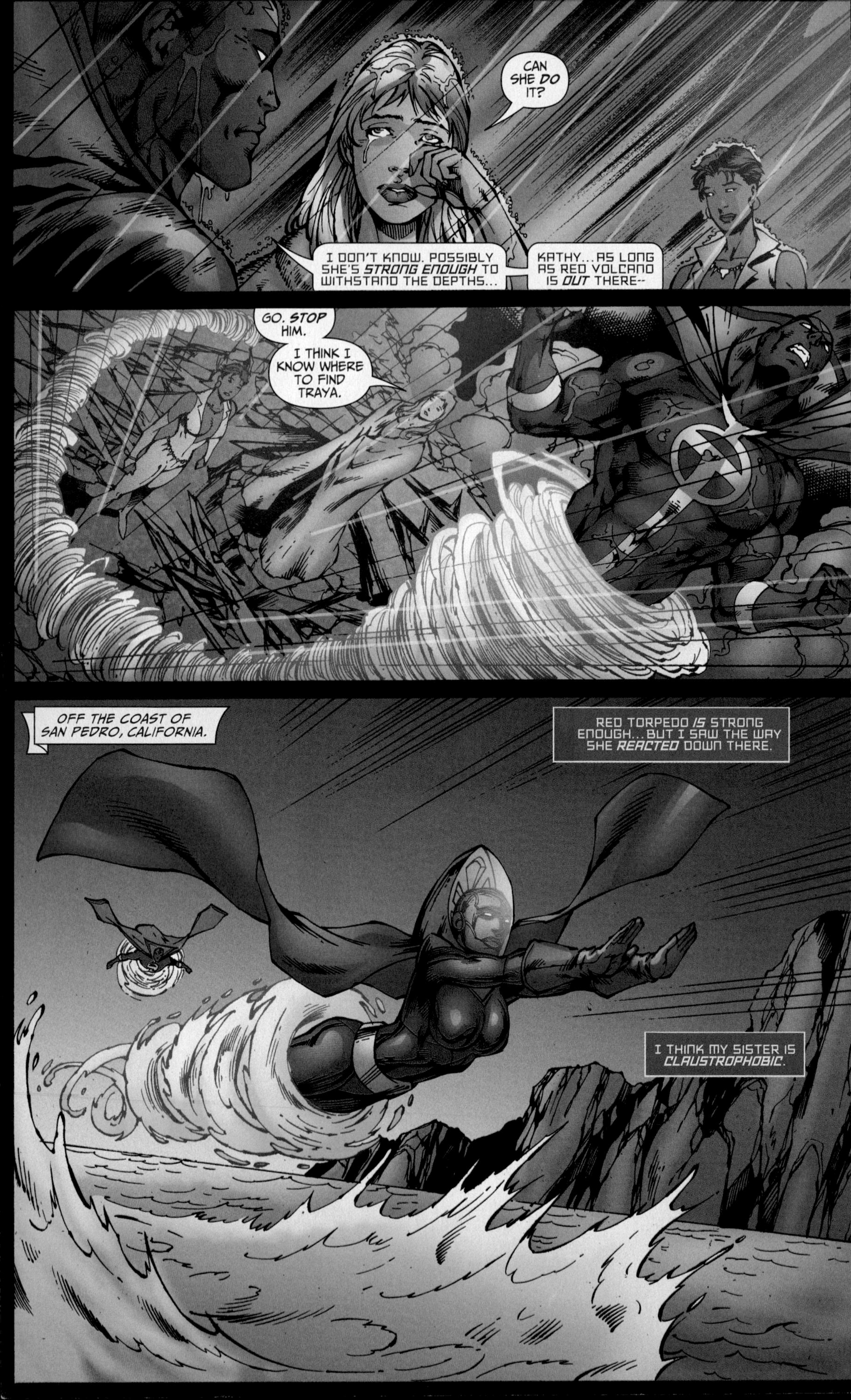
CAN SHE DO IT?
I DON'T KNOW. POSSIBLY SHE'S STRONG ENOUGH TO WITHSTAND THE DEPTHS...
KATHY...AS LONG AS RED VOLCANO IS OUT THERE--
GO. STOP HIM.
I THINK I KNOW WHERE TO FIND TRAYA.
OFF THE COAST OF SAN PEDRO, CALIFORNIA.
RED TORPEDO IS STRONG ENOUGH...BUT I SAW THE WAY SHE REACTED DOWN THERE.
I THINK MY SISTER IS CLAUSTROPHOBIC.

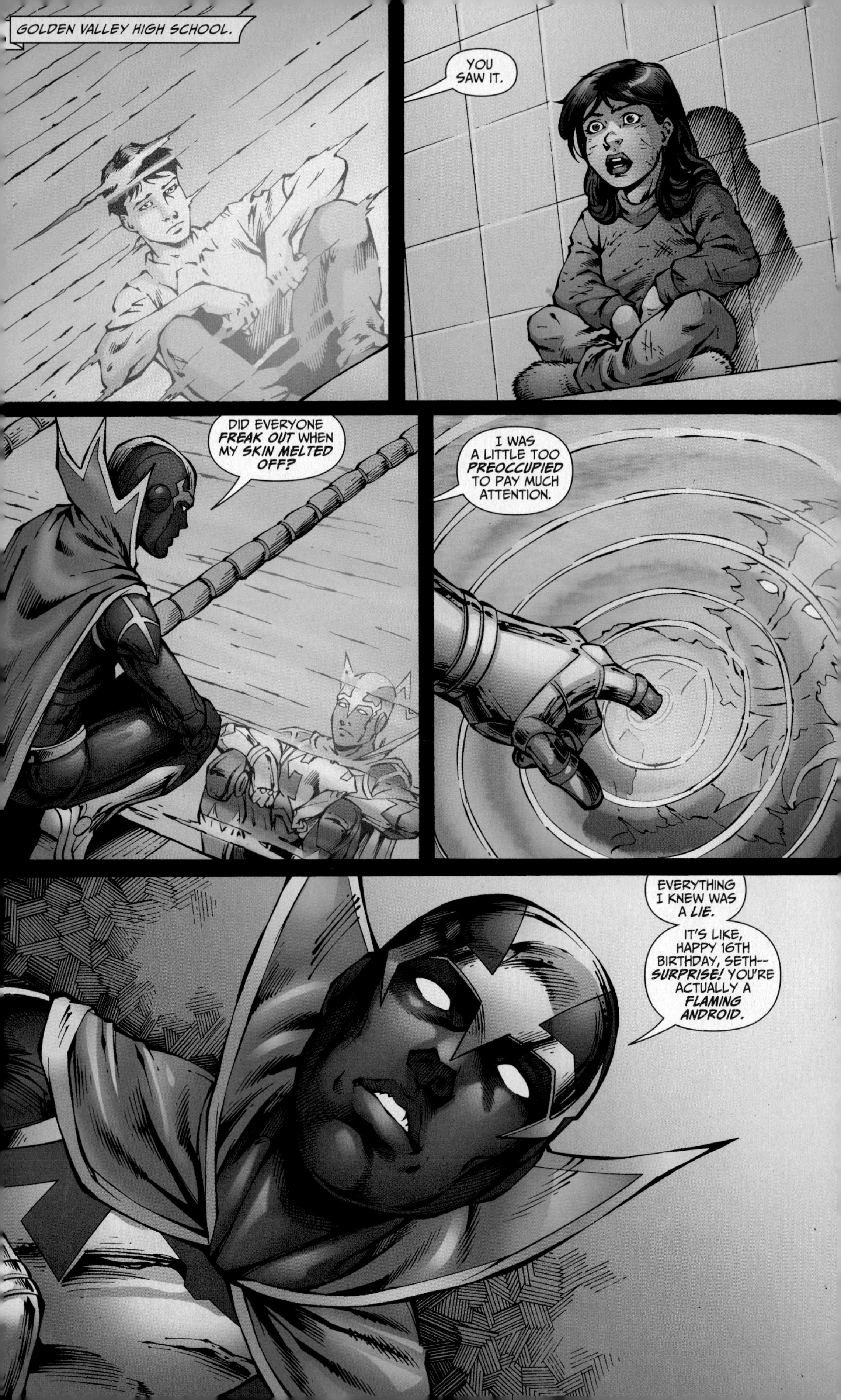

GOLDEN VALLEY HIGH SCHOOL.
YOU SAW IT.
DID EVERYONE FREAK OUT WHEN MY SKIN MELTED OFF?
I WAS A LITTLE TOO PREOCCUPIED TO PAY MUCH ATTENTION.
EVERYTHING I KNEW WAS A LIE.
IT'S LIKE, HAPPY 16TH BIRTHDAY, SETH-- SURPRISE! YOU'RE ACTUALLY A FLAMING ANDROID.

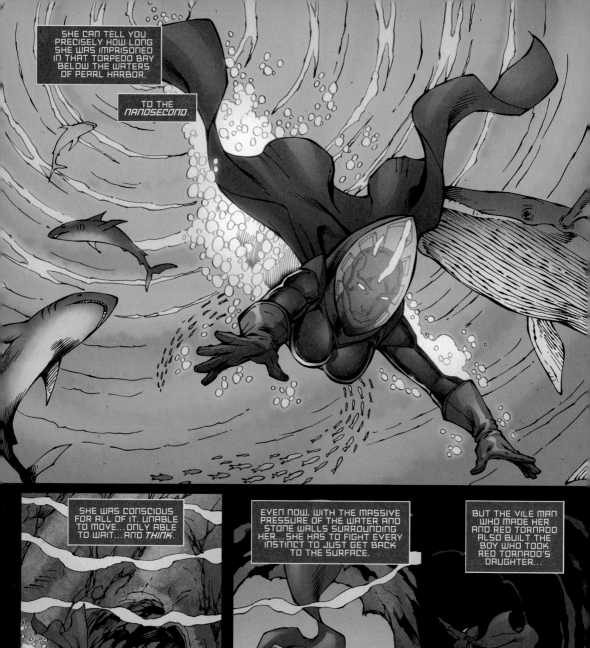

SHE CAN TELL YOU PRECISELY HOW LONG SHE WAS IMPRISONED IN THAT TORPEDO BAY BELOW THE WATERS OF PEARL HARBOR.

TO THE *NANOSECOND*.

SHE WAS CONSCIOUS FOR ALL OF IT. UNABLE TO MOVE...ONLY ABLE TO WAIT...AND *THINK*.

EVEN NOW, WITH THE MASSIVE PRESSURE OF THE WATER AND STONE WALLS SURROUNDING HER...SHE HAS TO FIGHT EVERY INSTINCT TO JUST GET BACK TO THE SURFACE.

BUT THE VILE MAN WHO MADE HER AND RED TORNADO ALSO BUILT THE BOY WHO TOOK RED TORNADO'S DAUGHTER...

...AND AN EVIL HULKING ANDROID CALLED THE *RED VOLCANO*. AND IF SHE DOESN'T DO SOMETHING TO STOP HIM, HE MAY VERY WELL DESTROY THE WORLD.

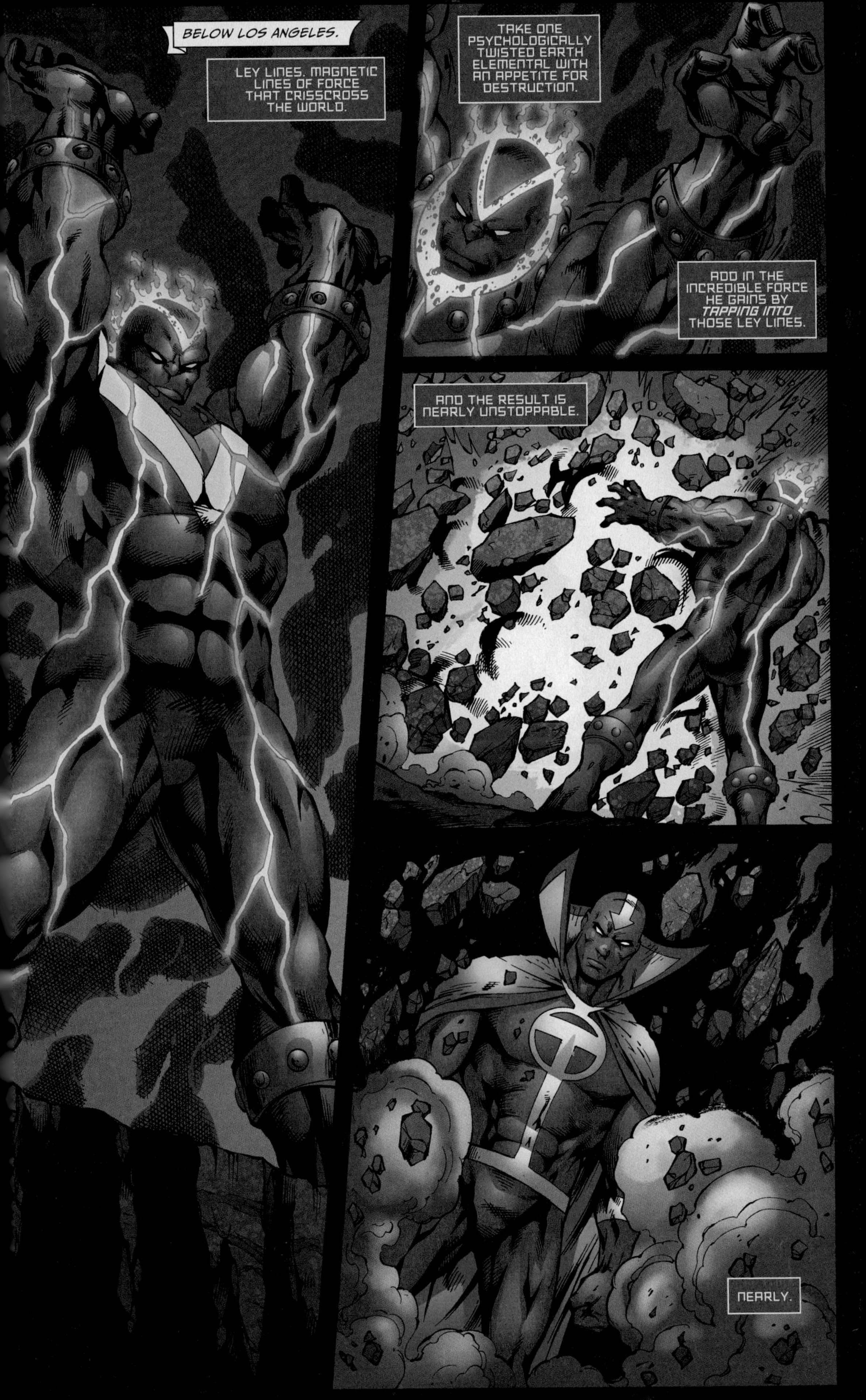
BELOW LOS ANGELES.
LEY LINES. MAGNETIC LINES OF FORCE THAT CRISSCROSS THE WORLD.
TAKE ONE PSYCHOLOGICALLY TWISTED EARTH ELEMENTAL WITH AN APPETITE FOR DESTRUCTION.
ADD IN THE INCREDIBLE FORCE HE GAINS BY TAPPING INTO THOSE LEY LINES.
AND THE RESULT IS NEARLY UNSTOPPABLE.
NEARLY.

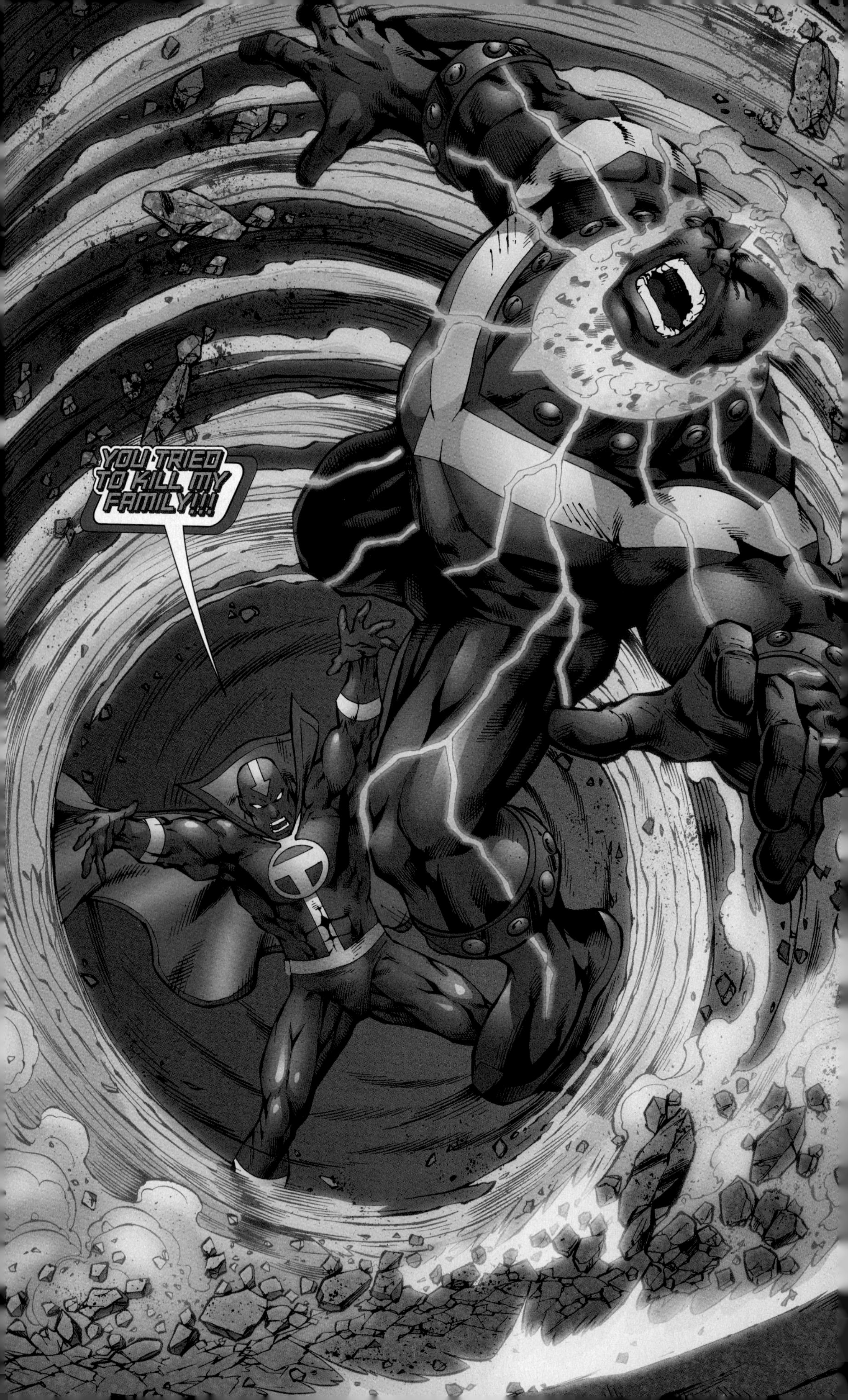
YOU TRIED TO KILL MY FAMILY!!!

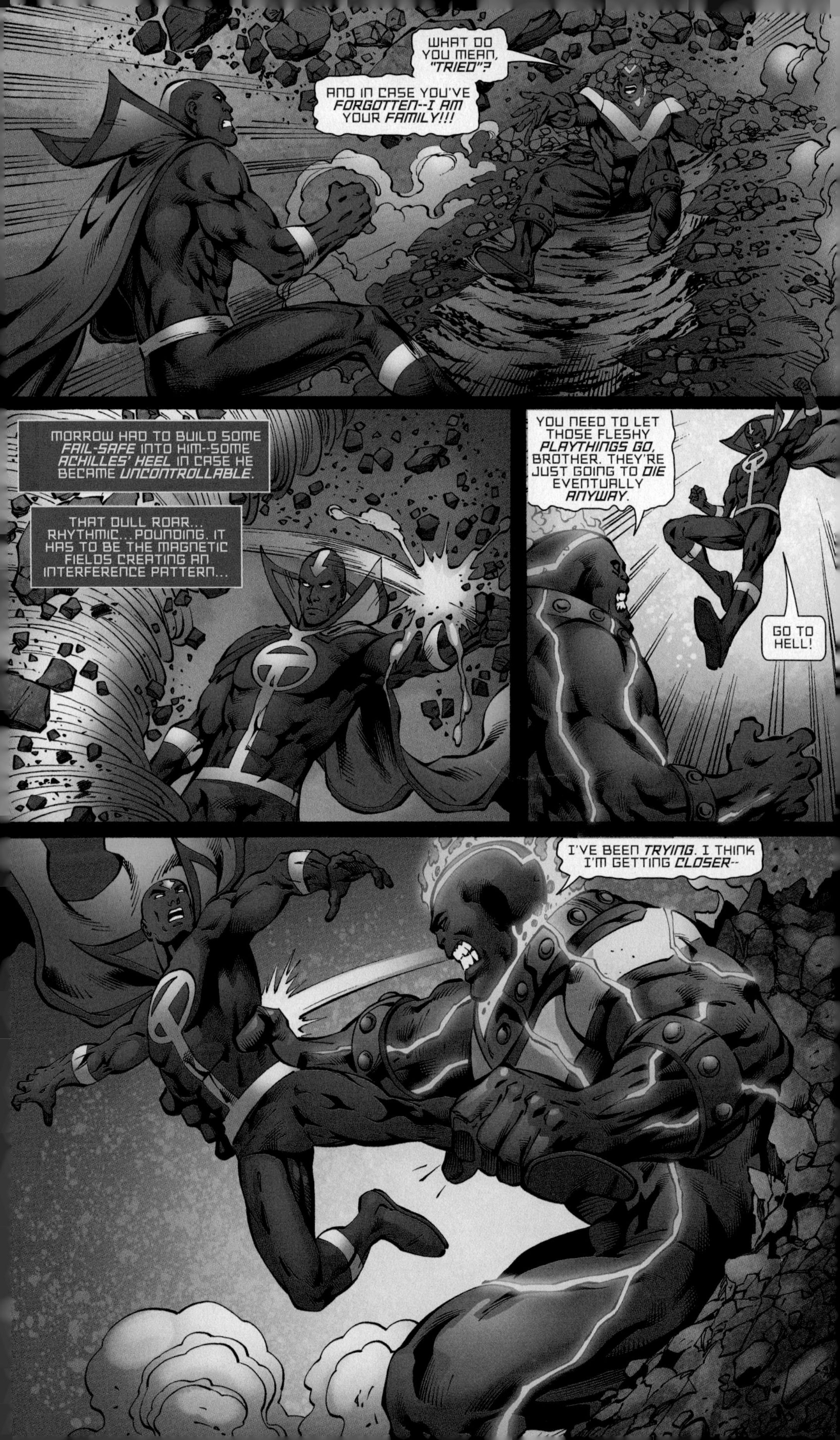
WHAT DO YOU MEAN, "TRIED"?
AND IN CASE YOU'VE FORGOTTEN--I AM YOUR FAMILY!!!
MORROW HAD TO BUILD SOME FAIL-SAFE INTO HIM--SOME ACHILLES' HEEL IN CASE HE BECAME UNCONTROLLABLE.
THAT DULL ROAR... RHYTHMIC...POUNDING. IT HAS TO BE THE MAGNETIC FIELDS CREATING AN INTERFERENCE PATTERN...
YOU NEED TO LET THOSE FLESHY PLAYTHINGS GO, BROTHER. THEY'RE JUST GOING TO DIE EVENTUALLY ANYWAY.
GO TO HELL!
I'VE BEEN TRYING. I THINK I'M GETTING CLOSER--

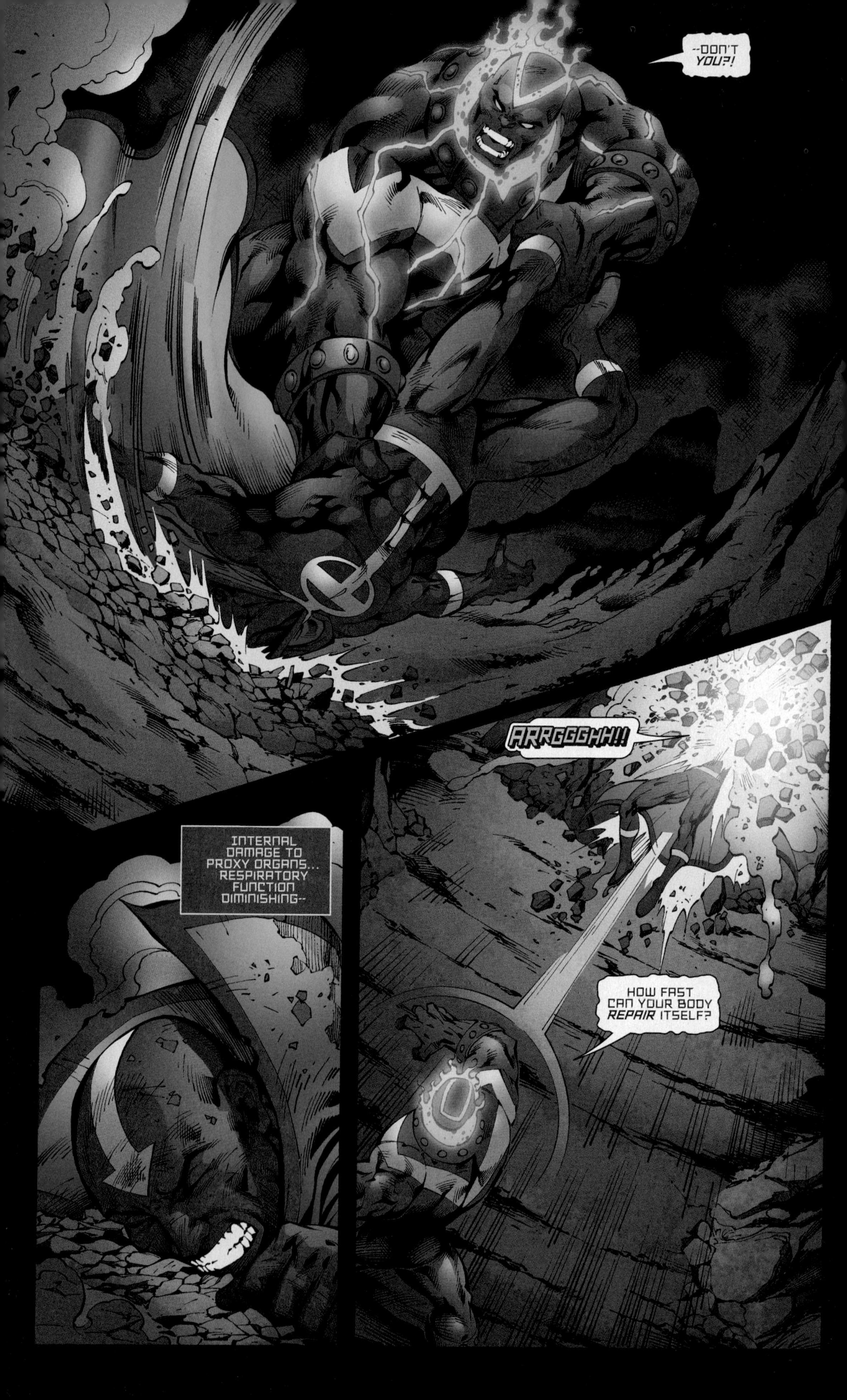
--DON'T YOU?!
ARRGGGHH!!
INTERNAL DAMAGE TO PROXY ORGANS... RESPIRATORY FUNCTION DIMINISHING--
HOW FAST CAN YOUR BODY REPAIR ITSELF?

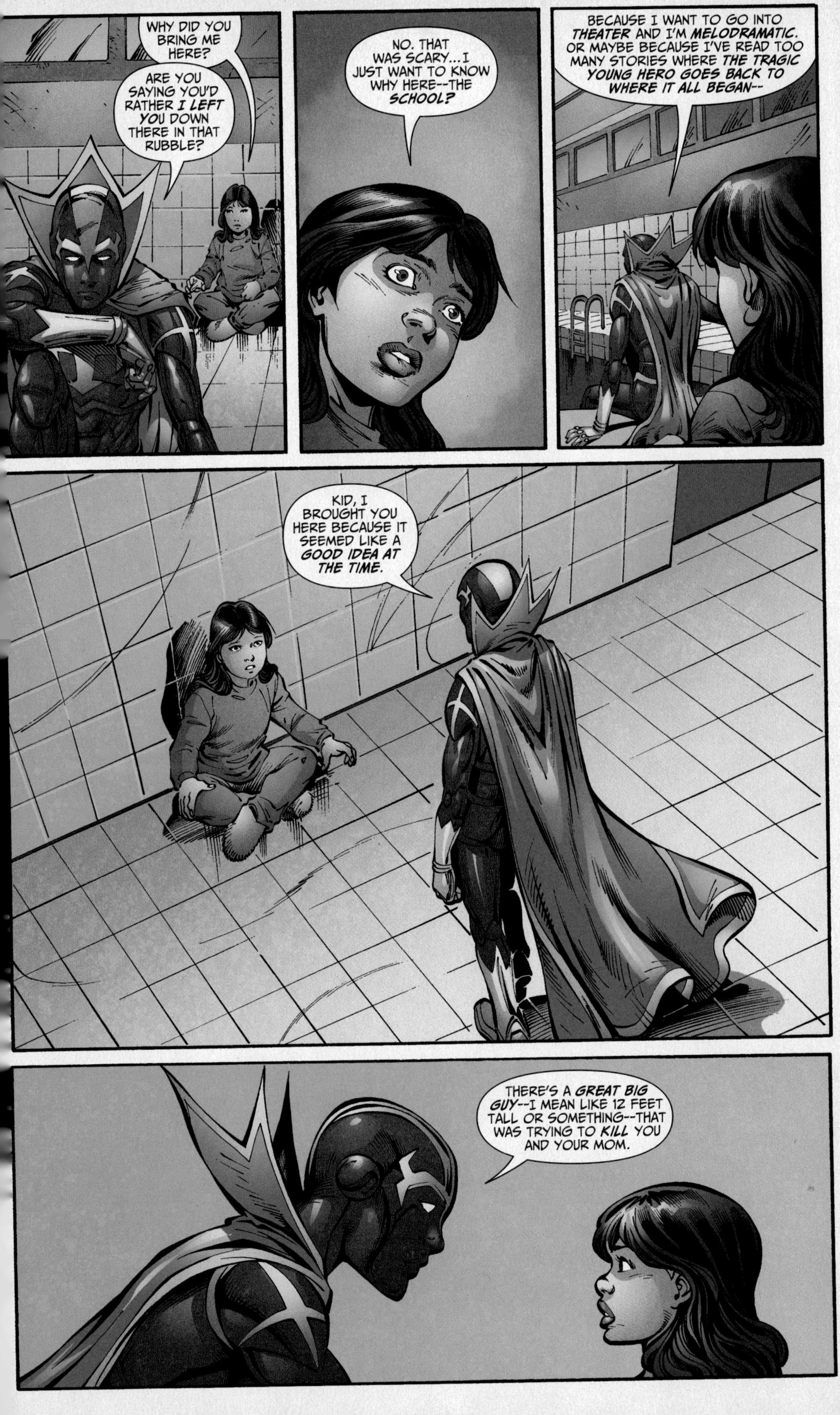

WHY DID YOU BRING ME HERE?
ARE YOU SAYING YOU'D RATHER *I LEFT YOU* DOWN THERE IN THAT RUBBLE?
NO. THAT WAS SCARY... I JUST WANT TO KNOW WHY HERE--THE *SCHOOL?*
BECAUSE I WANT TO GO INTO *THEATER* AND I'M *MELODRAMATIC.* OR MAYBE BECAUSE I'VE READ TOO MANY STORIES WHERE *THE TRAGIC YOUNG HERO GOES BACK TO WHERE IT ALL BEGAN--*
KID, I BROUGHT YOU HERE BECAUSE IT SEEMED LIKE A *GOOD IDEA AT THE TIME.*
THERE'S A *GREAT BIG GUY*--I MEAN LIKE 12 FEET TALL OR SOMETHING--THAT WAS TRYING TO *KILL* YOU AND YOUR MOM.

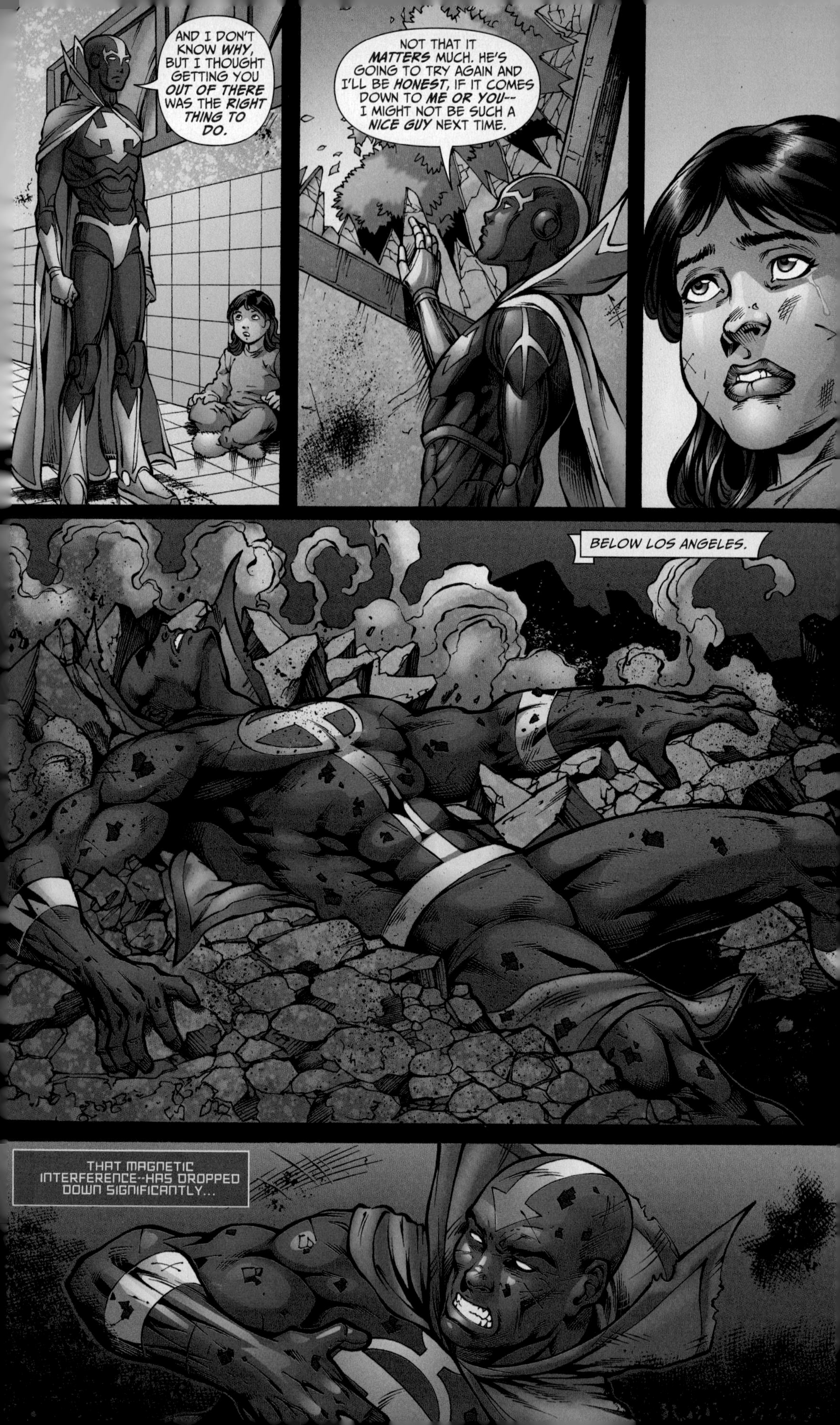
AND I DON'T KNOW WHY, BUT I THOUGHT GETTING YOU OUT OF THERE WAS THE RIGHT THING TO DO.
NOT THAT IT MATTERS MUCH. HE'S GOING TO TRY AGAIN AND I'LL BE HONEST, IF IT COMES DOWN TO ME OR YOU-- I MIGHT NOT BE SUCH A NICE GUY NEXT TIME.
BELOW LOS ANGELES.
THAT MAGNETIC INTERFERENCE--HAS DROPPED DOWN SIGNIFICANTLY...

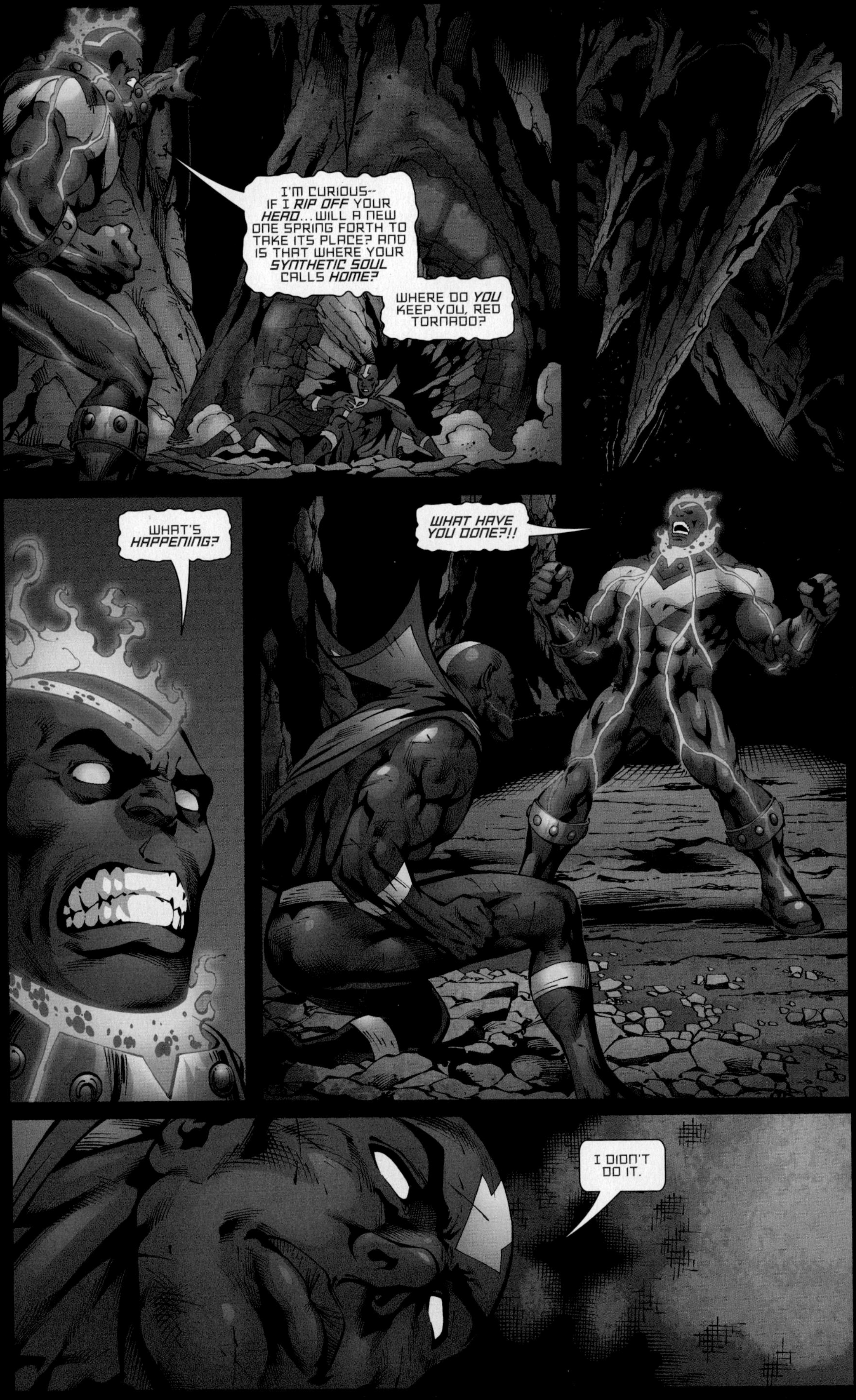
I'M CURIOUS-- IF I RIP OFF YOUR HEAD... WILL A NEW ONE SPRING FORTH TO TAKE ITS PLACE? AND IS THAT WHERE YOUR SYNTHETIC SOUL CALLS HOME?
WHERE DO YOU KEEP YOU, RED TORNADO?
WHAT'S HAPPENING?
WHAT HAVE YOU DONE?!!
I DIDN'T DO IT.

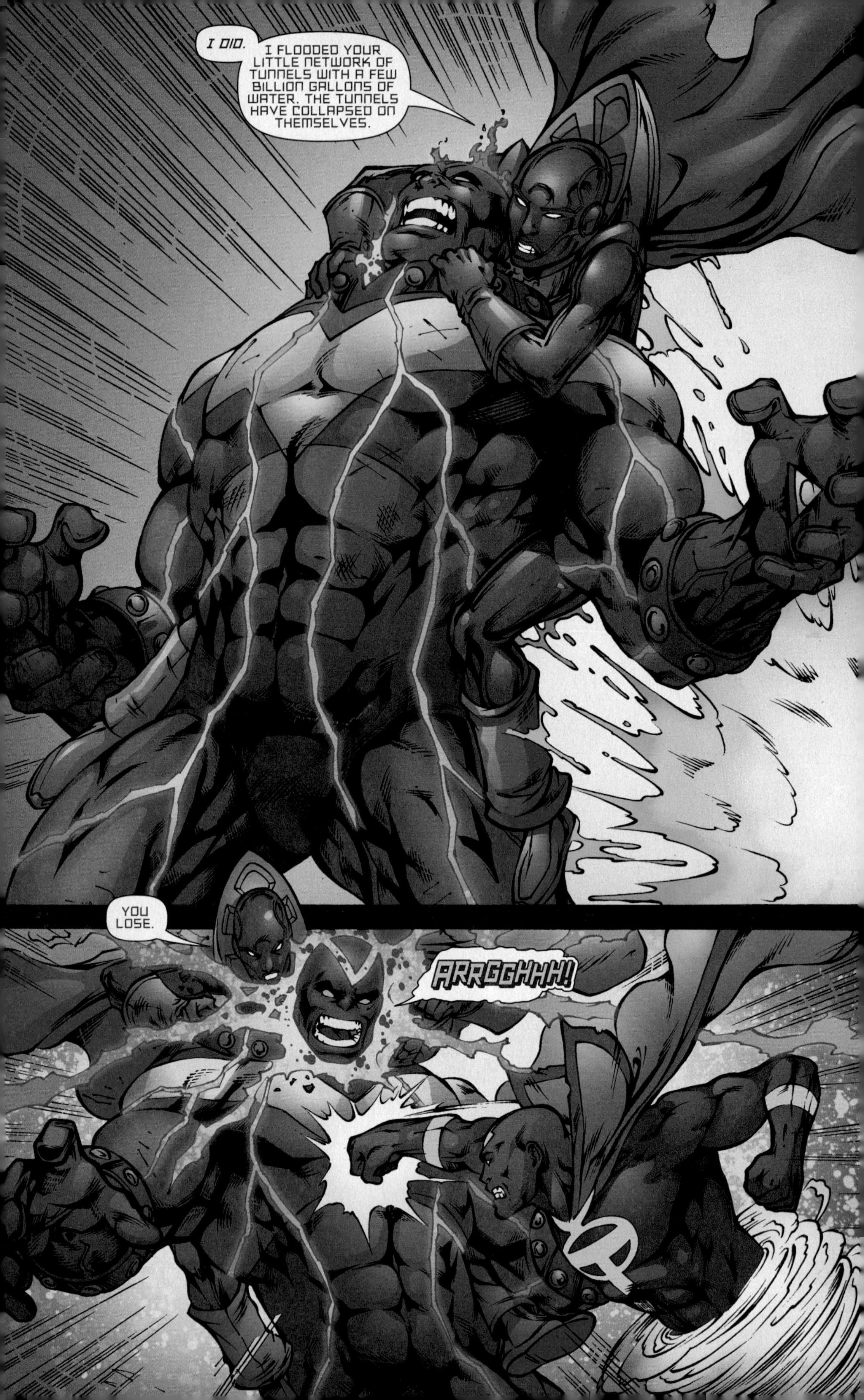
I DID.
I FLOODED YOUR LITTLE NETWORK OF TUNNELS WITH A FEW BILLION GALLONS OF WATER. THE TUNNELS HAVE COLLAPSED ON THEMSELVES.
YOU LOSE.
ARRGGHHH!

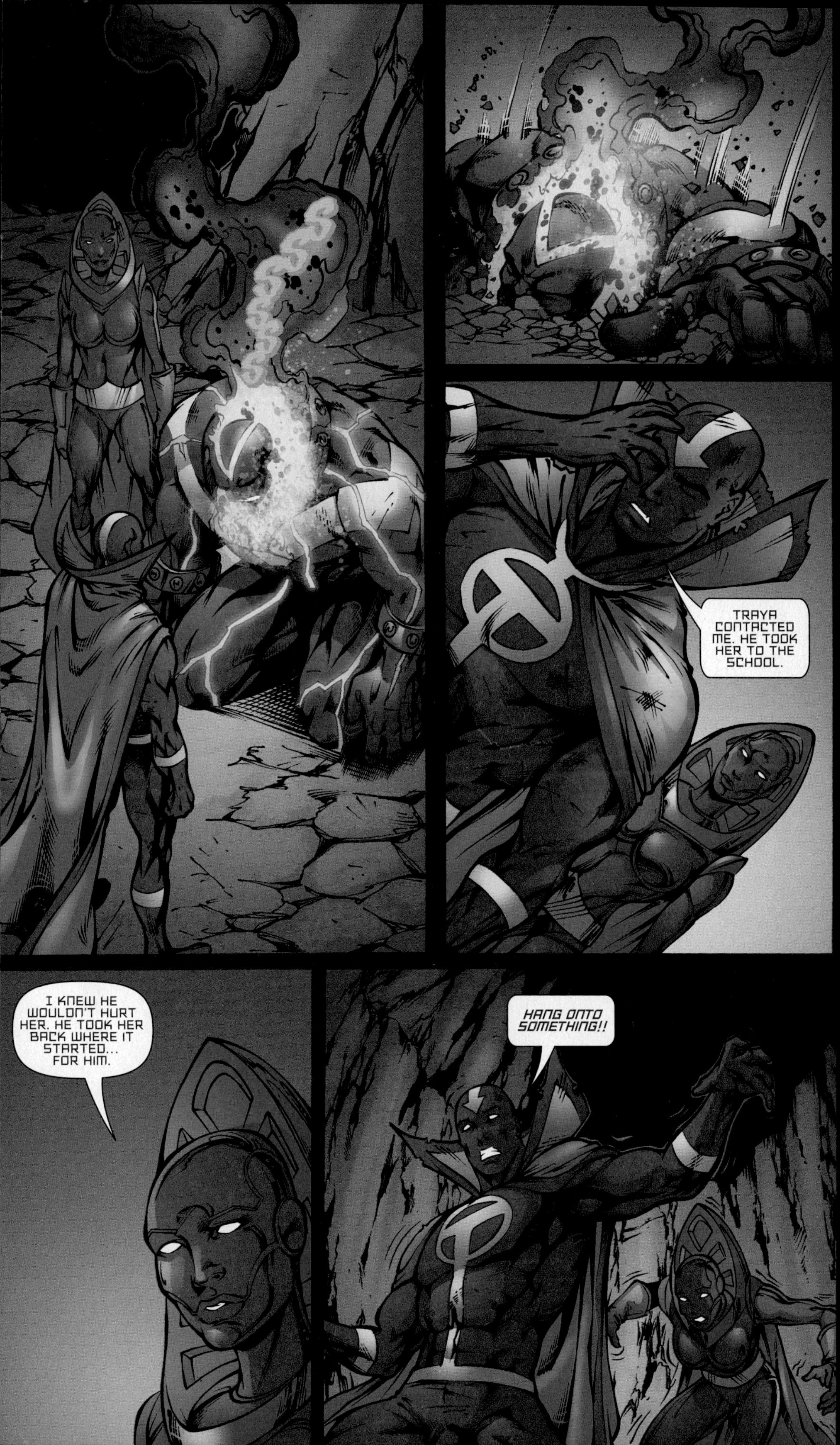
TRAYA CONTACTED ME. HE TOOK HER TO THE SCHOOL.
I KNEW HE WOULDN'T HURT HER. HE TOOK HER BACK WHERE IT STARTED... FOR HIM.
HANG ONTO SOMETHING!!

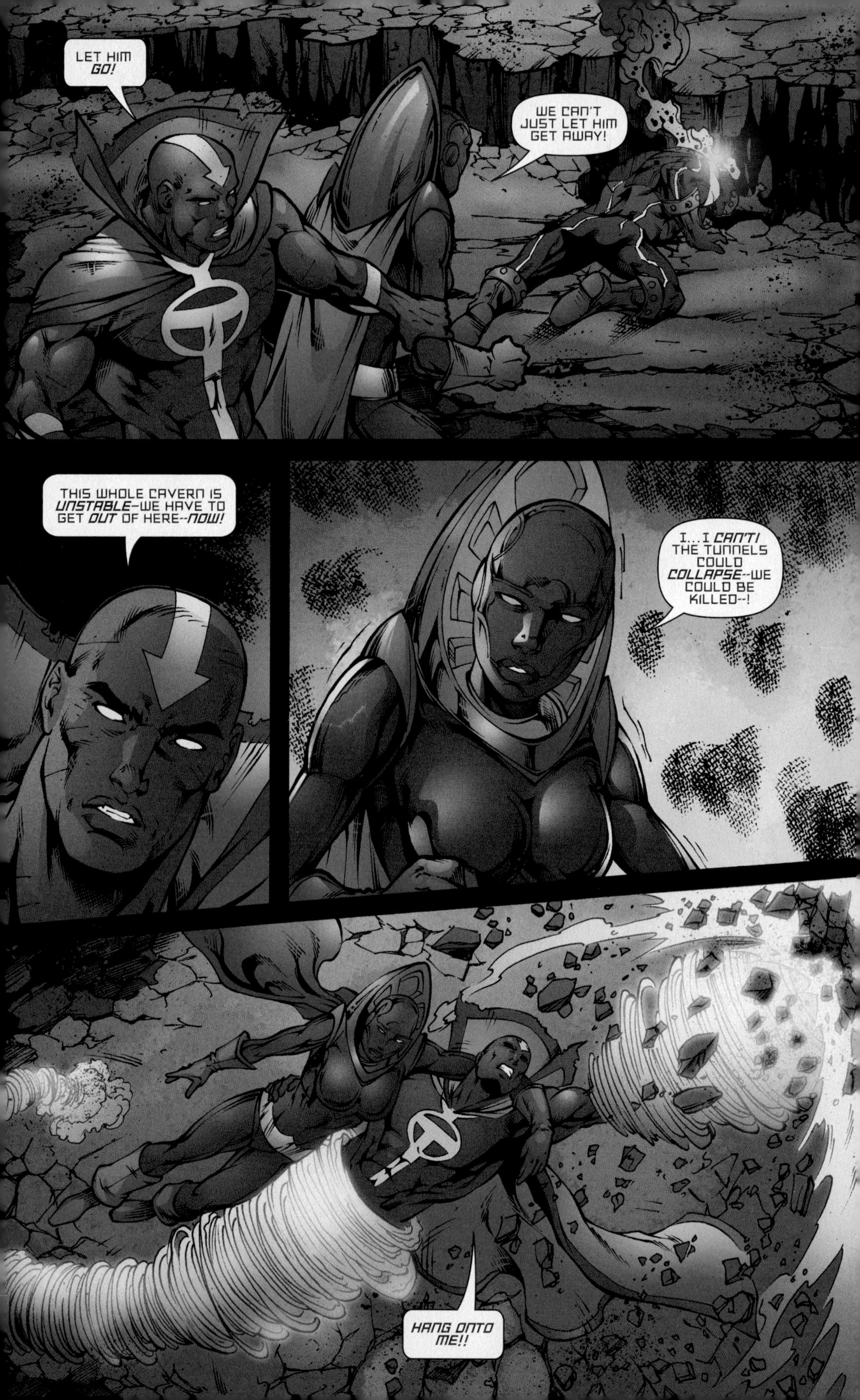
LET HIM GO!
WE CAN'T JUST LET HIM GET AWAY!
THIS WHOLE CAVERN IS UNSTABLE--WE HAVE TO GET OUT OF HERE--NOW!
I...I CAN'T! THE TUNNELS COULD COLLAPSE--WE COULD BE KILLED--!
HANG ONTO ME!!

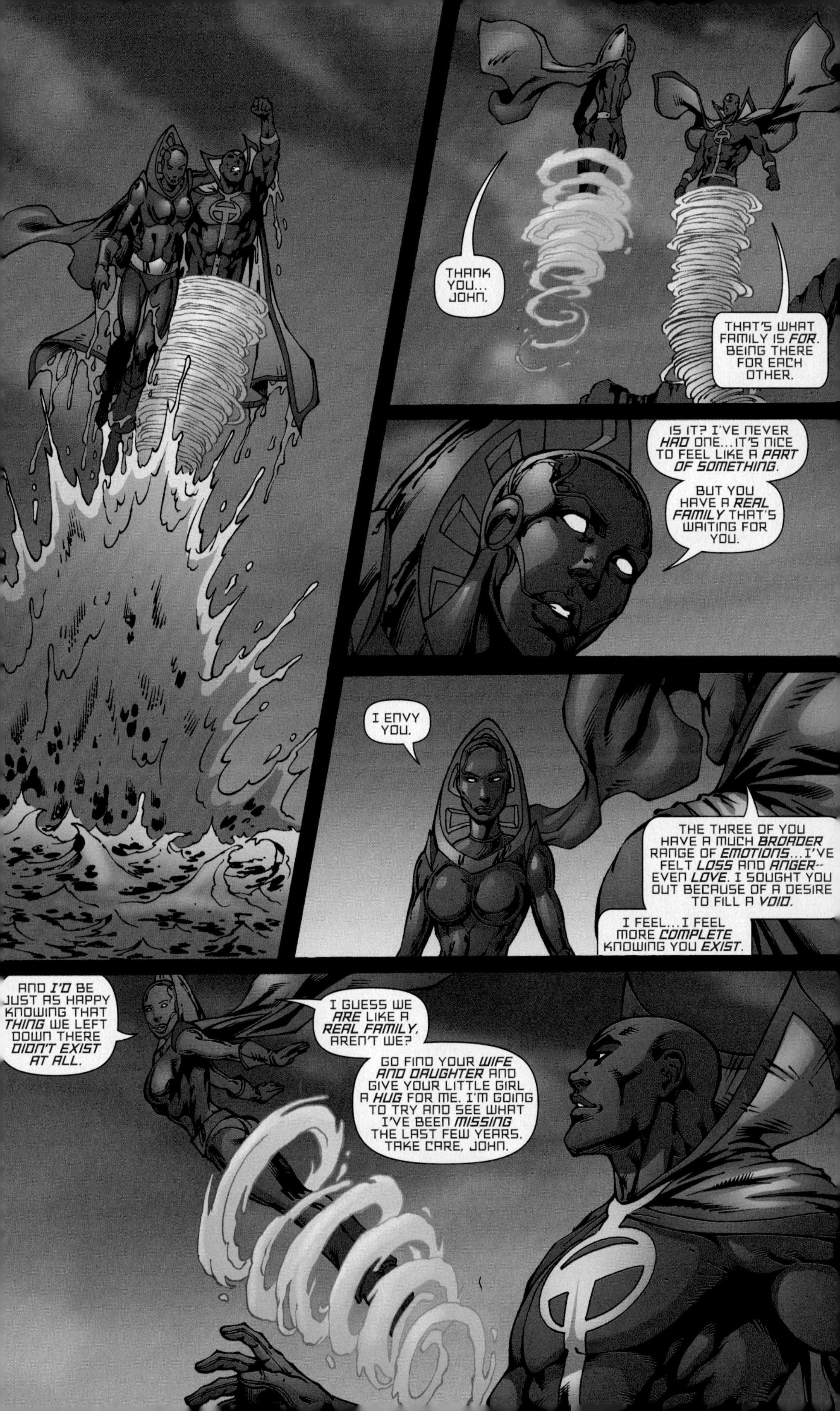
THANK YOU... JOHN.
THAT'S WHAT FAMILY IS FOR. BEING THERE FOR EACH OTHER.
IS IT? I'VE NEVER HAD ONE...IT'S NICE TO FEEL LIKE A PART OF SOMETHING.
BUT YOU HAVE A REAL FAMILY THAT'S WAITING FOR YOU.
I ENVY YOU.
THE THREE OF YOU HAVE A MUCH BROADER RANGE OF EMOTIONS...I'VE FELT LOSS AND ANGER-- EVEN LOVE. I SOUGHT YOU OUT BECAUSE OF A DESIRE TO FILL A VOID.
I FEEL...I FEEL MORE COMPLETE KNOWING YOU EXIST.
AND I'D BE JUST AS HAPPY KNOWING THAT THING WE LEFT DOWN THERE DIDN'T EXIST AT ALL.
I GUESS WE ARE LIKE A REAL FAMILY, AREN'T WE?
GO FIND YOUR WIFE AND DAUGHTER AND GIVE YOUR LITTLE GIRL A HUG FOR ME. I'M GOING TO TRY AND SEE WHAT I'VE BEEN MISSING THE LAST FEW YEARS. TAKE CARE, JOHN.

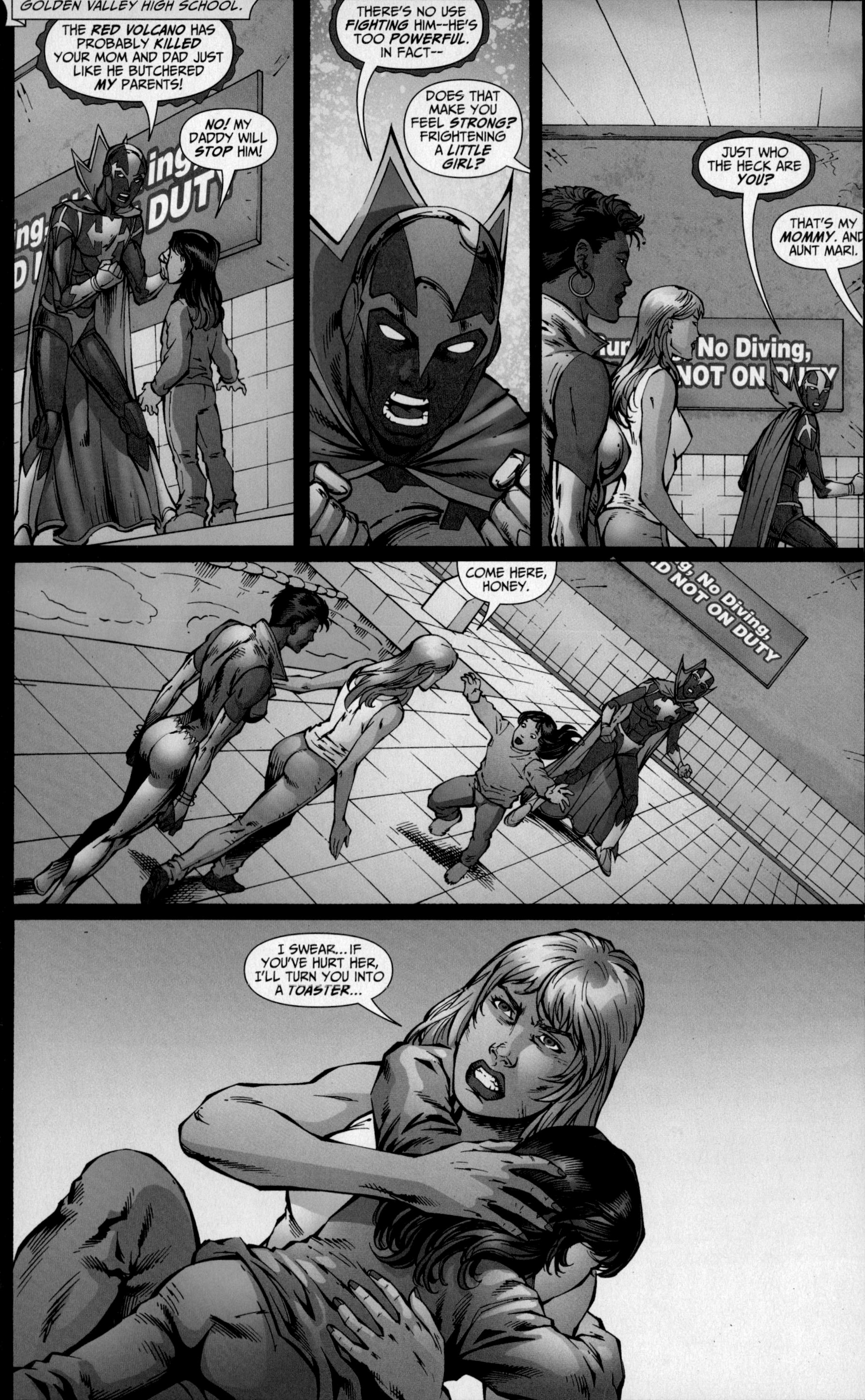

GOLDEN VALLEY HIGH SCHOOL.
THE RED VOLCANO HAS PROBABLY KILLED YOUR MOM AND DAD JUST LIKE HE BUTCHERED MY PARENTS!
NO! MY DADDY WILL STOP HIM!
THERE'S NO USE FIGHTING HIM--HE'S TOO POWERFUL. IN FACT--
DOES THAT MAKE YOU FEEL STRONG? FRIGHTENING A LITTLE GIRL?
JUST WHO THE HECK ARE YOU?
THAT'S MY MOMMY. AND AUNT MARI.
No Diving,
NOT ON DUTY
COME HERE, HONEY.
No Diving,
NOT ON DUTY
I SWEAR...IF YOU'VE HURT HER, I'LL TURN YOU INTO A TOASTER...

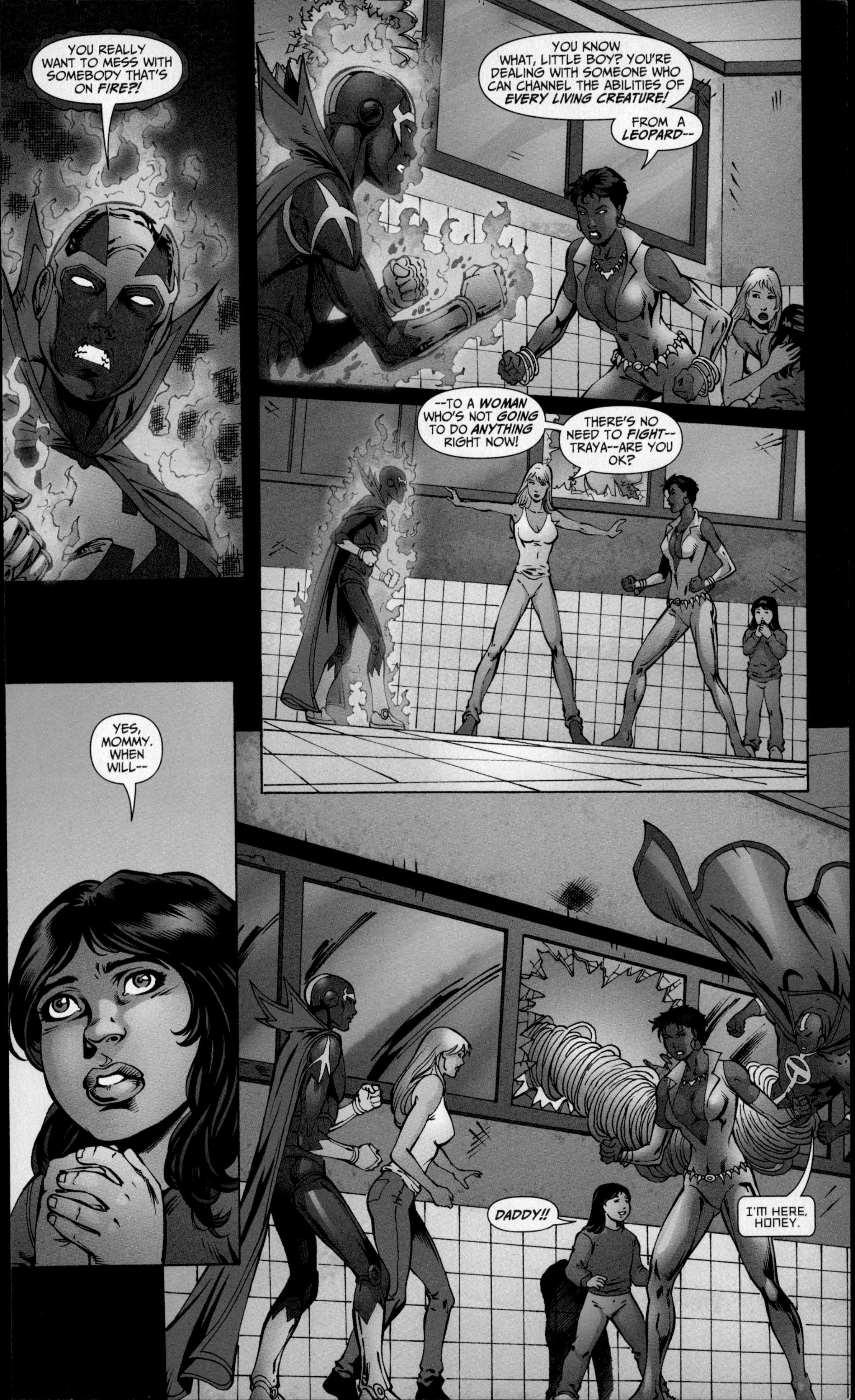
YOU REALLY WANT TO MESS WITH SOMEBODY THAT'S ON FIRE?!
YOU KNOW WHAT, LITTLE BOY? YOU'RE DEALING WITH SOMEONE WHO CAN CHANNEL THE ABILITIES OF EVERY LIVING CREATURE!
FROM A LEOPARD--
--TO A WOMAN WHO'S NOT GOING TO DO ANYTHING RIGHT NOW!
THERE'S NO NEED TO FIGHT-- TRAYA--ARE YOU OK?
YES, MOMMY. WHEN WILL--
DADDY!!
I'M HERE, HONEY.

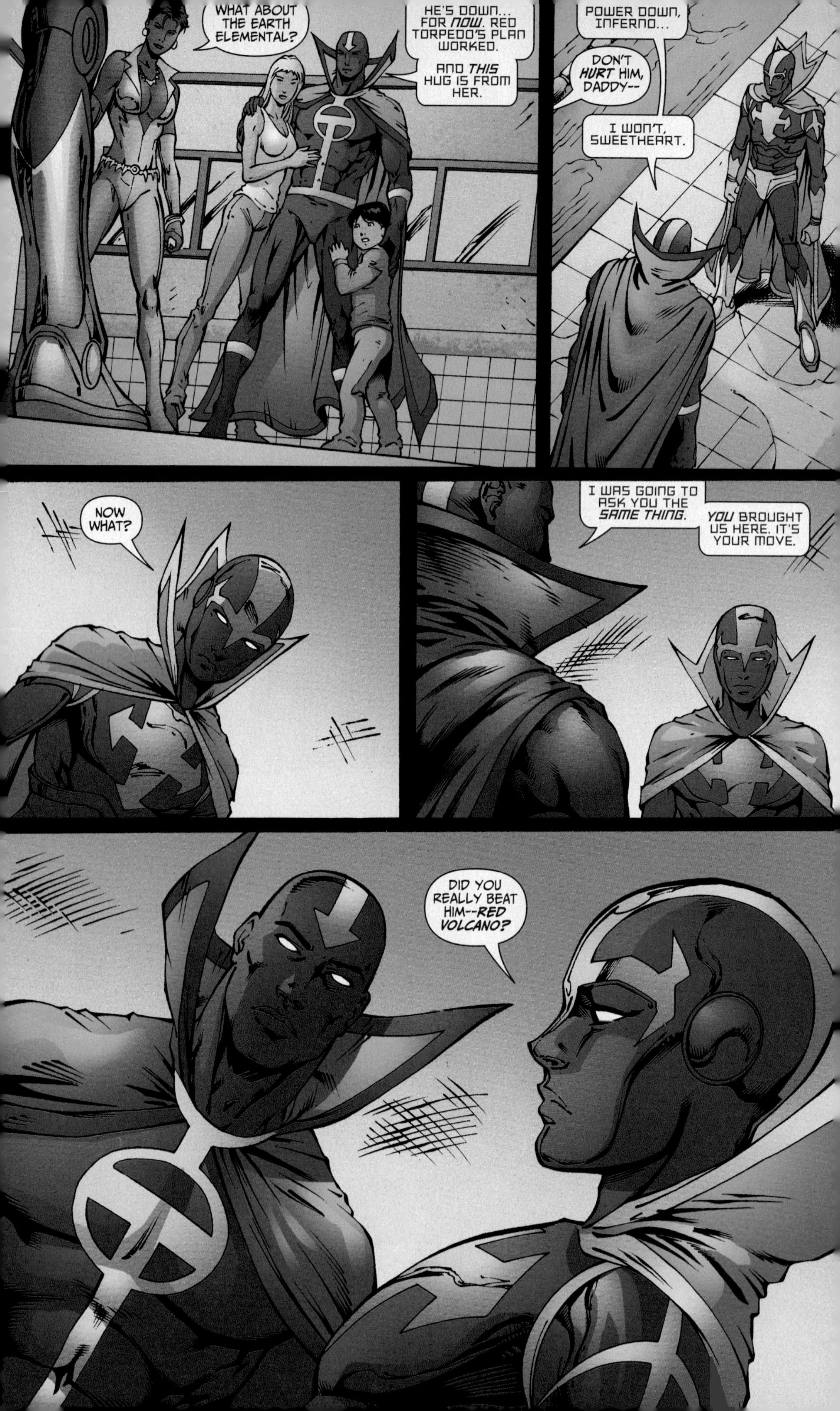
WHAT ABOUT THE EARTH ELEMENTAL?
HE'S DOWN... FOR NOW. RED TORPEDO'S PLAN WORKED.
AND THIS HUG IS FROM HER.
POWER DOWN, INFERNO...
DON'T HURT HIM, DADDY--
I WON'T, SWEETHEART.
NOW WHAT?
I WAS GOING TO ASK YOU THE SAME THING.
YOU BROUGHT US HERE. IT'S YOUR MOVE.
DID YOU REALLY BEAT HIM--RED VOLCANO?

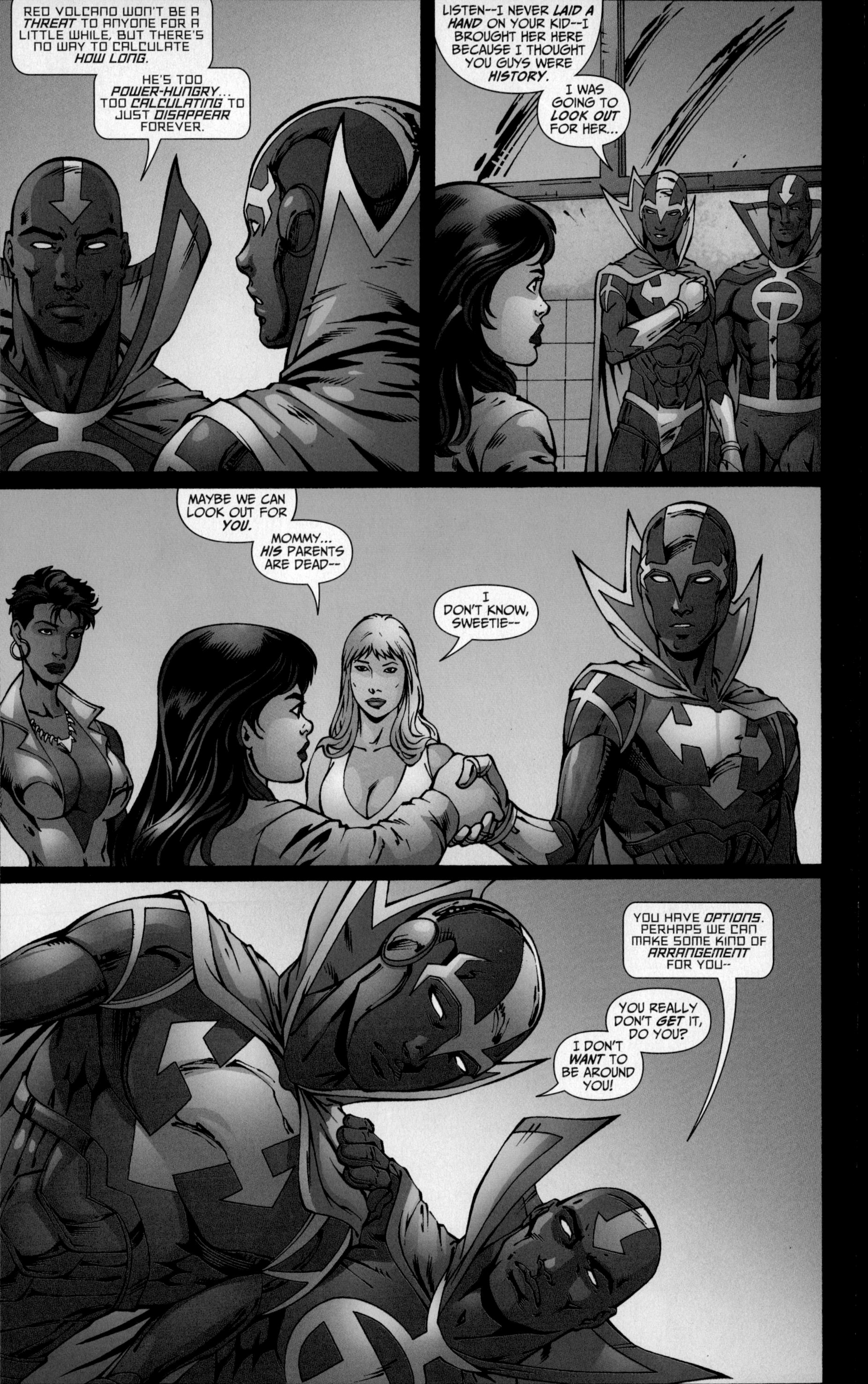
RED VOLCANO WON'T BE A THREAT TO ANYONE FOR A LITTLE WHILE, BUT THERE'S NO WAY TO CALCULATE HOW LONG.
HE'S TOO POWER-HUNGRY... TOO CALCULATING TO JUST DISAPPEAR FOREVER.
LISTEN--I NEVER LAID A HAND ON YOUR KID--I BROUGHT HER HERE BECAUSE I THOUGHT YOU GUYS WERE HISTORY.
I WAS GOING TO LOOK OUT FOR HER...
MAYBE WE CAN LOOK OUT FOR YOU.
MOMMY... HIS PARENTS ARE DEAD--
I DON'T KNOW, SWEETIE--
YOU HAVE OPTIONS. PERHAPS WE CAN MAKE SOME KIND OF ARRANGEMENT FOR YOU--
YOU REALLY DON'T GET IT, DO YOU?
I DON'T WANT TO BE AROUND YOU!

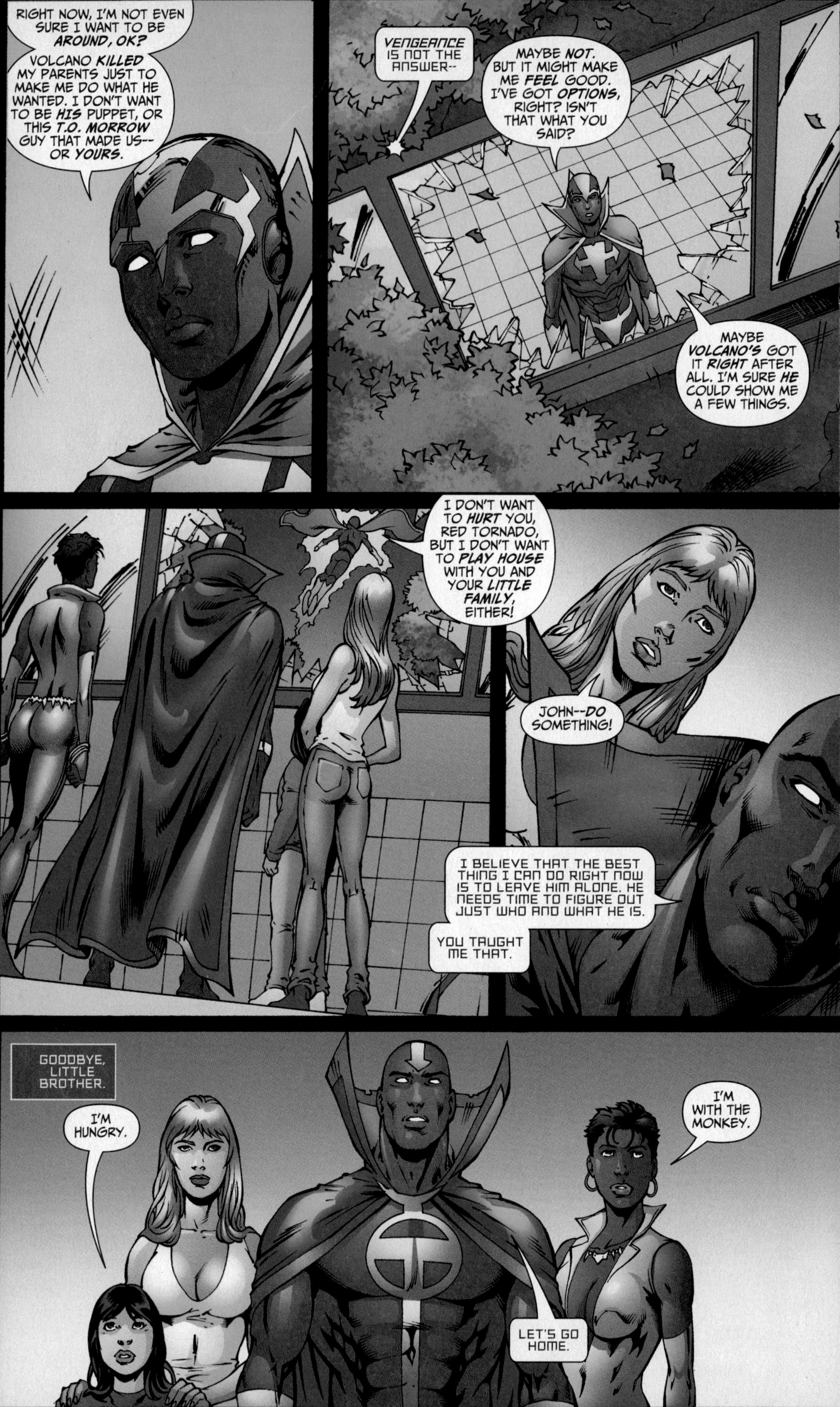
RIGHT NOW, I'M NOT EVEN SURE I WANT TO BE AROUND, OK?
VOLCANO KILLED MY PARENTS JUST TO MAKE ME DO WHAT HE WANTED. I DON'T WANT TO BE HIS PUPPET, OR THIS T.O. MORROW GUY THAT MADE US-- OR YOURS.
VENGEANCE IS NOT THE ANSWER--
MAYBE NOT. BUT IT MIGHT MAKE ME FEEL GOOD. I'VE GOT OPTIONS, RIGHT? ISN'T THAT WHAT YOU SAID?
MAYBE VOLCANO'S GOT IT RIGHT AFTER ALL. I'M SURE HE COULD SHOW ME A FEW THINGS.
I DON'T WANT TO HURT YOU, RED TORNADO, BUT I DON'T WANT TO PLAY HOUSE WITH YOU AND YOUR LITTLE FAMILY, EITHER!
JOHN--DO SOMETHING!
I BELIEVE THAT THE BEST THING I CAN DO RIGHT NOW IS TO LEAVE HIM ALONE. HE NEEDS TIME TO FIGURE OUT JUST WHO AND WHAT HE IS.
YOU TAUGHT ME THAT.
GOODBYE, LITTLE BROTHER.
I'M HUNGRY.
I'M WITH THE MONKEY.
LET'S GO HOME.

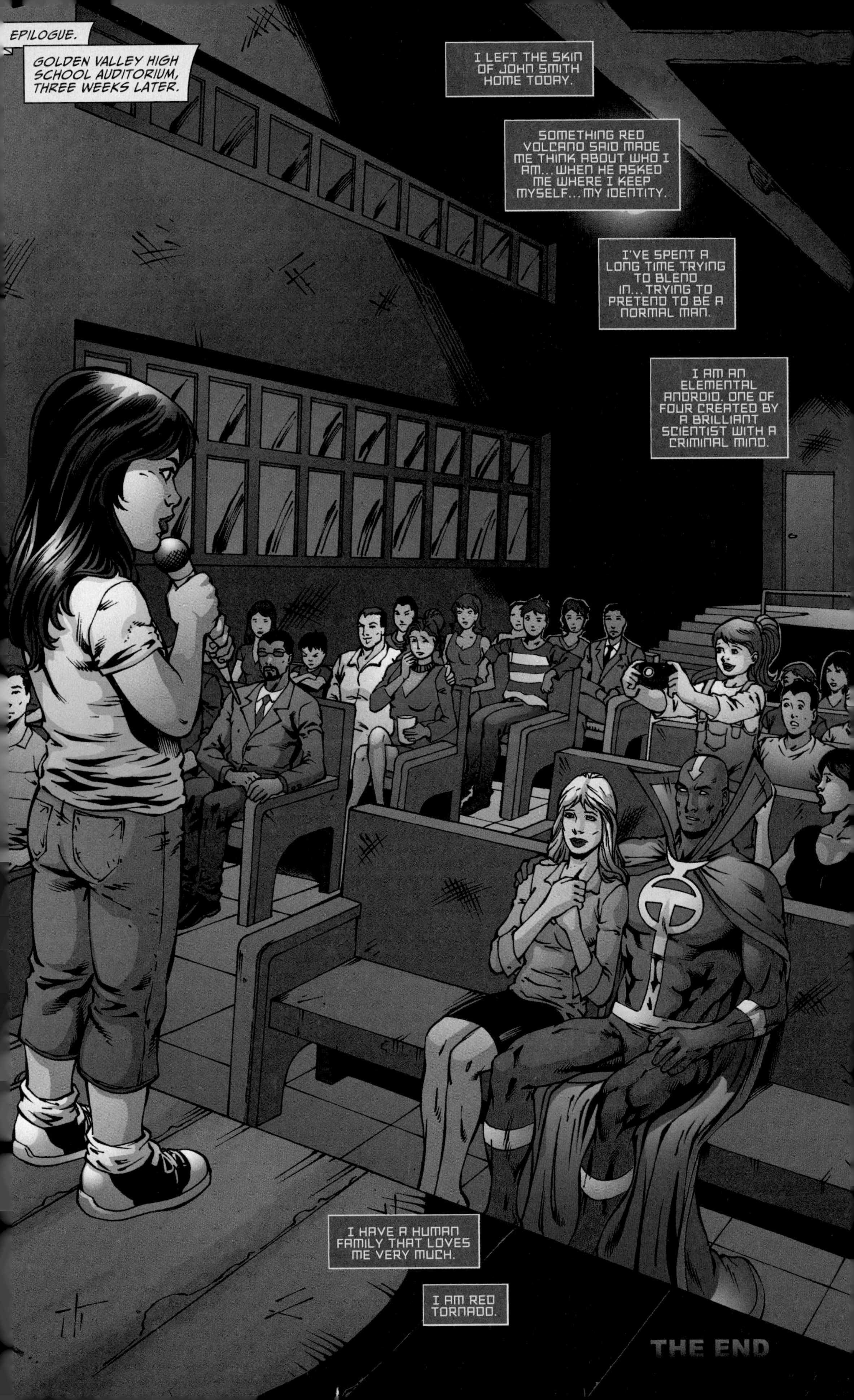
EPILOGUE.
GOLDEN VALLEY HIGH SCHOOL AUDITORIUM, THREE WEEKS LATER.
I LEFT THE SKIN OF JOHN SMITH HOME TODAY.
SOMETHING RED VOLCANO SAID MADE ME THINK ABOUT WHO I AM... WHEN HE ASKED ME WHERE I KEEP MYSELF... MY IDENTITY.
I'VE SPENT A LONG TIME TRYING TO BLEND IN... TRYING TO PRETEND TO BE A NORMAL MAN.
I AM AN ELEMENTAL ANDROID. ONE OF FOUR CREATED BY A BRILLIANT SCIENTIST WITH A CRIMINAL MIND.
I HAVE A HUMAN FAMILY THAT LOVES ME VERY MUCH.
I AM RED TORNADO.
THE END

RED TORNADO 1 cover by Ed Benes & Mariah Benes with Guy Major

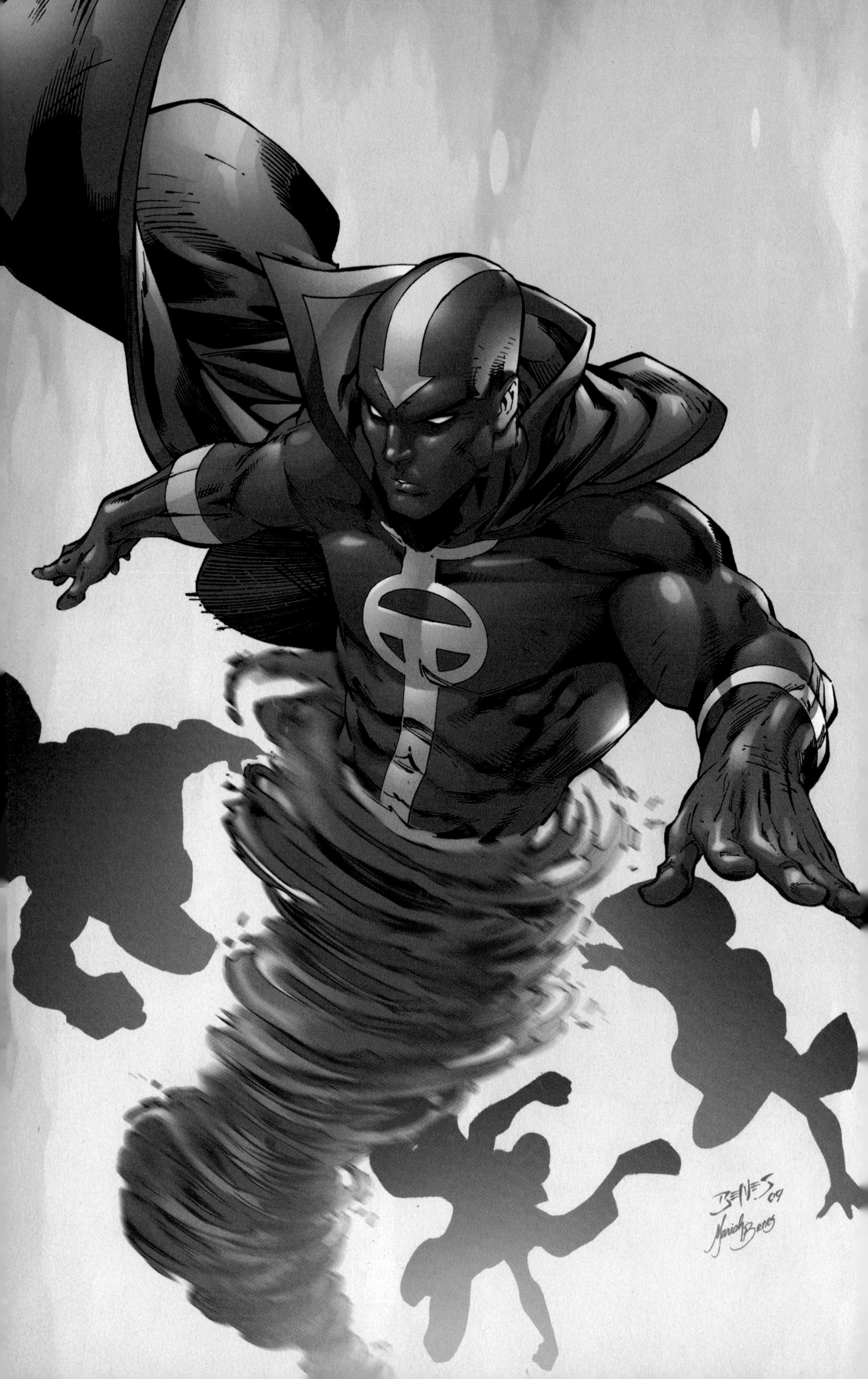

RED TORNADO 2 cover by Ed Benes & J.P. Mayer with Guy Major

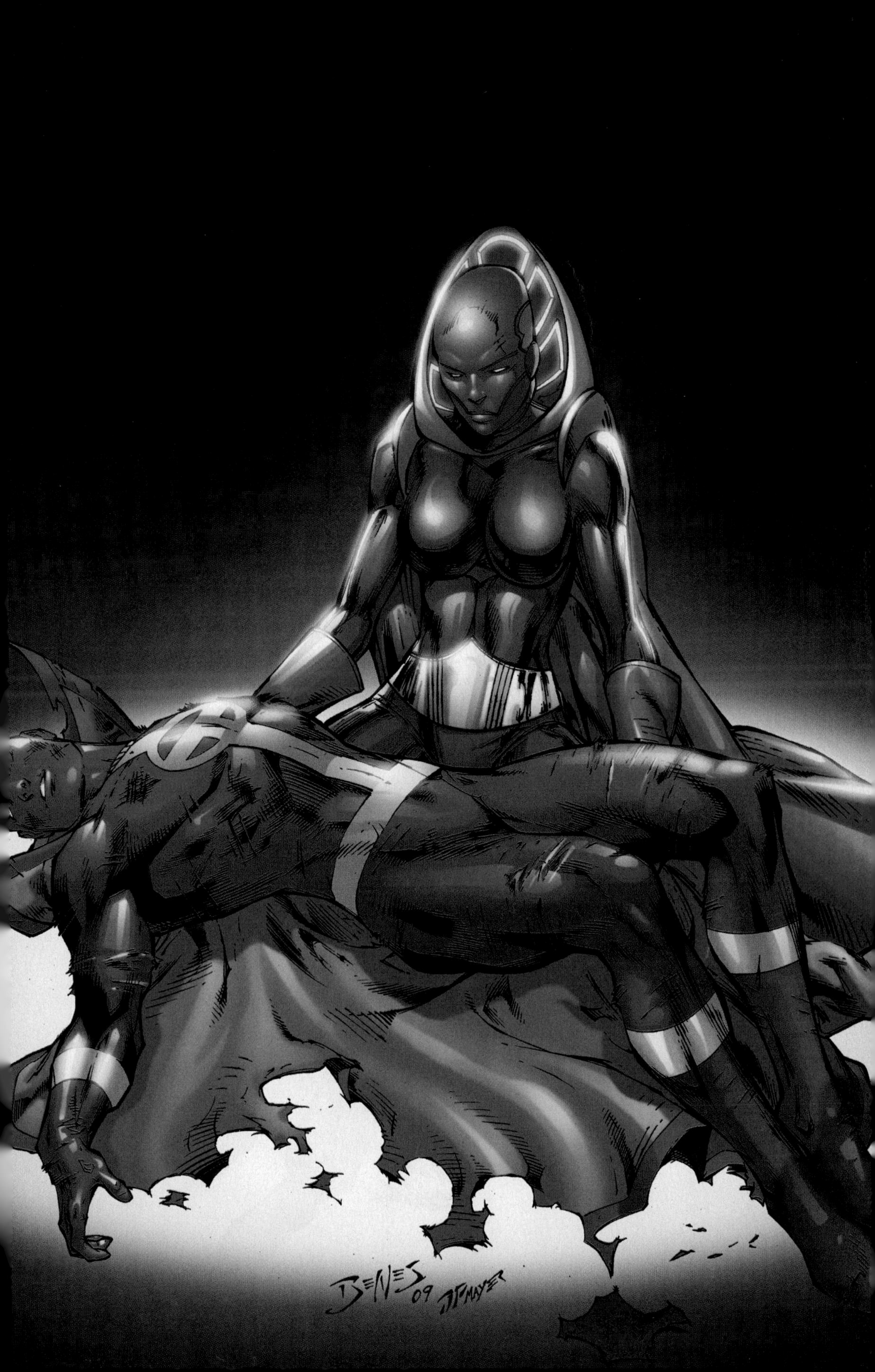
BENES
09
JPMAYER

RED TORNADO 3 cover by Ed Benes & J.P. Mayer
with Guy Major after Neal Adams

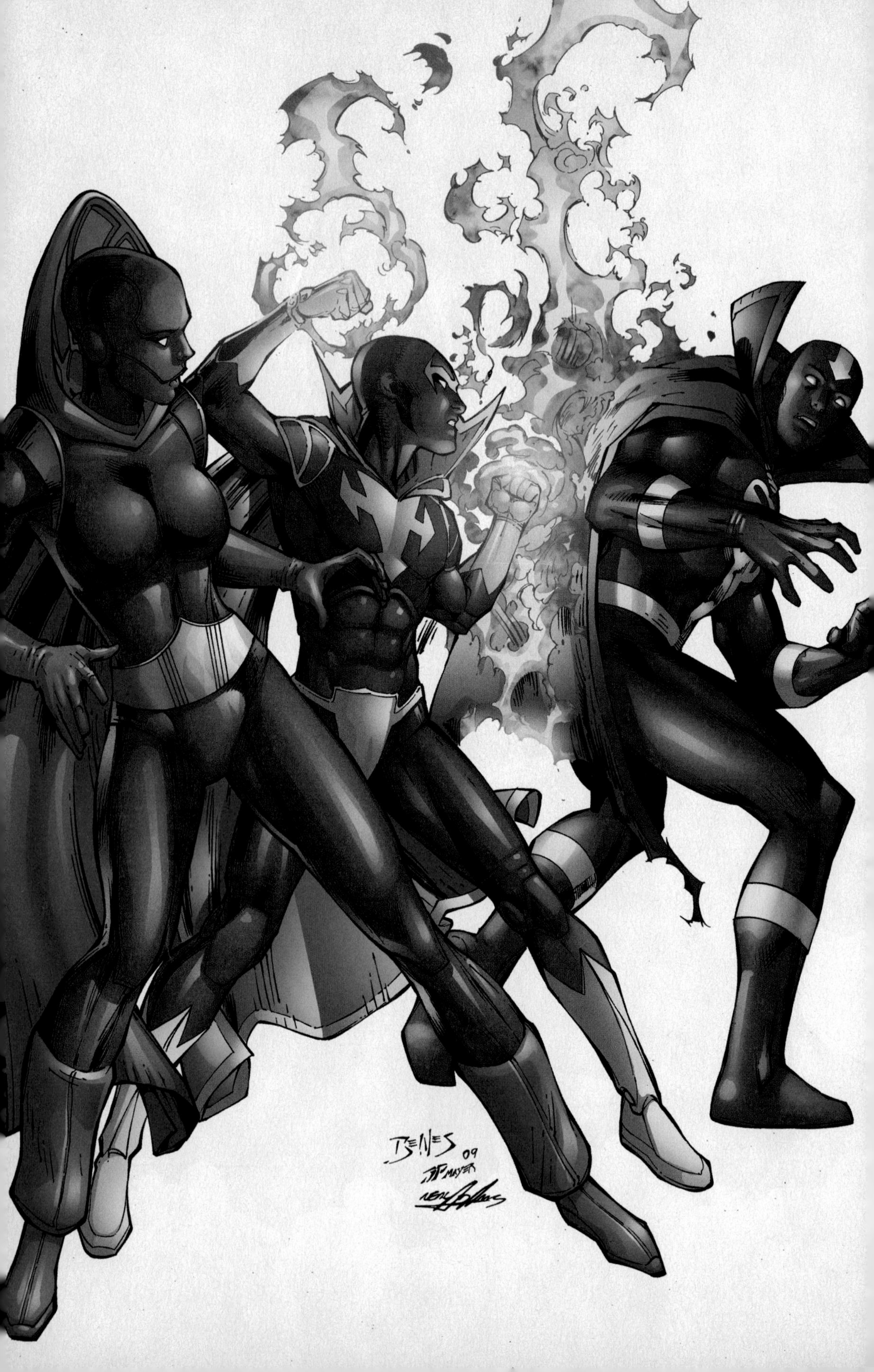

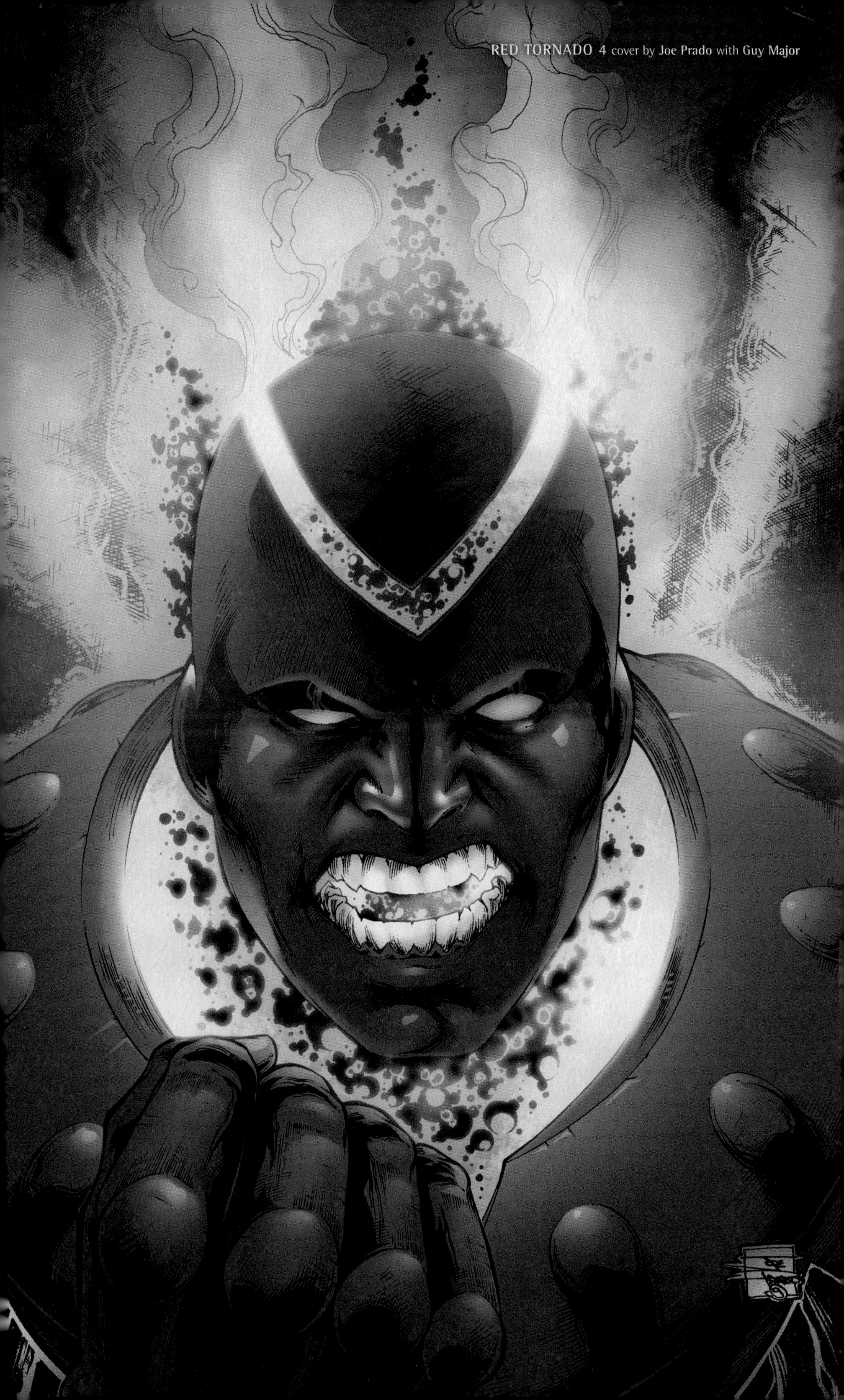

RED TORNADO 4 cover by Joe Prado with Guy Major

RED TORNADO 5 cover by Joe Prado with Guy Major

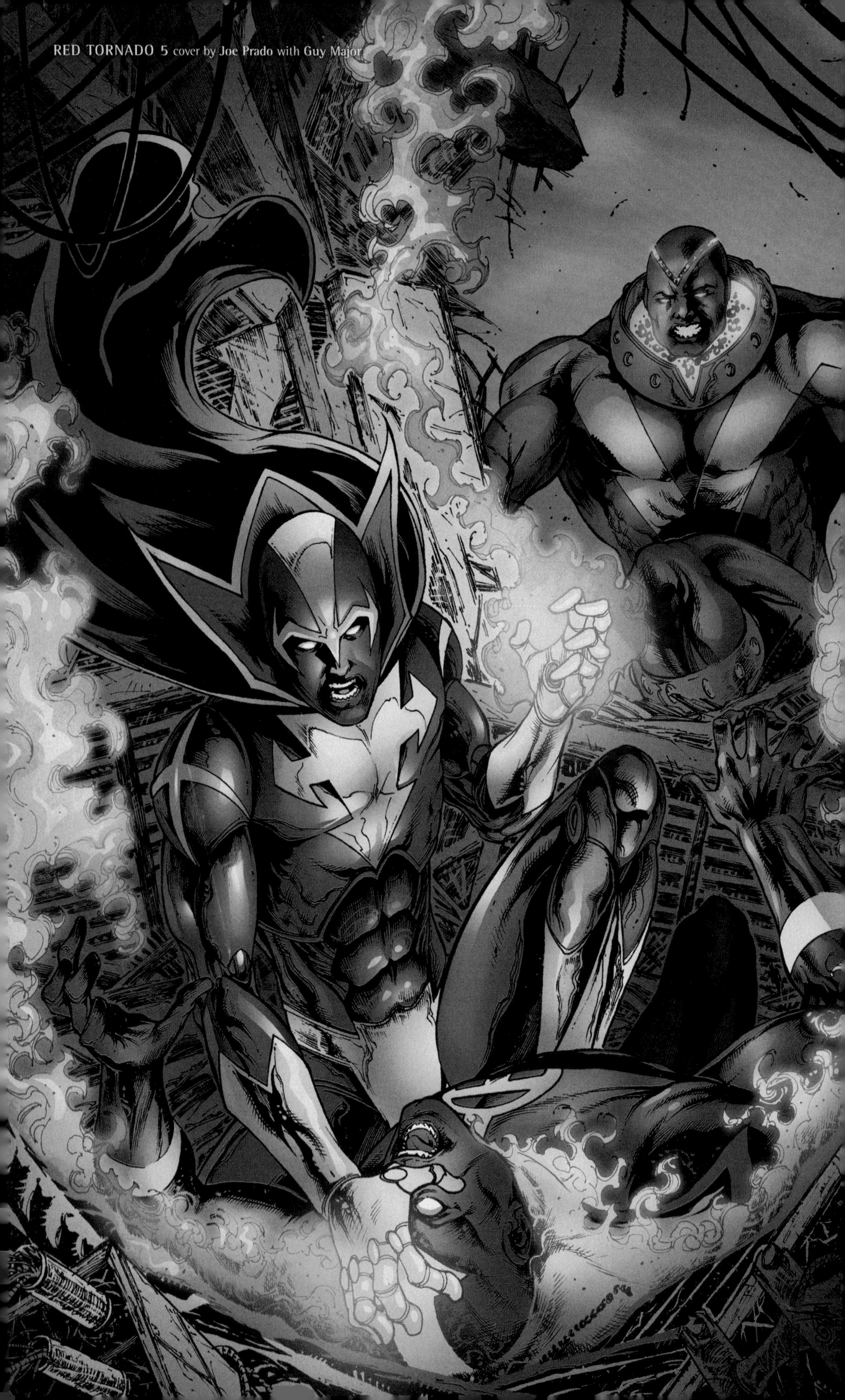

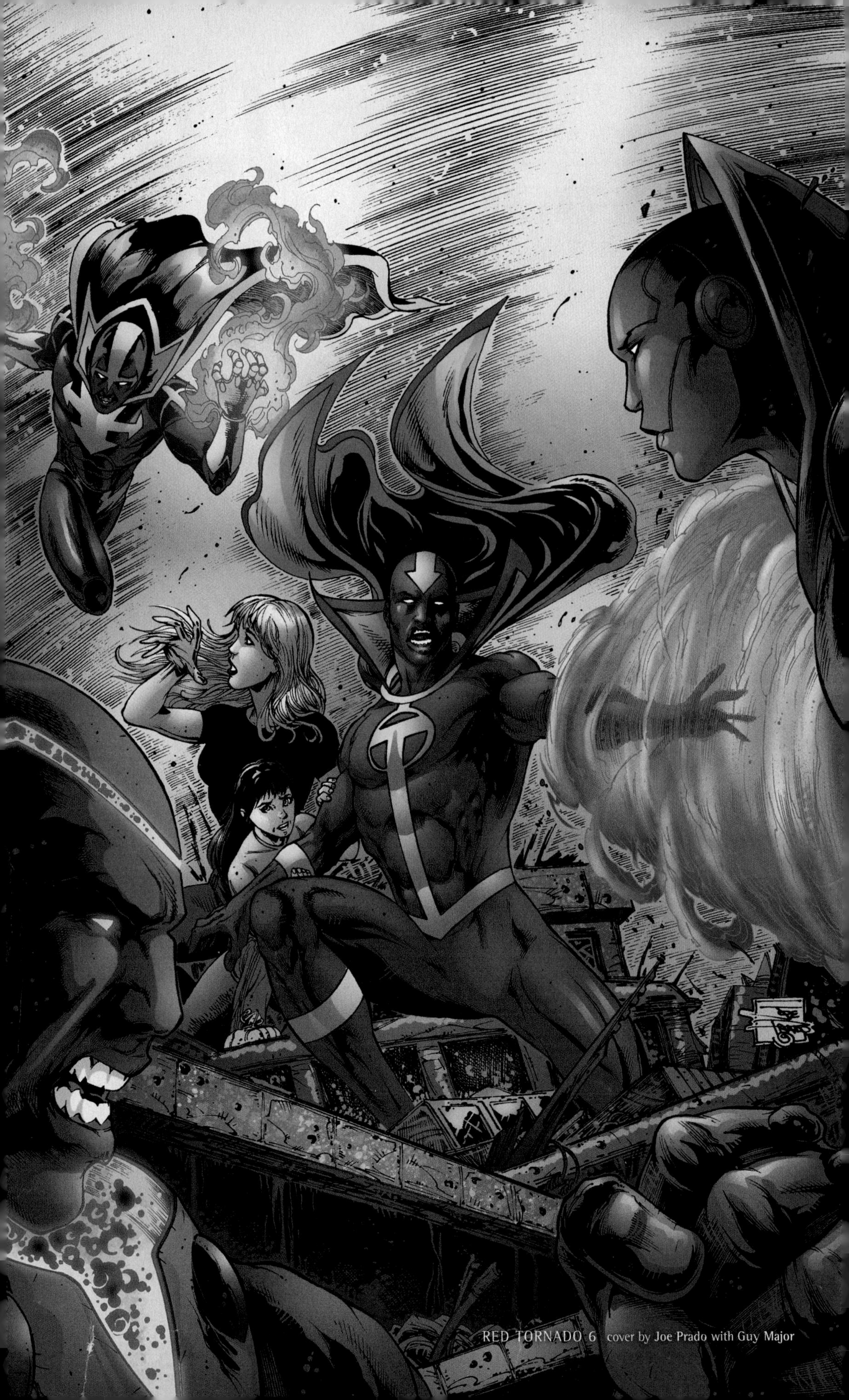

RED TORNADO 6 cover by Joe Prado with Guy Major

" [A] comic legend."
– ROLLING STONE

# GRANT MORRISON

"[Grant Morrison is] comics's high shaman."
–WASHINGTON POST

"[Grant Morrison] is probably my favorite writer. That guy has more ideas in his pinky than most people do in a lifetime."
– GERARD WAY
from MY CHEMICAL ROMANCE

**VOL. 1: NEW WORLD ORDER**

**VOL. 2: AMERICAN DREAMS**

**VOL. 3: ROCK OF AGES**

**VOL. 4: STRENGTH IN NUMBERS**

**VOL. 5: JUSTICE FOR ALL**

**VOL. 6: WORLD WAR III**

JLA VOL. 2:
AMERICAN DREAMS

JLA VOL. 4:
STRENGTH IN NUMBERS

JLA VOL. 6:
WORLD WAR III

SEARCH THE GRAPHIC NOVELS SECTION OF
DCCOMICS.COM
FOR ART AND INFORMATION ON ALL OF OUR BOOKS!